ONE MORE WARBLER

MILDRED WYATT-WOLD SERIES IN ORNITHOLOGY

One More Warbler

A LIFE WITH BIRDS

Victor Emanuel

WITH S. KIRK WALSH

UNIVERSITY OF TEXAS PRESS, AUSTIN

Requests for permission to reproduce material
from this work should be sent to:
    Permissions
    University of Texas Press
    P.O. Box 7819
    Austin, TX 78713-7819
    http://utpress.utexas.edu/index.php/rp-form

The paper used in this book meets the minimum
requirements of ANSI/NISO Z39.48-1992 (R1997)
(Permanence of Paper). ∞

Library of Congress Cataloging-in-Publication Data

Names: Emanuel, Victor, author. | Walsh, S. Kirk, author.
Title: One more warbler : a life with birds / Victor Emanuel
    with S. Kirk Walsh.
Description: First edition. | Austin : University of Texas Press,
    2017. | Includes index.
Identifiers: LCCN 2016027775
  ISBN 978-1-4773-1238-4 (cloth : alk. paper)
  ISBN 978-1-4773-1239-1 (library e-book)
  ISBN 978-1-4773-1240-7 (non-library e-book)
Subjects: LCSH: Bird watchers—Texas—Biography. |
    Bird watching. | Birds.
Classification: LCC QL31.E54 E33 2017 | DDC
    598.072/34764—dc23
LC record available at https://lccn.loc.gov/2016027775

doi:10.7560/312384

In memory of my mentors:
Joe Heiser
Armand Yramategui
Edgar Kincaid Jr.

All the way to heaven is heaven.
—ST. CATHERINE OF SIENA

Only birds
Sing the music of heaven
In this world
—KOBAYASHI ISSA

A friend may well be reckoned the masterpiece of nature.
—RALPH WALDO EMERSON

Contents

Prologue

I am sitting on the porch of my cottage on the Bolivar Peninsula. It is six-thirty in the morning. The stars have mostly disappeared. The sky brightens over the Gulf of Mexico. Hundreds of dark shapes are moving in the inlet thirty yards from my cottage porch. Some are swimming. Some are walking. There is not enough light to see colors or patterns, but I know that most of these shapes are American Avocets, a portion of the ten thousand that spend the winter here.

An intense band of red appears, stretching along the entire eastern horizon. After about fifteen minutes, it changes to orange. It soon grows paler and disappears, except in one spot where the sun will soon appear. My anticipation builds. I focus my binoculars on that red spot. No clouds sit on the horizon. Just before the sun rises, I see a flash of intense green. It lasts only a few seconds. I drop my binoculars and see the sun ascending until soon it is completely above the horizon.

Now the avocets are in clear view. Through my scope, I admire their black-and-white plumage, cinnamon necks, and long, upcurved, delicate black bills. Some feed alone, but a hundred or more assemble in a compact mass and swim counterclockwise, moving their bills from side to side. Along the shores of the inlet, dozens of egrets and herons gather. A flock of cormorants arrives and forms a triangular platoon. They swim up the inlet, dipping their long necks into the water. When they raise their heads, a few drops drip from the end of their bills. A small gathering of egrets discovers a school of fish that has congregated in an indentation off the inlet. Soon, many other egrets and herons join the feeding frenzy. Then, a Roseate Spoonbill drops in among the snow-white egrets and blue-gray herons. The spoonbill is mostly pink with a white back and neck. Its shoulders are deep red.

A lone female Northern Harrier flies low over the marsh. She holds her wings in a pronounced dihedral, flaps a few times, and then glides. Overhead appear six Brown Pelicans, coming from their roosting sites. The first pelican flaps seven deep wing beats and then glides. The next pelican in line flaps and glides, then the next, until the last one flaps. A few minutes later, eight huge White Pelicans fly over.

Now that the sun is up, I take in this remarkable vista. Up the inlet, hundreds of avocets and egrets converge. Directly across the inlet, there are more avocets, egrets, and herons. Toward the jetty, the panorama is even more spectacular. More than five thousand birds of twenty or more species are feeding. Most are American Avocets and Laughing Gulls, but buff-colored Marbled Godwits also walk along the shallow waters, probing the mud with their long, upcurved, black-tipped pink bills.

A black-and-white American Oystercatcher alights nearby. A Long-billed Curlew, a large shorebird, rests on a small patch of mud. The curlew is light brown with a very long, decurved bill. The most abundant medium-sized shorebirds are the Willets, which are a uniform light gray. When they fly, their black-and-white wings are prominent. Hundreds of brown Short-billed Dowitchers also probe the mud with their long bills. Nearby are a few Whimbrels. Sanderlings, Least and Western Sandpipers, Semipalmated and Black-bellied Plovers, and other smaller shorebirds are scattered across the shallows.

There is so much going on. It is hard to know where to look. The densest groups of birds consist of the Laughing Gulls, Forster's Terns, and American Avocets. All of a sudden, a large flock of Black Skimmers flies in and alights near the gulls, forming a large dark mass. These skimmers are black above and white below with a long, black-tipped red bill. A few fly up the inlet, passing right in front of me. The tips of their lower bills skim the water as they search for fish. A few moments later, all the skimmers fly up into an explosion of birds. They settle back down on the mudflats and shallows. Throughout the morning, the birds lift up again, over and over.

ONE MORE WARBLER

1

Early Days

Male Cardinal

RUTH STREET, HOUSTON

I was eight years old and getting ready for school. I looked out the dining room window of our house. There, on the bright green moss carpet under our fig tree, I spotted a brilliant red male Cardinal and its brown-clad mate feeding on sunflower seeds. My mother had scattered the seeds there a few days earlier. Bright and beautiful against the green backdrop, the red bird captivated me. I had never appreciated the beauty of birds until that spring morning.

As I was walking to school on another morning, I spotted a tiny bird in a small live oak tree next to the sidewalk. This bird was almost at eye level and only a few feet from me. It was entirely made up of shades of gray, black, and white. The bird featured no dramatic colors, yet I was struck by its bold pattern of feathers—its intense black cap and throat bordered its stark white cheek. Later, I learned that this bird was a Carolina Chickadee.

One afternoon at our house, I observed a Ruby-throated Hummingbird feeding on the red blossoms of a mimosa bush that grew near our screened-in porch. When the angle of the sun was right, the throat of the hummingbird glowed an iridescent red, almost like a jewel. It was a much different shade of red than that of the male Cardinal.

For a long time, I stood there, my nose pressed against the meshed squares of the screen, looking at this tiny bird as it zipped from flower to flower. Birds had become an integral part of my life.

I grew up in Houston during the forties and fifties. At that time, the city's population was about four hundred thousand. Only a few tall buildings, including the Gulf Building and the Rice Hotel, defined its spare skyline. No freeways intersected the city.

My father, Victor Emanuel, was a sportswriter for the *Houston Post* and worked part-time occasionally in the campaigns of various Democratic politicians, such as Harris County Commissioner Squatty Lyons and Congressman Albert Thomas. During the Depression years, my mother, Marian Williams Emanuel, worked in the offices of the Works Progress Administration (or WPA) as a secretary, assisting in the building of the San Jacinto monument. After living on Ruth Street, we moved into a modest two-story house on Chenevert Street, just west of the Third Ward, an African-American neighborhood where our maid, Myrtle Turner, lived. Her husband was a "minister" and sold sassafras roots that we used to make tea.

My parents came from very different backgrounds. My maternal grandmother, Sallie Williams, and my mother were born in Indianola in the Mississippi Delta. Sallie had grown up on a farm along the Sunflower River, a tributary of the Mississippi. As a child, I loved hearing her stories about life on the farm. There was the enormous flood that forced the family to retreat to the roof of their house. She told of eating only the hearts of their plentiful watermelons and throwing the rest to the hogs. I felt a deep kinship with Sallie. In some ways, I felt closer to her than I did to my own parents. She and her husband, Crawford, moved to Houston in 1922 with their children. Her husband passed away in 1935 before I was born. Initially, Sallie lived near us on Chenevert, and a few years later, she moved to a house on Westheimer Road where she opened an antique store.

My paternal grandfather, Benjamin Emanuel, was born into a Jewish family in St. Louis. His parents had emigrated from Worms,

Germany, in 1823. Benjamin married Elizabeth Schwarzkopf, who was also Jewish. She was born in Austria and immigrated to the United States in 1895. They moved to Fayetteville, Arkansas, where, in 1906, my father was born. His family moved to Iola, Kansas, where his father ran a general store for a couple of years. Benjamin moved the family again, this time to Nordheim in south Texas, in order to manage his cousin's store. The Emanuels were the only Jewish family in this small German-American Texas town.

Benjamin eventually started his own business in Nordheim. He and Elizabeth had two children, my father and his younger sister, Evelyn. Evelyn attended Southwest Texas State Teachers College in San Marcos, where Lyndon B. Johnson was one of her classmates. She became a Spanish teacher in the public schools of San Antonio. My father attended the University of Texas and was a sportswriter for the *Daily Texan*. It was his ambition to go to law school, but, unfortunately, he was thrown out of the university when it was discovered that he and some friends had been drinking and gambling at their boardinghouse.

My father landed a job as a sportswriter for the *Galveston Daily News* and subsequently moved to Houston, where he was also a sports journalist for the *Houston Post*. My mother's oldest brother, Crawford Williams Jr., worked as a police reporter for the *Houston Press*. He and my father met at the city's press club and became friends. Crawford told my mother about this interesting man, Victor Emanuel. When she learned that my father had been hospitalized with yellow jaundice, or hepatitis, she decided to visit him. After his discharge from the hospital, he invited her on a date to the Balinese Room, a legendary establishment located at the end of a six-hundred-foot pier off the Galveston seawall. (It was built on the pier so that nightclub staff could alert the customers and hide the gambling apparatus before the police reached the end of the pier.) A few years later, my parents married. My sister, Marilyn, was born in 1938, and I arrived two years later.

My father worked many nights at the newspaper, so my mother was home alone for many long hours with my sister and me. A friend of hers lived down the street, and my mother often pushed the baby carriage to her house for daily visits and companionship. Unfortunately, this friend was an alcoholic, and my mother also started to drink excessively. Depression soon followed.

One night when I was two and my sister was four, my mom became so depressed that she decided to slit her wrists. But she thought of my sister and me, lying in our beds, and decided that she needed to live for us. She called her sister-in-law, Margaret, who took her to the hospital. When we woke up, Marilyn and I were told that our mother had suffered a nervous breakdown. When she got out of the hospital, she joined Alcoholics Anonymous and never took another drink. Alcoholism had ravaged her family; her older brother, Crawford, died of cirrhosis of the liver. AA saved my mother.

Soon after my mother got sober, my sister and I developed severe ear infections that required surgery. This was before penicillin had been developed and even sulfa drugs were not widely used. The doctor punctured holes in our eardrums and then in our mastoids behind our eardrums in order to drain our ears. Post-surgery, my sister and I were wrapped in sheets with our hands bound along our sides to stop us from picking at the bandages around our ears. When the infections subsided, the hole in the eardrum of my left ear remained. This caused a significant loss of hearing.

This loss had several effects. It was difficult for me to determine the direction of a sound. It also affected my speech. I had great difficulty pronouncing certain words. My parents sent me to a speech therapist who helped me to overcome these problems. Later, as a teen, I found it hard to discern the lyrics of popular songs, which is one of the reasons I, unlike my peers, was never drawn to this kind of music. (I did like Simon & Garfunkel; one of my favorite songs was "I Am a Rock" because it spoke to my status as a loner.) Fortunately, I could hear well with my right ear, and could enjoy birdsong and other natural sounds.

Like some young boys, I was interested in just about anything that was alive—birds, butterflies, crayfish, snakes, turtles, fish. I remember discovering a large snapping turtle that had crawled out of a ditch onto the sidewalk. It was about two feet long and probably weighed about five pounds. My friends and I found a broom handle and poked it. The turtle proceeded to snap the broomstick in two. We came to the quick realization that the broomstick could have been one of our fingers or arms and that we'd better leave the turtle alone.

Open ditches bordered the urban streets for the draining of rainwater. I somehow discovered that crayfish lived in these muddy ditches. I spent hours with a bit of bacon secured to the end of a long piece of string, doing my best to catch the freshwater crustacean. I wasn't interested in cooking and eating the crayfish. It was just the thrill of being perched on the edge of this four-foot-deep ditch, trying to catch them.

Given the wet weather of Houston summers, many of these ditches were often at least halfway full of water, attracting swarms of mosquitoes. Pesticide trucks made regular rounds many nights throughout the neighborhoods, spraying large, noxious clouds of DDT in order to decimate the ever-growing mosquito population. Much like the recognizable jingle of an ice-cream truck, the rumbling motors of the spraying vehicles drew my friends and me outside and into the streets to run directly behind the foggy cascades of pesticide. We thought this was fun; neither we nor our parents had any idea that we were breathing in vaporous clouds of poison.

Just across the street from our house was a city lot choked with dewberry vines. My father nicknamed that lot "the jungle." My friends and I spent countless hours there, exploring the paths that traversed through the untamed property. In late April, it was a wonderful spot to pick dewberries, a close relative of the blackberry, for my mother's delicious dewberry pies.

Back then, many blocks of Houston were vacant and overgrown with weeds and bramble. In these empty lots, we discovered that if you picked up a decaying board, an old piece of linoleum, or even a flimsy slip of cardboard, there might be a snake underneath. In fact, in those days, there were many snakes (Texas brown snakes, bull snakes, rat snakes, green snakes), and we loved catching them.

I accumulated an impressive collection of snakes. My parents allowed me to keep them in cages in our garage, and in no time, I converted the entire space into a serpentarium of slithering rep-tiles. Looking back on it, I don't know what we fed all those snakes; I imagine that we fed mice to the larger ones.

This snake collection emphasized two important aspects of my childhood. First, my entrepreneurial spirit took flight as I decided it would be a good idea to charge the neighborhood children five cents to come and see all my snakes. Second, that experience underscored what a wonderful mom I had. She couldn't bear to look at even a photograph of a snake. She was terrified of them. And yet she allowed her intrepid son to collect more than fifty and house them in her garage.

My father, in contrast, had a passionate interest in snakes. Over the years, he made friends with John Werler, a herpetologist who later became the director of the Houston Zoo. At that time, though, he managed the Snake House and would arrange for us to visit off-hours to watch as rats were fed to the snakes.

My father loved taking me to the zoo. At that time, admission was free. Later, when the city proposed that a fee be charged, my father was outraged, feeling that such a fee would make it more difficult for low-income families to bring their children for a day of entertainment. Despite his efforts, an admission fee was instituted, but the zoo remained free one day a week.

Despite our shared enthusiasm for snakes and the zoo, my father didn't understand my newfound fascination for nature and birds. He would have preferred that I play baseball, football, or some other sport, rather than spend hours outside, looking at birds and other creatures. He was concerned that I wasn't like other boys. It irritated him that I had trouble getting up in the morning to go to school, but would spring out of bed on the weekends when I went birding.

From a young age, I was keenly aware that I was different from other children. I was the product of a mixed marriage between a Christian and a Jew, though neither parent was religious. My father was agnostic, but deeply steeped in Jewish culture. He had never attended Hebrew school because he and his family were the only Jews in Nordheim. On High Holy Days, they traveled to San

Antonio to attend services at a synagogue there. My father told my mother that, as far as religion was concerned, it was up to her to decide how my sister and I would be raised. My mother had us both christened in the Presbyterian church, but we only attended services on Easter Sunday. Early on, I came to feel that nature was my church.

I continued to feel set apart into my teenage years. When I was in middle school, I asked a young woman for a date. She was Jewish and said that she could not go out with me because I was not Jewish. Subsequently, I asked another young woman who was a Christian for a date, and she said that she could not go out with me because I was Jewish. I was not, it seemed, a member of any tribe.

I did find friends on the school debating team. My father encouraged me to join because of his own interests in politics and oratory. As I honed my speaking skills, I began to take debating quite seriously and did my best to win. In hindsight, I recognize a few intersections between an effective debater and a birder: both activities require attention to detail and research. That said, none of my debate colleagues cared about birds.

My lack of skill and interest in sports also contributed to my isolation. This was, after all, Texas, and sports reigned supreme. Coaches were much more interested in helping boys who, unlike me, were athletically gifted. While other children were competing in sports, I wandered around the schoolyard among the trees, looking at nature.

On one of those schoolyard walks, I spotted some small blue flowers with three propeller-shaped petals that were parallel to the ground. I was entranced by their shape and the beauty of their colors. I couldn't find any information about these flowers in the library—and no one I knew could tell me what they were. Twenty years later, I received a newsletter from the Armand Bayou Nature Center in Houston that contained a sketch of this very flower. It was identified as Herbertia, a small iris found only in Louisiana and southeast Texas. Every spring when I see this little flower, it reminds me of the hours that I spent alone, wandering around the schoolyard and finding a refuge and a home in nature and birds.

Not long after the Cardinal sighting in our backyard, I saw my very first warbler. I had been given my first pair of binoculars for Christmas. I spotted a Myrtle Warbler (now called the Yellow-rumped Warbler) on Christmas Day near where my aunt Claudine and my uncle Shelby lived on Saulnier Street, just west of downtown Houston.

We had celebrated the holidays at their house that year. It was a gray, cold day, and a few warblers were perched in Chinese Tallow trees. At the time, I didn't own a comprehensive field guide, but my grandmother had given me a copy of John James Audubon's *The Birds of America*, which features full-size color plates of Audubon's paintings, but with no descriptive text related to the various species. By referencing this book, I was able to identify my first Myrtle Warbler.

Back then, I didn't have any friends who shared my passion for birds. I did, however, talk some of my young friends into exploring Hermann Park. It was the first large natural area where I spent time as a child. Numerous live oaks, sweet gum, pecan, and other trees populated the park, and Brays Bayou bordered its southern edge. Some parts of the park contained dense thickets. My visits to Hermann Park expanded my world and put me more intensely in touch with nature.

I tended to keep my birding activities a secret from most other boys because I knew that if they found out that I was a birder, they would make fun of me. I remember my horror when my mother, driving some of my classmates and me to school, told them that I was a birder.

One afternoon in Hermann Park, I spotted a Hermit Thrush, rich brown in color with its beige-speckled chest. None of my friends were interested in looking at this wonderful bird. Instead, they stood on a bridge over Brays Bayou, dropping a golf ball in hopes of hitting a large gar as it surfaced.

A few months later, a friend I knew in Cub Scouts, Sterling Dickinson, told me about the Outdoor Nature Club, which met in the downtown public library. At my first meeting, I felt at home, despite the fact that all the members were quite a bit older; most were in their fifties, sixties, and seventies. The club was organized by interest, and a different member led each subgroup.

It was in the Outdoor Nature Club that I found two of my mentors, Armand Yramategui, who led the ornithology group, and Joe Heiser. At twenty-seven years old, Armand was one of the younger members of the group. He still lived with his parents and taught electrical engineering part-time at Rice. Armand was a kind, gentle man with a head of thick black hair and an olive complexion. His parents were from Mexico, and his father was of Basque descent (this explained his unusual last name). Not surprisingly, I joined the ornithology group.

My other mentor Joe Heiser was one of the founders of the Outdoor Nature Club, which began in 1923. Heavyset and balding, Joe worked as an accountant for the Texas Company (which later became Texaco) and lived with his three brothers and sister at their family home. His passions, outside of nature, included opera and the circus. He told me that he had a wonderful collection of circus posters. He loved listening to the Metropolitan Opera performances that were broadcast on the radio on Saturdays. Joe and Armand held a deep appreciation for all living things and enjoyed seeing all birds, common as well as the more unusual ones.

Both men frequently took me out and taught me about birds and nature. Early on, I became aware that they enjoyed sharing nature with me as much as I enjoyed sharing with them. It was a two-way street, a true mentorship. Neither Armand nor Joe had children or wives. It was almost as if they were "married" to nature. Looking back, I see clearly that our relationships provided some of the satisfaction and richness that parents likely experience through their own children. Joe and Armand truly cared about me.

In addition to being all-around naturalists, Joe and Armand were also conservationists, with an interest in preserving pristine stretches of land to protect natural habitats. They would spot pieces of land that were slated for development and would try to raise the money to purchase the property. It might only be a small bog, but this was their way of preserving nature. Both men were among the founders of the Texas Nature Conservancy.

Greater Prairie Chicken

LA PORTE, TEXAS

During the spring of 1950, I went on my first field trip with the Outdoor Nature Club to La Porte, Texas, on northwest Galveston Bay. By this time, I owned a Peterson's field guide. Our goal for this trip was to observe the Greater Prairie Chicken and the male mating dance during the early dawn hours. This mating ritual is called "booming," a term inspired by the sound that the males produce during this impressive exhibition. About five to ten males gather for the dance in an area of short grass. Such an assemblage of male birds displaying is called a "lek." In an effort to attract a female, the birds cock their tails, lean forward, and raise the feathers that hang down over their ears, creating a crest-like formation above their heads. The males stamp their feet repeatedly against the ground and vocalize their low three-syllable hollow calls (*oo-loo-woo*), which they produce by sucking air into the bright orange air sacs on either side of their necks and then slowly releasing it. The males face off, charging toward each other and leaping into the air, in hopes of winning over one of the females. The female chickens choose the male who appears to be the best dancer, the idea being that the best dancer will likely produce the most robust offspring. The Blackfoot and Plains Cree peoples imitated the display movements of prairie chickens in some of their ceremonial dances.

Our group met in a parking lot before sunrise. The sky was just beginning to brighten as the sun emerged over the horizon. I had read in my Peterson field guide that the sound produced by a male prairie chicken resembles the sound made by blowing over the opening of a Coke bottle. So, I searched for a Coke bottle in and around the parking lot, and then I took my find into the restroom to wash it out so I could blow over it. When I returned to the parking lot, everyone was gone. They had forgotten me. I nearly started to cry, but then I recovered and went into the nearby restaurant and ordered breakfast. Just as my order arrived, one of the club members returned and retrieved me, so I didn't get a chance to eat my breakfast.

By the time we arrived at the lek, the birds had finished dancing, and I only saw one of the prairie chickens fly away over the distant meadow of tall grasses. The entire morning was a bust: I didn't get to eat breakfast, I didn't get to blow over my Coke bottle, and I didn't get to see the Greater Prairie Chickens dance. As I learned during the coming years, disappointment is a part of birding, and timing is everything. But that lesson was especially tough for a young boy to accept.

Vermilion Flycatcher
SAN JACINTO ORDNANCE DEPOT

When I was ten years old, I went on my first Christmas Bird Count with Frank Watson, one of the top birders in the Outdoor Nature Club. The Christmas Bird Count was established in 1900 by Frank M. Chapman, the editor of *Bird-Lore* magazine and an early officer of the then-nascent Audubon Society. He decided it was time to create an alternative to the traditional Christmastime "Side Hunt," where hunters spent the day out in the woods attempting to kill as many animals and birds as possible. The goal of the Side Hunt was to generate the highest tally by the day's end. Chapman's first Christmas Count included twenty-seven people. There were other teams in twenty-five different localities across the country. The counters spent varying lengths of time in the field—anywhere from a half-hour to nine hours—with each team surveying birds within a fifteen-mile diameter. The largest list of birds spotted came from Pacific Grove, California (thirty-six species), and the second largest came from Chapman's region around Englewood, New Jersey (eighteen species). Over the past hundred-plus years, the Audubon Christmas Bird Count has grown considerably, with more than fifty thousand participants identifying and counting birds between December 14 and January 5 throughout the country.

For our count, Frank and I traveled to the San Jacinto Ordnance Depot on the north bank of the Houston Ship Channel, where it converges with the San Jacinto River, about fifteen miles east of

Houston. The San Jacinto Ordnance Depot was originally a World War II facility, which primarily received, stored, and inspected a variety of ammunition, handling up to 329 million pounds throughout its decade-plus of operations. Sallie Williams, my grandmother, had worked there during the war, grinding binocular lens. After the war, the coastal area was transformed into a 4,954-acre reserve, heavily wooded with pine trees, water oaks, and cypresses.

With our binoculars around our necks and field guides in hand, Frank and I walked along a narrow trail that bordered one of the many swampy stretches. He advised me to stay quiet and alert as we attempted to add more bird species to our list. At one point, Frank paused, tapped my shoulder, and nodded in the direction of a small cypress. Its delicate branches arched over the reeds that fringed the pond's edge, and on one of those branches perched a bird with brilliant red upperparts and cap. Its bright feathers almost glowed against the somber browns, greens, and grays of the marshy landscape. I lifted my binoculars to get a closer look: The bird's vivid tufted crown fluttered in the winter breeze. It was a startling sight. Here was a bird that was an even more intense shade of red than the Cardinal on Ruth Street. I was mesmerized by its sheer brilliance. Frank informed me that it was a male Vermilion Flycatcher. Much smaller than the Cardinal, the Vermilion Flycatcher, with its black mask and red underparts and cap, is considered one of the most beautiful birds in North America. On this morning of my first Christmas Bird Count, I watched this bird sally out and snatch insects before returning to its perch in the cypress.

Later, we walked on a trail that bordered the reedy shoreline of an inlet of the river. At one point, we rounded a bend that overlooked the slate-gray waters of the inlet. A wintry breeze gusted into our faces as we stared out over the cattails in front of us. The waters were solidly blanketed with ducks. Hundreds, hundreds, and hundreds of ducks. I had never seen so many birds in one place. This enormous collection looked like an undulating quilt on the choppy waters. The ducks dipped their heads in and out of the water as they searched for food. Others floated peacefully among the masses. To this day, this remains the most impressive congregation of ducks that I have ever seen.

After this experience, I participated in the Houston Bird Count every year for another twenty-five years. When I was thirteen, I was assigned to an area with fellow birder Arlie McKay. Arlie wasn't married and lived with his father, who had a farm along the west side of Trinity Bay. Carl Aiken, a friend of mine from Bellaire High School, and I would spend the night at Arlie's farmhouse the night before the count. At the time, Arlie was about fifty years old, and his father was in his late eighties. Much earlier in his life, Arlie's father was a market hunter. He would go out on Trinity Bay and set up a line of guns and kill hundreds of ducks, which would then be sold in the markets. He told us that when he was a very young man, he was riding with a friend and they saw a Native American. His friend raised his gun to kill the man. Arlie's father pushed the barrel down, and the man escaped. That must've been around the late 1800s.

A keen observer, Arlie taught me a lot about identifying birds. For example, I learned from him that the small, delicate Bonaparte's Gull—a species named after Charles Lucien Bonaparte, a leading ornithologist in the 1800s and a nephew of Napoleon—can be picked out by how it sits in the water. Most gulls' bodies tend to be halfway submerged, but a Bonaparte's Gull rides high in the water.

Hooded Warbler

LITTLE THICKET NATURE SANCTUARY

When I joined the Outdoor Nature Club, Joe Heiser was heading up an effort to acquire 655 acres in San Jacinto County, which is about two hours north of Houston in East Texas. The acreage was at the headwaters of the San Jacinto River and near the San Jacinto National Forest. Joe used his own savings (in 1950, the property was valued at $39 per acre) to buy the property in order to establish the Little Thicket Nature Sanctuary, and then sold it to the club at the purchase price, with no interest, over an extended period of time. Joe had a very outgoing personality, which helped him reach out to the local people who owned land adjacent to the Little Thicket Nature Sanctuary.

As I entered my teenage years, I went to this sanctuary with Joe almost every weekend, and sometimes my friend David Safley joined us, too. My parents knew I enjoyed my time at the sanctuary with Joe and were happy to allow me to spend weekends there. Most kids were going to parties or rock concerts or were involved in sports, but here I was, out with this old man at this nature sanctuary in the Piney Woods, north of Houston. Like my father, Joe had a strong interest in politics and history, and we often engaged in compelling conversations about these topics during our drives to and from the sanctuary.

Before Joe purchased the property, it had belonged to a man who owned a herd of cattle. His cattle had eaten virtually all the understory plants and young trees in the forest with the exception of the sweet gum, yaupon, and pine trees. Joe decided to re-establish the indigenous plants by gathering and scattering their seeds. And so, in my early teens, I became involved with habitat restoration. Over the years, four hundred species of plants were re-introduced and now thrive in the area. A part of Joe's motivation was to create an environment similar to what the Big Thicket Sanctuary had been before its diversity was steadily altered by cattle ranching and tree farms.

On the property, there was a giant tree called the "grandfather magnolia." I loved looking up at its intricate network of crooked branches and smelling its white fragrant blooms during the spring months. Pristine creeks traversed the land. Towering pines, holly, beech, and dogwood trees densely populated the forest. During our outings, I remember seeing all kinds of marvelous birds, such as Indigo and Painted buntings.

One afternoon, we discovered a Hooded Warbler's nest. The nest was constructed of dead leaves, bark, fine grasses, spider webs, and other natural debris. Four small birds huddled in the open cup, their opened mouths tilted toward the sky as they produced a soft chirping chorus in hopes of being fed by their parents. I was immediately taken by the striking black-and-yellow plumage of the male birds. The male's yellow face was framed by black as though it was wearing a hood. The yellow enclosed by the hood was an even richer and brighter shade than that of the bird's underparts. It looked like a bright swath of sunshine.

We also spotted a Swainson's Warbler, a secretive bird that is plain brown above and grayish below with a long pale bill. Found almost exclusively in the southeastern United States, the Swainson's Warbler was discovered new to science in 1832 by the Reverend John Bachman in Charleston, South Carolina, and named by his friend, James Audubon. It remained a "lost" species to science for nearly forty years because no one could find another one.

In 1955, I met Edgar Kincaid Jr., at a gathering of the Texas Ornithological Society. He was to become another one of my mentors. The nephew of the folklorist and writer J. Frank Dobie, Edgar was a legendary figure among birders in Texas. He edited Harry C. Oberholser's massive tome, *The Bird Life of Texas*. Edgar spent fourteen years researching and then editing the three-million-word manuscript down to the one-million words that were finally published as a two-volume set in 1974. He was also one of the charter members of the Travis Audubon Society and the Texas Ornithological Society in Austin, Texas.

Edgar was a tall, slouched man with a pockmarked complexion. His eccentric ways were the stuff of legend around Austin. There was his hoarding habit, for example. Vast piles of magazines, clothes, and other items crowded his home and car. When his car became too cluttered to drive, he would just buy another car.

Over the years, Edgar developed a tradition of bestowing bird names on his close friends. He had christened himself "Cassowary," a large, flightless bird of Australia and New Guinea known for its bellicose behavior. He favored this bird—similar in size to an ostrich—because with its sharp inner toenail, it could disembowel a human with a swift kick. Edgar felt that with all of the grief that birds endured from man, it was good that here was a bird that could strike back. His name later evolved to "World's Oldest Cassowary" or simply "Casso." It was acceptable to suggest a name for yourself if Edgar thought it might be appropriate. I first suggested that my name should be "Green Violetear" because I found this hummingbird to be beautiful with its brilliant colors. A few years later, however, I decided to change my name to "Hooded Warbler." I love all warblers. It seemed appropriate for me because, like warblers, I don't stay in one spot for very long. I'm somewhat peripatetic and full of energy. From then on, my close friends started calling me "Warbler."

Cerulean Warbler
BRAYS BAYOU

I experienced my first "fallout" of warblers when I was a junior at Bellaire High School in 1957. I had heard about fallouts from Joe Heiser and some of the other members of the Outdoor Nature Club. Joe kept a second house on the shore of Galveston Bay, near Kemah. I never visited there, but I remember Joe telling me about the fallouts on certain days during the spring migration, when the area surrounding his home teemed with migrating birds. They stopped there to feed and rest after their long flights over the Gulf of Mexico from Latin America. Strong north winds and rain triggered these fallouts, forcing hundreds and hundreds of birds to land temporarily. These natural events seemed almost unreal to me. A tree harboring ten kinds of warblers was something that I couldn't imagine.

At the time, our house was just a half-block north of Bellaire Boulevard, near the intersection of Bellaire and Buffalo Speedway. Across the street, just south of our house, there was a thirty-acre field. One winter (I walked across the field almost every day after school), I was heading to a dense woodland that bordered Brays Bayou. There I spotted a variety of birds, including titmice, chickadees, woodpeckers, and sparrows. As late March approached, large numbers of Blue-gray Gnatcatchers suddenly populated the woodlands near the edge of the field. In my memory, there were more than a hundred of them. At that point in my life, I had never seen any small bird in such great numbers.

I saw the gnatcatchers for several days in a row. Then, one day, a bright yellow bird appeared among these blue-gray birds. I quickly realized that it was a Blue-winged Warbler, a yellow bird with grayish-blue wings with white wing bars and a black line from the base of its bill through its black eye. It was the first one that I had ever seen, and I was struck by the beauty of this brightly colored bird with its intricate markings.

A few weeks later, on April 9, a heavy rainstorm made its way through Houston one night. The next day after school, I followed my familiar route across the nearby field to the woodland. At that point, I didn't understand the effect that a rainstorm might have on the migrating bird population and that this type of weather might cause a fallout. As I entered the woods, I was aware of a transformation. An energy was present all around me, something I had never before experienced. Everywhere I looked, there were small birds. They were, I realized, warblers. More than fifty moved through the branches of the trees, looking for insects. Adrenaline rushed through my system. I was experiencing my first fallout.

In particular, I remember looking up and seeing a warbler whose upperparts were a remarkable shade of sky blue. Below, it was all white, but across the upper chest was a blue band. The bird reminded me of a miniature Blue Jay, but no Blue Jay embodied the swift movements and lightness of this tiny bird. It was a Cerulean Warbler. Now, this beautiful bird, which figures prominently in Jonathan Franzen's novel, *Freedom*, is one of the most endangered warblers in North America.

I recall that I saw about fifteen different warblers that afternoon, including the beautiful American Redstart. The Cubans call this bird *La Candelita*, the "little candle," because the male Redstart reminds them of a candle's glowing red flame. That afternoon it was hard to pull myself away and walk home.

2

The Tropics

Blue-crowned Motmot
XILITLA, MEXICO

In December 1955, when I was fifteen years old, Armand Yramategui invited my friend, Carl Aiken, and me to travel with him to Mexico for the Xilitla Christmas Bird Count. Xilitla (pronounced *Hill-eet-la*) is a small village nestled amid the limestone mountains and coffee plantations of San Luis Potosí in northeastern Mexico, about 350 miles from the Texas border.

It was my second trip to Mexico. I had taken a trip to Mexico City with my Aunt Claudine's mother, Hazel, and my maternal grandmother, Sallie, but they had been unwilling to stop anywhere for me to look at birds because they were afraid of being attacked. It was frustrating to me to glimpse interesting birds perched on telephone wires and not have the opportunity to look at them.

In contrast, Armand was thoroughly at ease in Mexico. He spoke fluent Spanish and reached out to many of the people we encountered during our travels. The trip was ten hours from Houston to Monterrey, and we were packed, along with Armand's parents, into his blue Nash Rambler. We drove nonstop except to buy gas, eat, and use the restroom. Carl and I sat quietly in the back seat with Armand's mother, surrounded by piles of bulging suitcases, clothes, and gifts. His parents were spending the Christmas holiday with his mother's relatives in Monterrey.

From there, Armand, Carl, and I continued an hour south to Montemorelos, arriving at a small motel after dark. The next morning I woke up, walked outside, and took in the smells of the tropical landscape, not at all like those of Houston. The air was sweet and fragrant, like the scent of flowers blooming or oranges ripening. A lizard skittered across my path. The air felt vibrant and alive. I felt like I had crossed over into another world, a tropical world.

That morning, we drove south for about two hundred miles to a little town called Tamazunchale, which is right where the Pan-American Highway begins to climb into the Sierra Madre Oriental.

The eminent naturalists Roger Tory Peterson and James Fisher had visited Xilitla in 1953 on the coast-to-coast excursion chronicled in *Wild America: The Record of a 30,000-Mile Journey Around the Continent by a Distinguished Naturalist and His British Colleague* (1955). This memoir details the two men's travels from Newfoundland to Mexico and from Texas to Alaska.

Xilitla was known for its variety of habitats, a requirement for any successful bird count. The Xilitla count area represents a typical strip across the mountain range. It receives abundant rain, about a hundred inches annually during the late summer and autumn. Within a short distance from the banks of the Axtla River, the dirt road traverses various habitats that include a diverse mix of plants and birds. There are habitats ranging from lower elevations at about five hundred feet along the lush banks of the Axtla River to elevations of twenty-two-hundred feet, where there are patches of remnant cloud forests. These different bands, or slices, of elevations are referred to as "life zones," a concept first developed by the scientist Alexander von Humboldt. Every thousand feet or so, the plant life and animals change due to shifts in climate and temperature.

A longtime birder, naturalist, and the founder of the Xilitla Christmas Bird Count, Irby Davis had helped start a local chapter of the Audubon Society in the Rio Grande Valley. He was an expert on Mexican birds and one of the first amateur ornithologists to record bird songs for the Cornell Laboratory of Ornithology. In summer 1958, right after I graduated from high school, Carl and I worked as assistants to Davis. We recorded bird sounds for the Library of Natural Sounds at Cornell University during a two-month, five-thousand-mile expedition from Harlingen, around the Gulf of California, down the entire length of Baja, California, and later farther north to British Columbia.

During Davis's inaugural count in 1950, the birders listed 230 species in a single day within a fifteen-mile circle centered in Xilitla; this was the largest Christmas count recorded in Mexico or North America. On the day before the 1955 count, we drove up a dirt road from the river into the mountains and stopped at a spot where there was a deep ravine. A steady stream trickled down the side of the mountain. In the trees above the road, we spotted a flock of eight Emerald Toucanets. It was the first member of the toucan family that I had ever seen. The Emerald Toucanet is a beautiful light-green bird with a long black-and-yellow bill. It makes a loud, harsh barking call. This toucanet—like a number of toucans—eats the eggs and the young of other birds, as well as wild figs and other fruit. A researcher discovered that it was one of the main predators of the eggs and young of the Resplendent Quetzal. Toucanets roost and nest inside the holes of trees; in fact, more than one toucanet will roost in a hole, one piling on top of the other.

I was immediately taken by the lovely color of these toucanets. The birds hopped from branch to branch. The giant trees were laced with bromeliads, mosses, and orchids. Later, we spotted clear-winged butterflies fluttering along the roadside. Their wings were entirely transparent except for a cinnamon-colored border. (In Spanish, this kind of butterfly is called *espejitos*, which means "little mirrors.")

While we were participating in the count on Christmas Day, I wandered off the trail into the cloud forest. This was primary forest, so there was very little undergrowth, making it easy to maneuver through the enormous stands of trees. As I walked along, I flushed a bird from the forest floor and it rocketed off with a great explosion. It turned out to be a Thicket Tinamou. After this startling encounter, I decided it might be a good idea to head back to the trail and find Armand and Carl. As I walked through the old-growth forest, I didn't know which way to go to get back to the trail. All the trees and growth looked the same to me. Later, I would learn that this can be a common experience in tropical forests. If you don't keep a close watch on where you're going, it's easy for the forest to close behind you. It might not be clear where you came from because everything looks the same. Often there is a dense canopy of trees overhead, so you can't discern the sun to figure out where you started.

As I was wandering, lost, at age fifteen, in the cloud forest, I grew increasingly anxious. I was worried about finding my friends. At that exact moment, I spotted a bird in a nearby bush. Through my binoculars, I could see only its head, framed by leaves and branches. Its crown was iridescent blue. Soon, I was able to see more of this enchanting bird: Its breast was a rich cinnamon, and a black mask, bordered by turquoise, surrounded its red eyes. The bird had a heavy beak that was serrated, looking as though it bore sharp teeth. I realized I was looking at a Blue-crowned Motmot (now called Blue-capped). It was sitting only thirty feet away from where I stood. My anxiety quickly transformed into excitement.

The Blue-capped Motmot belongs to the family by the same name (*Motmotidae*). They are in the order of the Coraciiformes. This order includes some of the most striking and beautiful birds in the world, such as the kingfishers, rollers, and bee-eaters. Like most members of this family, motmots nest in holes that they dig in a bank along a hillside. Sometimes an observer might notice mud on a motmot's beak because it has been digging a burrow. Many motmots grow central tail feathers that are longer than their other tail feathers. These feathers are often iridescent blue and green. When the motmots are young, they don't have the longer feathers. As they get older, these central feathers grow longer than the bird's other tail feathers. As they preen these feathers to clean them, the central section falls away, resulting in long central tail feathers that end in racquets. Sometimes, they swing their tail like the pendulum of a grandfather clock.

I continued to gaze at this motmot. It was a striking bird. During this moment, I became totally absorbed in admiring the beauty of the motmot. This was one of the best presents I had ever received, and I received it on Christmas Day in this wild, magnificent place. After reveling in the beauty of the Blue-capped Motmot, I walked in the direction where I thought the trail was—and to my great relief, I found it, and then Carl and Armand, and we continued the count.

The day after the count, we were birding near Xilitla. Armand initiated a conversation with a farmer. He told the man that we had come to his region to look for birds. This man told Armand that three days walking to the west was a valley that contained a forest with trees so large that it would take three men to reach around their trunks. He also said there were monkeys in the forest. Armand told Carl and me what the man had said. We all wished that we could go there, but that was not possible. At that point in my life, I had never thought of experiencing such a wild place, and this conversation planted a seed in my mind. I began to dream of being able to walk among the giant trees of a pristine tropical forest.

We drove north and stayed in Nuevo Morelos along the Pan-American Highway. As we traveled west toward the Sierra Madre Oriental, we came to a small town called El Naranjo. Armand explained that he had something special to show Carl and me as he drove down a gravel side road. Near the end of the road, we arrived at a spectacular waterfall. Pristine water cascaded a hundred feet down from its narrow precipice. Having grown up in Houston, I had never seen a waterfall before. I was transfixed by the continuous movement of the water, the loud rush and tumble of it all, the churn produced in the sparkling pool below.

"Let's go on farther down the road—and see what else we see," Armand said.

We rounded a bend in the road—and there was El Salto, a three-hundred-foot waterfall, about two hundred feet across, with white water pouring down dramatic cliffs into a series of crystal-clear pools that flowed over travertine terraces. Large Montezuma cypress trees bordered the river. A flock of two hundred or more White-collared Swifts circled above the waterfall. We soon realized they were nesting behind the falls. As we quietly stood there, we witnessed the birds plunge through the tumbling waters to their nests. Their movement was as dramatic and spectacular as the waterfall itself. This species was a large black swift with a distinctive white collar and pointed black wings. Small flocks of Green Parakeets, a brilliantly colored medium-sized parrot, flew overhead.

We also spotted a Bat Falcon perched in the trees below the falls. I later learned that these small dark falcons launch aerial attacks on the swifts and eat them as part of their diet, which also includes large insects and bats. Bat Falcons are adept and powerful flyers. They can accelerate and turn quickly, making it difficult for their prey to outmaneuver them. With a rusty breast, white throat, and yellow bare skin around the eye, this species is among the most beautiful of falcons.

The waterfalls—and all these birds—were a truly awesome sight. Sadly, El Salto is now dried up due to the building of a hydroelectric plant. And though I traveled to the area on multiple occasions, I only had a chance to see these dramatic falls a few more times.

The next day, we drove farther west on the Pan-American Highway. We climbed along a low range of hills into the Sierra Madre. During this drive, we stopped on the side of the road and took in the expansive valley completely filled with sabal palms. A Common Black Hawk sat in the lower branches of one of the palm trees. The trees hadn't been cut for agriculture yet, giving us the opportunity to see an area of Mexico that was relatively unchanged at that point.

Armand continued to drive higher into the mountains. We reached a region where some of the land had been cleared for crops. At this point, we entered a dense fog. We could hardly see for more than twenty yards. When we got out of the car to stretch, we heard the call of a bird that sounded like a parrot some distance away. I decided to walk toward the sound and found myself behind a small house with a chinaberry tree in its backyard. A magnificent pair of Military Macaws, with long beautiful tails of red, blue, and green, rested on its branches, feeding on the fruit of the tree just above my head. Their bodies were bright green, with bare white facial skin, and small red feathers immediately above their beaks. Carl and Armand joined me in marveling at this pair of wonderful birds, the first macaws any of us had ever seen.

The great ornithologist Frank M. Chapman expressed best how I feel about the tropics. In his book, *My Tropical Air Castle: Nature Studies in Panama* (1929), he wrote:

> For my own northern woods and fields I have the affection born of long and close association; but they lack the romance, the mystery, the enchantment, the inexhaustible possibilities of tropical forests. . . . One forms a lasting and intimate friendship with nature in the north, but falls hopelessly in love with her in the south. But even while she lures she repels and perhaps herein lays her endless fascination. One is never quite sure of her. Her most winsome aspect may be deceptive, or it may be a dream of rare delight.

3

Freeport Christmas Count

Rose-breasted Grosbeak

FREEPORT, TEXAS

One beautiful Saturday morning in spring 1957, I was birding with Carl Aiken and Armand Yramategui in Galveston. The sun was coming up as we stood on the beach at the southeastern tip of Galveston Island, looking at hundreds of shorebirds. A flock of Brown Pelicans flew over San Luis Pass, the body of water that separates Galveston Island from the mainland. Armand said, "Someone should start a Christmas Count at Freeport."

As we continued to look at this myriad of birds, Armand pointed across the water toward Freeport and explained why he thought this was a good idea. The Freeport area offered a wide array of habitats due to its unique geographic location bordered by the Gulf Coast, beaches, and the jetties on either side of the mouth of the Brazos River. The terrain also included open cattle-grazing fields, dense woodlands, old groves of live oaks and salt-cedar thickets, and swampy marshes. The town of Lake Jackson, which had been developed for employees of the Dow Chemical Company in 1942, was close to Freeport and encompassed about five thousand acres of the former Abner Jackson Plantation. Because of this varied landscape, a Freeport count circle could include many different kinds of habitat, which would offer enormous potential for sightings of land and water birds.

Armand's suggestion sounded like a good idea to me, so I started to organize the very first Freeport Count. I chose December 31, 1957, for our count day. I recruited seven other birders to join me. Like other Audubon Christmas Bird Counts around the state and country, we followed a similar set of rules. Our area consisted of a circle of fifteen miles in diameter. The southern part of the circle was the Gulf of Mexico, near the mouth of the Brazos River, including a small portion of the Gulf, and then went north to about five miles south of Angleton, Texas. Our primary emphasis was on accurate identification and census of all birds seen, so I encouraged our group to cover their count area slowly and methodically. With unusual sightings, it was recommended that birders record all the species' field marks on the spot.

We started at dawn, and our small group of eight formed two parties: Some of us went east of the highway and the rest traveled to areas to the west. We covered as much territory as we could before dusk. Although we only traversed a fraction of the approximately 175 square miles, we counted 110 species and came in fourteenth in the United States that year. Some of the highlights of that first count included a sighting of a Bald Eagle, two Snowy Plovers, and an Eastern Towhee. Reflecting back on this time of my life, I am surprised that, at age sixteen, I was able to organize an important Christmas Count.

Then again, perhaps the personal characteristic that has helped me most in my life is persistence. After the first count, I continued to organize and compile the Freeport Count year after year. I recruited more people, including birders from other parts of Texas and the country. To draw observers from other parts of the state, I emphasized the goal of making a Texas count the number one in the country. Over the next fifteen years or so, the count grew from eight observers to more than a hundred. Even after I transferred from Rice University to the University of Texas to study zoology and botany and then went to Harvard to study government, I continued to organize and compile the Freeport Count with help from Nancy and Jerry Strickling. The Stricklings were avid birders and close friends of mine. They were devoted to the Freeport Count, playing a significant role in keeping the count going when I was away at school.

Over the years, I developed a basic strategy to ensure repeated success: To cover the Freeport area, the participants were divided into about eight groups, each led by an expert. Each group was given a geographic area approximating about fifteen square miles, which they would cover by car and on foot. First, most of the bread-and-butter birds must be sighted. Since about 1960, the same basic 136 species have turned up every year, which illustrates the huge diversity of this area's common bird population. Second, there is a group of essential species, birds that are seen on most counts in low numbers and require work to locate. These essential species are key to a successful high count. Finally, there are the few bonus birds that are rare and unexpected. During the past forty-five years, these birds usually send the day's total over the two-hundred-species mark.

Over time, I have developed a standard protocol for these unusual sightings: A committee of four experts cross-examines every birder who has reported a rare species. The answers to these questions reveal whether or not he or she knew the bird well enough to have recognized it and had sufficient time and light for an accurate observation. If the committee feels that wasn't the case, the bird is not recorded in the count total.

Our number of annual birders increased due to more people moving to Lake Jackson in order to work for Dow Chemical. Some of these employees were interested in birds and started to join us on the count year after year. Also, Dow Chemical opened up their land to the Freeport Count so we could also survey those areas. Because of these efforts, the Freeport Count often listed among the top two or three in the United States in the total number of species sighted. During the late sixties into the seventies, the competition for the highest count was among three places in California (San Diego, Santa Barbara, and Point Reyes); Cocoa Beach, Florida, where wildlife photographer and naturalist Allan Cruickshank was the field marshal; and our count in Freeport, Texas. As one 1965 recruiting flier for the Freeport Count advertised: "We Shall Overcome. Down with Cruickshank and Cocoa."

In 1971, we sighted birds that normally winter farther south. We saw western birds that had wandered farther east. We saw birds from the north that sometimes don't reach our area until later in the winter. It was a perfect situation for a record count. We had a large number of people. Among those participating were some very distinguished birders from around the state and the country, including Bill Graber, who has participated in our count for more than fifty years; Joe Taylor, treasurer of the American Birding Association (ABA); and Jim Tucker, who started the ABA in 1969. Another participant, Ted Parker, eighteen at the time and one of the top young birders, was hoping to break the Big Year record that year. (A Big Year is an informal competition among birders to see who can identify the most species of birds within a single calendar year in North America.) He set the new North American record with 627 species.

Ted and I birded together that day. We saw the rarely observed Greater Scaup, a medium-sized diving duck, at the end of the rocky jetty in Freeport. I had met Ted the previous year when he was birding in Texas, but never had the opportunity to go birding with him. It was a treat to spend a day in the field with such an accomplished and enthusiastic young birder. Like me, Ted appreciated every bird we saw.

That night, we assembled at a roadside café called Jack's Restaurant in Rosharon, which is halfway between Freeport and Houston. We sat at long tables arranged in rows. The air was full of anticipation as I read aloud the birds sighted that day. I was astounded to find that 235 species were reported, the highest total ever recorded in any Christmas Count in North America. Upon cross-examination, the committee decided that details submitted for nine species were not adequate. As a result, our official count was lowered to 226, but that number was still an all-time national record.

This impressive milestone led to another fortuitous moment in my life. The editor of *Audubon Magazine*, Les Line, decided to send

George Plimpton to Freeport the following year to write about the count. George was interested because he practiced participatory journalism, taking readers inside specific worlds. He "tried out" a variety of professions: professional athlete (boxer, pitcher, quarterback, tennis player, golfer, ice hockey goalie); musician for the New York Philharmonic; and circus aerialist, among others. His participation as a backup quarterback at the Detroit Lions preseason training camp was the subject of his well-known book, *Paper Lion* (1966). Les decided that George should not only go on the Freeport since it had set a new national record, but also on a bird count in Maine where very few species were seen.

In the opening of his November 1973 article about the Freeport Count, George wrote:

> I should admit at the outset that my credentials as a birdwatcher are slightly sketchy. True, bird-watching *is* a hobby, and if pressed I tell people that I truly enjoy it: on picnics I pack along a pair of binoculars and the Peterson field guide. But I am not very good at it. . . . As a birder, I have often thought of myself as rather like a tone-deaf person with just a lesson or two in his background who enjoys playing the flute—it's probably mildly pleasurable, but the results are uncertain.

I picked George up at the Houston airport. He was a tall and lanky man who was, I quickly discovered, very pleasant and personable. We drove to Surfside, a small Gulf Coast town, where some of the participants were staying in rental beach cottages. (We had ninety-five birders participating in our count that year.) The next morning, I decided that George and I would cover various sections of the count circle. We woke up before the first light and drove to an area known as Big Slough, a narrow waterway that widens into a small lake. As dawn brightened the morning sky, we walked along a levee that bordered the slough. We spotted a variety of different ducks— including Gadwalls, Canvasbacks, and Northern Pintails—on the pond's rippled surface.

During the day, we visited a number of other areas in the count circle. Late in the afternoon, we walked along the west bank of the

Brazos River in an area that we called "Sheriff's Woods" because the property was owned by the Brazoria County sheriff who gave us permission to observe birds there. We spotted a small flock of Myrtle Warblers (now called Yellow-rumped Warblers) feeding on the ground. To my amazement, among these mostly gray birds was a brightly plumaged male Magnolia Warbler, which had never before been sighted on the Freeport Count. This species normally winters in southern Mexico and Central America.

"My God, no, look," I said to George.

George peered through his binoculars.

"It's a Magnolia Warbler," I exclaimed. "Don't you see it? It's a first ever on this count. I can't believe it."

Shortly thereafter, we walked into an open field surrounded by woodlands on all sides. Sitting near the top of a tree on the other side, I spotted a male Rose-breasted Grosbeak. The sun hit its red breast, enhancing its already beautiful color. Once again, this was a very rare species that normally winters in southern Mexico. By this point, I was even more transfixed and excited. George wrote of this encounter in his *Audubon* article:

> In midafternoon Emanuel spots a bird in the top of a tree. He begins swaying back and forth in his excitement. "Oh my." Without taking his eyes from his binoculars, he motions me forward.
>
> "A Harris's Sparrow?" I ask.
>
> "It's better," he whispers. "Much better. It's a Rose-breasted Grosbeak. No one else will get this. Oh, terrific. It's only been seen once before on the count." We stare at the bird. I can see the wash of pink at its throat. When it flies, the sun makes it blaze, and then oddly, a barn owl floats out of the trees behind it.

Reagan Bradshaw, the photographer from *Texas Monthly*, captured a picture of me when I discovered the grosbeak. Later a friend of mine, Nadine Eckhardt, was looking at the same image and commented, "You looked like you just saw Jesus Christ." And I said, "Actually, it was a Rose-breasted Grosbeak."

That evening, we congregated at Jack's Restaurant again for the tabulation dinner. As we went through the list and confirmed the two-hundredth bird (a Parula Warbler), everyone cheered and applauded with great enthusiasm. That year, Freeport and Cocoa Beach matched up with the same tally of 209 species in an unprecedented tie. (The three major counts in California had been hurt by cold weather; San Diego and Santa Barbara tied with 195 species each.)

The following year, in 1973, Kenn Kaufman, age sixteen, decided to come on the Freeport Count. After much consideration, I assigned him to spend the day at the end of the Surfside Jetty and gave him Edgar Kincaid's fine Balscope to use. I determined that it would be an ideal spot for observing such seabirds as jaegers and gannets, as well as various species of scoters that were only present offshore, making it difficult to record them. This jetty is mostly made up of massive stone blocks and extends for about a mile out into the Gulf of Mexico. It runs parallel to another similar jetty about a hundred yards away, creating a ship channel that leads into the inner harbor. It was a windy day, and the waves were crashing violently. Kenn positioned himself and Edgar's Balscope at the very tip of the jetty. Herring and Ring-billed Gulls hung on the strong updrafts. Then, as the breakers grew higher, he spotted a Black-legged Kittiwake, a rare bird in Texas. As Kenn describes in his wonderful book *Kingbird Highway* (1997), a rogue wave suddenly crashed over the jetty and swept him and Edgar's prized Balscope into the Gulf of Mexico. The scope was lost, but, fortunately, Kenn was able to pull himself up over the rocks that lined the jetty. He was soaked, and the barnacles on the rocks had sliced his hands. Kenn walked back to the shore and into a nearby café. The waitresses were a bit stunned to see this thoroughly soaked young man with bloody hands.

After cleaning up, he returned to the jetty to spend the rest of the day trying to spot more birds. "The borrowed telescope was gone, my hands were bandaged, and my cheap binoculars were clouded with salt water, but I was keeping my vigil," Kenn wrote in *Kingbird Highway*. "I could still see rare seabirds if they came in close. As the afternoon waned, the sun might find a break in the clouds, and then it would be low in the western sky behind me—flooding everything in front of me with perfect light."

Like his good friend Ted Parker, Kenn set a new national record with 671 species identified during a Big Year, which he concluded in Freeport with our bird count. I was honored to have him participate in our count despite his encounter with the turbulent sea. That day, Kenn exhibited two of the key characteristics of any good birder on a Christmas count—perseverance and endurance.

4

The Bird of My Life

Eskimo Curlew
GALVESTON ISLAND, TEXAS

On the evening of March 22, 1959, Ben Feltner, another Houston-based birder, called me. It was a call that I'll never forget: Ben told me that he and Dudley Deaver had spotted a bird in a short-grass prairie on West Galveston Island that they had identified as an Eskimo Curlew. It was among a flock of Long-billed Curlews and Golden-Plovers, but was noticeably smaller in size. Also, its bill was much thinner and shorter than the bill of a Whimbrel.

This was stunning news! I had read in bird books about this small curlew, and often the account ended with the phrase "probably extinct." A sighting of this extremely rare bird hadn't been documented in the United States since April 17, 1915, in Norfolk, Nebraska. In the late 1800s, the Eskimo Curlew had become the target of choice for market hunters, with often thousands being killed during a single hunt. The result: near extinction. My mentor Joe Heiser and two other observers had seen two Eskimo Curlews on West Galveston in spring 1945, but no photographs were obtained to document their sighting.

Ben had moved to Houston from England a few years earlier. We had met through the Outdoor Nature Club and he was a few years older than I was. Because of our common interests, we became fast friends and often birded together. So I knew that Ben was a careful and skilled observer. Since he did not own a car, his birding was often confined to the Jacinto City and Galina Park area, where he lived. One of his friends, Dudley Deaver, did own a car, and although Dudley was not a birder, he offered to take Ben on his first trip to Galveston Island. One of the birds that Ben was hoping to see on that trip was a Whimbrel, a species that breeds in Canada and Alaska and is found during migration mainly in coastal areas. On West Galveston, they located Ben's lifer Whimbrel in a marshy wetland area.

Then they drove farther out onto the island. In those days, West Galveston was still a relatively underdeveloped area, with very few houses or other buildings populating its windswept landscape. They came across a coastal prairie grazed by cattle, making it the perfect habitat for American Golden-Plovers and Upland Sandpipers. Ben and Dudley stopped to take a look at a flock of Golden-Plovers that fed in the short-grass field not far from the road's shoulder. Among the Golden-Plovers, they spotted a small curlew that resembled the Whimbrel they had seen earlier in the day, but it was buffier, smaller, and had a less decurved bill. Based on these field marks, they concluded it was an Eskimo Curlew.

I decided *not* to go look for the bird Ben and Dudley had seen. It was the spring of my freshman year at Rice University. I was a full-time student, studying biology, history, German, and English, and I was still trying to figure out exactly what I wanted to major in. The academic demands made it difficult for me to get away. Moreover, I knew Ben's observational skills, so I didn't doubt his identification.

After hearing this news, I called Armand to report Ben's sighting. The next day, he drove to Galveston, but didn't find the bird that Ben had seen. I thought it must have moved on and was perhaps now somewhere in the Great Plains, en route to the tundra of northwestern Canada. On April 5, I drove to Galveston with Ben, Ronald Fowler, and a few other friends from the local ornithology group. We weren't looking for the Eskimo Curlew that Ben and Dudley had seen; we were just going birding for the day.

We had driven only a few miles west of the city when we encountered a field teeming with shorebirds about six miles east of the field where Ben and Dudley had observed the Eskimo Curlew. I pulled over to the side of the road so we could scan the field and see what species were there. The short-grass pasture was dotted with fresh cow pies and surrounded by a barbed-wire fence. Among the many shorebirds in the field were American Golden-Plovers, Black-bellied Plovers, Upland Sandpipers, Killdeer, Whimbrels, Long-billed Curlews, Buff-breasted Sandpipers, Lesser Yellowlegs, and Pectoral Sandpipers. Thanks to the recent dairy cattle droppings, the field was rich in invertebrate life, which provided an abundance of food for these birds. When I put up my binoculars, I immediately saw a small buffy curlew. I told my friends that we needed to get out of the car and set up our Bushnell scopes. It was about ten o'clock in the morning, and the sun was shining brightly. Looking at this small curlew through our scopes, we all agreed that it looked very different from the nearby Whimbrels. As we continued to study the bird and then rotated our scopes fifteen degrees to look at a Whimbrel, we became even more excited. We thought that maybe this was the Eskimo Curlew that Ben and Dudley had seen almost two weeks earlier.

One of my mentors, Edgar Kincaid, taught me to look for every possible field mark when identifying a rare bird. Our Peterson field guide emphasized that in contrast to the Whimbrel's gray legs, Eskimo Curlews had darkish green legs. (This description was written by Ludlow Griscom, an American ornithologist who pioneered the field of ornithology and often was referred to as the "Dean of Birdwatchers.") The book also described the call of Eskimo Curlew as a clear whistling sound. Because we couldn't see the leg color from where we were standing, we decided to climb through the fence and walk out into the pasture. In our eagerness to nail down this unusual sighting, we trespassed, a cardinal sin for which one can be arrested or shot in Texas.

Once we got closer to the bird, we could see that it had bluish-gray legs. Our approach disturbed the birds and caused some to take flight, including the small curlew. Ben said he heard the bird call and that it sounded something like a Whimbrel. Then I thought I heard a gunshot. We left the field as quickly as possible and drove away.

We spent the rest of the day birding Galveston, but I couldn't get that small curlew out of my mind. "What was it?" I thought. "It couldn't have been a Whimbrel. It looked too different." As we drove back to Houston in the dark, I thought, "You have blown it. You drove away from the rarest bird you will ever see." I was kicking myself.

The next day, in Rice University's Fondren Library, I read the account of the Eskimo Curlew in *Birds of Massachusetts and Other New England States* (1925) by Edward Howe Forbush, a noted Massachusetts ornithologist, prolific writer, and one of the founders of the Massachusetts Audubon Society. I was surprised to read Forbush's description of the leg color of the Eskimo Curlew as bluish-gray. That convinced me that the bird we had seen was, in fact, an Eskimo Curlew.

Two days later, I decided to return to Galveston, hoping to spend more time studying the small curlew we had seen. I drove there alone, wondering all the way if the bird would still be there. Often in the spring, migrating birds only stop for a day or two since they are eager to reach their breeding grounds. To my great relief, when I arrived at the field, the small curlew was still there. This time, I approached the dairy farmer who owned the property and asked for permission to wander into his field. He readily granted it. Later, the farmer told me that, as a boy in the late 1800s, he regularly saw and hunted flocks of the small curlews in these fields. Doubtlessly, those were Eskimo Curlews. I wish that I had asked him for more details about the curlew flocks that he saw.

Slowly, I walked out into the field, taking care not to scare away the birds, especially the small curlew. Its richly colored buff feathers were different from any other curlew that I had ever seen. It was feeding in the southeastern corner of the field. I edged closer. In one extraordinary moment, I managed to get a Whimbrel, a Long-billed Curlew, and the small curlew in the view of my scope. How I wish I had photographed that unforgettable scene—one that perhaps no birder or scientist had ever seen or will ever see again.

After spending two hours observing the small bird, I was convinced that it was an Eskimo Curlew. As I drove back to Houston, I thought, "No one may ever accept this observation, but I know I have seen an Eskimo Curlew." Back then, few birders took photographs of birds, and it didn't occur to me to find someone who would try to obtain photographs.

What did occur to me was to show the bird to George Williams. George taught English at Rice University, but was also passionate about ornithology. He wrote many articles about birds and migration for scientific journals, helped to establish the Houston Museum of Natural Science, and started a newsletter in the forties called *The Gulf Coast Migrant*. For a number of years, he and George Lowery, a professor of zoology, director of the Louisiana State University Museum of Natural Science, and one of the preeminent ornithologists, wrote articles in *The Auk*, the official quarterly journal of the American Ornithologists' Union, debating the question of circum-Gulf versus trans-Gulf migration. Williams defended the position that most migrants travel around the Gulf, while Lowery supported the idea that most birds migrate over the Gulf. I thought that if I could show the small curlew to George Williams, the record might be accepted.

On April 10, George and I drove to Galveston. The bird I thought was an Eskimo Curlew was still in the field where, a few days earlier, I had observed it. After a lengthy study of the small curlew, George agreed with my conclusion that it was probably an Eskimo Curlew, but felt that we could not conclusively rule out the possibility that it was the first North American record of a Little Curlew, an Asian species that in the fifties was known as the Least Curlew, Pygmy Curlew, or Little Whimbrel.

At that time, some ornithologists listed Little Curlew as a subspecies of Eskimo Curlew. Edgar Kincaid owned a book on Japanese birds that contained a description of Little Curlew. The book was written in Japanese, and Edgar had asked a Japanese woman to translate the Little Curlew account. The text mentioned two distinguishing features:

- The scales on both sides of the tarsi (or the long foot bones that lead to a bird's toes) of a Little Curlew are arranged in horizontal plates, whereas in an Eskimo Curlew, the scales on the posterior side of the tarsi are hexagonal in shape, resulting in a pattern that resembles a fishing net. (Obviously, we couldn't observe this pattern in the field, even with high-powered scopes.)
- Eskimo Curlew has reddish-cinnamon axillars (the feathers located at the "armpits" of a bird's wing), while the axillars of Little Curlew are pinkish buff. (Our bird had reddish-cinnamon axillars.)

George decided to write a note, which was published in *The Auk*, titled "A Probable Record of an Eskimo Curlew." Over the next few weeks, an Eskimo Curlew continued to be observed either in the pasture where we had first seen it on April 5 or in the field where Ben and Dudley had discovered it on March 22. When Ben saw the bird in the pasture, he commented that it looked different from the bird that he and Dudley had found two weeks earlier. That bird had a shorter, straighter bill than the bird we found on April 5. It seems very likely that two were present in 1959, though neither was photographed nor seen at the same time.

Remarkably, only about two dozen avid birders made the journey to Galveston to see the Eskimo Curlew. Today birders can refer to multiple numbers and websites prior to making a trip into the field, but in the fifties, there was no hotline alerting birders to rare bird sightings. Most of the observers who saw the Eskimo Curlew lived in Houston, but a handful of birders traveled from Austin, including my friends Edgar Kincaid, Fred and Marie Webster, Frank Oatman, Rose Ann Rowlett, and John Rowlett. (I had met Frank, Rose Ann, and John at a meeting of the Texas Ornithological Society in 1955, and was thrilled to meet a trio of fellow birders close to my age.) Happily, Armand did see the curlew on April 26, 1959—in fact, he was the last person to see it that year on Galveston Island.

My most memorable observation of the curlew came on April 10, 1960. I drove to Galveston with my friend, Ernest P. (Buck) Edwards, an ornithologist who had recently moved to Houston to become the associate curator of the Houston Museum of Natural Science. We drove first to the pasture at the junction of 7 Mile Road and Stewart Road where the Eskimo Curlew was seen on April 5, but the bird was nowhere to be found. Then we drove farther out on the island to the field where Ben and Dudley had first found it on March 22. No luck.

As we started back to Houston, I suggested to Buck that we check the 7 Mile Road pasture again. Again, no luck. We were just about to return home when we spotted a flock of ten Golden-Plovers flying along the dune line in our direction. They were traveling from the western end of the island. Even at a distance, I could see that there was a larger bird among them. Right away, I knew it was likely the Eskimo Curlew, as the species was known to migrate with Golden-Plovers. The flock flew closer and closer. Fortuitously, the birds landed in the field directly in front of us.

It was an extraordinary sight.

As the flock alighted, the small curlew raised its wings, enabling us to see clearly its reddish-cinnamon axillars. It was only twenty or thirty yards away. The bird probed its beak into a clump of bunch grass and then walked on. The late afternoon sun was behind us, bathing this small buffy bird in a lovely light. The curlew was, in fact, an Eskimo Curlew. Buck and I had seen a sight from the history of these two species—an Eskimo Curlew and a flock of Golden-Plovers flying together. It's likely that no one had witnessed such a sight for many years—and I doubt anyone will ever see this again.

As it turned out, at least one Eskimo Curlew was reported on Galveston Island each spring until 1964, when two Eskimo Curlews were last seen in the area. The birds weren't together but were observed at the same time in fields that were five to ten miles apart. In April 1962, Don Bleitz, a bird photographer, traveled to Galveston from Los Angeles and obtained the only photographs ever taken of the species. Careful analysis of those photographs confirms that potentially four different birds were present.

Despite searches later in the sixties and over the decades, no other Eskimo Curlews have been reliably reported from Galveston Island and none have been photographed since 1962. In succeeding years, there have been reports from various locations in the United States and Canada, but none of these birds were documented by photograph or specimen. In fact, the only other Eskimo Curlew documented in the sixties was a lone bird shot by a hunter on Barbados on September 4, 1963.

Since my last sighting on April 10, 1962, I have seen more than six thousand species of birds, including many stunning ones, but that small curlew will always be "the bird of my life."

5

Beginnings

Northern Bobwhite Quail
OUTSKIRTS OF HOUSTON

When I was young and people asked me what I wanted to do when I grew up, my answer was usually that I wanted to be a farmer or a forest ranger because I thought both these occupations would give me the chance to be outdoors. As I approached my college years, I realized that neither profession was what I really wanted to do with my life. At Rice, I decided to study biology, thinking that I might become a research scientist and teacher. After two years there, my biology professor, Dr. Joseph Davies, encouraged me to transfer to the University of Texas because its biology program included studies in zoology and botany. The biology program at Rice at that time emphasized pre-med.

After graduation from the University of Texas, I received a National Science Foundation scholarship. I decided to pursue graduate work in ornithology with Dr. Frank Pitelka, a leading ornithologist and expert in behavioral ecology at the University of California, Berkeley. That summer, before packing up and moving west, I experienced a moment of truth: I spent a significant amount of time reading articles in ornithological journals, and it became clear to me that my fascination with birds was more about appreciating them, watching them, enjoying their colors and songs, and not about doing the kind of research that required detailed observations to collect large volumes of scientific data. I recognized that my interest was more in the spirit of eighteenth-century individuals, like Gilbert White (1720–1793), who wrote *The Natural History of Selborne* (1789). White maintained a passionate fascination with birds—the kind of nests they built, their migration patterns, and their plumage markings—but not at the level that would involve many months studying one particular bird and writing a detailed paper based on those studies.

I turned down the scholarship and wrote to Dr. Pitelka, explaining my decision. Given all these changes, I still had a hard time figuring out what I wanted to do because I had so many interests. This has been a blessing in my life: I'm interested in history, politics, classics, languages, evolution, biology, social issues, and literature. In the end, I decided to study political science because my father had instilled in me an appreciation for the importance and the impact of current events and public affairs. He had encouraged me to get involved as a volunteer in political campaigns when I was a teenager. I attended many political events with him, including the first political gathering in Houston attended by both Anglos and African-Americans. It was there, at the Shamrock Hilton Hotel, that I met Eleanor Roosevelt.

Given this background, it seemed a natural choice to study political science with the intention of becoming a professor in that field. I decided to remain at the University of Texas as a fifth-year student taking courses in political science. Later that year, I was awarded a Woodrow Wilson Scholarship and accepted into graduate school in government at Harvard.

Although I loved many aspects of my years at Harvard, I came to realize that I wasn't well suited to academia. Long hours in the library doing research or in the classroom teaching did not satisfy my deep desire to be out in nature. While at Harvard, I met Peter Alden through the Massachusetts Audubon Society. About my age, Peter had saved his money and traveled the world, looking at birds. He later wrote about his adventures in *Finding Birds Around the*

World (1981). The book, written with John Gooders, became the first world travel guide for birders.

Peter and I sometimes birded at Mount Auburn Cemetery, a 174-acre stretch of rural, rolling hills on the geographical boundary between Cambridge and Watertown, Massachusetts. It's one of the best places in the Boston area for springtime birding. During one of our outings, Peter told me that the Massachusetts Audubon Society had established a natural history tour program and hired him as a tour leader. I was intrigued by the fact that he would be paid to travel to show birds to Audubon members.

In summer 1967, when it came time to work on my dissertation, I returned to Houston because my topic was the political culture of Dallas and Houston. Around the same time, an old friend, George Oser, asked me to manage his campaign for the Houston school board, and I accepted his offer. Then followed seven years working as a political organizer, concentrating on school board politics, and working with Citizens for Good Schools, a school reform movement that I helped to found. All the while, I continued my birding activities.

Toward the end of the sixties, when I was working at the Institute for Urban Studies at the University of Houston, Peter Alden passed through town on his way back from a trip. We had lunch together, and he recounted many stories about his most recent adventures. It was spring, and a rainstorm had caused some migrating birds to stop over in a wooded lot near my office. We decided to visit the area after lunch. As we walked through the leafing trees, Peter and I spotted a number of colorful small birds, including Scarlet Tanagers, Rose-breasted Grosbeaks, and a variety of warblers. As I returned to my window-less office, I found myself envying Peter for the life that he was living. I had no idea how I could fashion a life like that for myself.

Nonetheless, this was about to change. In 1970, I received a phone call from Dean Gorham, a sixty-five-year-old banker and financier from Decatur, Illinois, who was coming to Houston for a homebuilders' conference. That phone call changed my life. Mr. Gorham had gotten my name from my friend Russell Clapper, who was the manager of Anahuac National Wildlife Refuge, outside Houston, where I spent time birding. Mr. Gorham said, "If I pay you a hundred dollars, will you take my sister Helen and me out for a day of birding?" I was twenty-nine years old, living in a sub-letted room in my friends' rented house, unsure of what I was supposed to be doing, and not finding much satisfaction in my job. Nobody had ever offered me money to take them birding. I quickly accepted Mr. Gorham's offer.

We spent the day birding around the Houston and Galveston area. As I recall, there were five birds that they were particularly interested in seeing, including the White-faced Ibis and the Sprague's Pipit. In order to find the pipit, we drove out the Texas City Dike, which extends from Texas City for more than a mile into Galveston Bay. The grass on the shoulders of the road was very short, which created ideal feeding conditions for this uncommon bird. We had only driven partway out the dike when I spotted a small, buffy bird walking in the grass. We observed the pipit at such close range that we could see its bright yellow legs, which is one of its field marks that distinguishes this bird from the much more common American Pipit. That observation was one of the highlights of a very fine day of birding.

After this trip, it occurred to me that there might be other people interested in hiring me for a day or two of birding. My friend, Ben Feltner, who had discovered the Eskimo Curlew on West Galveston Island years before, was also interested in taking people on private birding tours. We decided to place an ad in *Birding*, the magazine of the American Birding Association. We shared the cost of the ad, but decided not to become partners. A number of people contacted me and hired me for a day of birding in and around the Texas coast. I requested a payment of $32 per day and 16 cents per mile, which was approximately the cost of a rental car (I used my own car). Thus, I was valuing my own services at zero, but I was earning some money and gaining experience.

Over the next five years, I took twenty or so people out each year. I often led these tours on the weekends or during my free time, outside of my full-time job at the Institute for Urban Studies.

During this period, I told my major professor, Dr. James Q. Wilson, that I wasn't going to complete my PhD. As a result, I received a master's degree from Harvard instead. This decision was difficult because my father wanted to see me pursue a political science career. I could tell he was deeply disappointed in this change in my career plans.

But my heart wasn't in being an academic and spending large amounts of time in libraries or classrooms. It was instead in being outdoors and, increasingly, in guiding bird tours. Among my early clients was Dr. Nicholas Halmi. An immigrant from Hungary, he taught physiology at Iowa State and was a prominent member of the American Physiological Society. Once or twice a year, he traveled to Galveston for work at the University of Texas Medical Branch, and during those visits, he hired me for a few days of birding.

On another occasion, I took a doctor from Seattle to northeastern Mexico on a weeklong trip. My most vivid memory from that excursion was being in the Sierra Madre Oriental above the town of El Naranjo. At the high point of forty-five-hundred feet, the road passes through a dense forest of sweet gum, oak, and other trees. Here, I played a tape recording of a Ferruginous Pygmy-Owl, a species that the doctor had never seen. The owl appeared, and then about two dozen songbirds, including ten Yellow-green Vireos and a pair of Elegant Euphonias, flew in to mob and harass the owl. This is what happens when small birds hear an owl during the daytime. It turned out that all these species were life birds for my client. The male Elegant Euphonia is a stunningly beautiful bird that is steel blue above with a deep orange breast and upperparts, a black throat, and a bright turquoise crown and hind neck.

In 1974, I received a phone call from Wiley Wilkinson, who lived near New Orleans and was a volunteer with the local chapter of the Audubon Society. The National Audubon Society was going to hold its convention in New Orleans in late March 1975, and, as Wiley explained, the regional chapter, Orleans Audubon, was in charge of organizing pre- and post-convention trips. One of these excursions was going to be in the Galveston area. A member of my local bird club, who had recently moved to New Orleans and joined Orleans Audubon, recommended me to Wiley. Wiley asked me if I would be willing to be a local leader for one day during a Galveston trip.

I said that I would be happy to do so, and I gave Wiley a suggestion for what I thought might be a more memorable birding adventure: pre- and post-convention trips to the Yucatán and Palenque. It is only a short flight from New Orleans across the Gulf to the Yucatán. Wiley thought this was an excellent idea and asked me to organize these trips. I contacted a travel company and they made all the necessary reservations and provided a local guide. The trips filled up quickly, with about twenty people signed up for each weeklong excursion. I co-led with my longtime friend John Rowlett, who became my business partner a couple years after I started Victor Emanuel Nature Tours (VENT) in 1976.

We visited Chichen Itza, Uxmal, and Palenque and saw many special birds, including Yucatan Jays, Turquoise-browed Motmots, and a brilliant flock of American Flamingos that we observed near the town of Rio Lagartos. Many of these birds were seen near the spectacular Mayan ruins that we toured. I was especially thrilled to see a Black-collared Hawk soaring above the marshes of Usumacinta River. A species I had long wanted to see, it is a very large hawk that perches near the water to catch fish. Once found as far north as Veracruz, the Black-collared Hawk features bright rufous upperparts, a white head and underparts, and a black collar.

Overall, the Yucatán and Palenque trips went well despite the fact that we tried to do too much within too little time. I certainly learned a lot about how to organize a tour, and the experience strengthened my resolve to pursue a career that involved organizing and leading birding trips. I later learned that these trips were the first birding and ecotourism tours ever operated in the Yucatán.

Following that trip in March 1975, I decided to expand Victor Emanuel Nature Tours by offering more excursions to other areas. At that time, there were very few firms offering birding and nature tours. I placed advertisements in a few birding magazines, including *Birding* and *Audubon Field Notes*, and listed a tour schedule for fall 1975 and spring and summer 1976.

Around this same time, I started Rockport Wildlife Tours as a way to use a Mercedes bus I had recently bought and to bring in some revenue for the new company. Trips were offered near Rockport, Texas, departing on a large boat that took about fifty participants to view the wintering Whooping Cranes and other birds. The boat trip usually afforded participants the chance to see Whooping Cranes at close range as these magnificent, huge white birds searched for blue crabs along the edge of the Intracoastal Canal. The Whooping Crane is one of the rarest birds in the world, and at that time, fewer than one hundred remained in existence. In a 1941 count, the species had declined to about sixteen birds, but thanks to protection and captive breeding programs, today this figure has increased to about six hundred.

The idea of Rockport Wildlife Tours was to provide people with a few hours of birding before or after the boat trip to look for birds that they didn't see on the water—including the Greater Prairie Chickens, Sandhill Cranes, hawks, geese, and other winter birds of the Central Texas coast. I asked John Rowlett to become my partner, and David Wolf and John's sister, Rose Ann Rowlett, joined our company as leaders. Each spent several weeks in Rockport, operating these tours. Although the Rockport Wildlife Tours attracted very few participants, some of them traveled on VENT excursions for many years.

In 1978, I moved my business to Austin. Houston was becoming so large and developed that I found it challenging to re-enter the bustling city after leading a trip to beautiful natural areas. It was also becoming increasingly difficult to access natural areas because Houston's urban sprawl continued to move west and encroach on natural habitats, such as the rice fields of Harris County. In addition, two of my friends, Sharon and Randy Green, had moved to Austin. Sharon told me that she was interested in becoming my part-time administrative assistant if I relocated my business to Austin. Having attended the University of Texas, I already knew that I liked the city.

But politics was to pull me back to Houston for a brief period after I started VENT. My close friend Mike Andrews was running in the 1980 Democratic congressional primary for the

Twenty-Second District in Houston. At a fundraising event, he told me that his campaign manager had quit the day before. As a result, Mike couldn't raise any money and asked if I would be willing to step into the position. I had a business to run in Austin, but I said yes—reluctantly.

During the week, I commuted from Austin to the campaign headquarters in a strip mall in southeast Houston, about thirty minutes out of the city on the way to Galveston. When in Houston, I lived with my parents in the Montrose area. Though I was helping out a friend, I still wasn't entirely enthusiastic about the work. One day at the campaign headquarters, I was working at my desk in the back office, dealing with some of the logistics related to the campaign when I heard the clear, loud sound of a bird— *bob-white, bob-white*. The office building was constructed of cinder blocks, and the whistling sound traveled loudly through the thick walls. I walked around the rear of the building where there was a field of grass. A wooden post was located directly behind my office. A Northern Bobwhite Quail was sitting on it. The bird calls were passing through the cinder block walls into my office!

I interpreted this moment as a sign: I was being called back to the natural world. I wanted to be completely immersed in that world, but instead, I was working in a tiny, smoke-filled office. The phones rang nonstop. Various employees often became very upset when the candidate called and they didn't get a chance to speak with him. It was not a pleasant work environment. Most of the time, I felt stressed out and exhausted.

In May 1980, I finished the campaign after Mike Andrews won the Democratic primary and returned to Austin to resume building my company full-time. That was my last hurrah in politics. Mike lost in the general election to Ron Paul, but later won in another district. He ended up serving in Congress for twelve years.

My ultimate decision to leave politics certainly bewildered some people. An avid birder named Lola Oberman, who had worked for the Democratic National Committee and later became a speechwriter for Senator Lloyd Bentsen, told me about a visit she had made to the senator's Houston office to meet with some of her colleagues. When she told them that she had traveled to Texas to do some birding, one of her colleagues responded, "You should meet Vic. Vic what's-his-name. We hoped he would go into politics, but he went into birding instead, and we haven't heard from him since. What a wasted life."

6

Meeting Curlew

Common Eider
MONTAUK, LONG ISLAND
STOCKHOLM, SWEDEN

Near the end of the Freeport Bird Count in 1972, George Plimpton said to me, "Victor, I'd like for you to meet my oldest friend, Peter Matthiessen." I had recently read *The Tree Where Man Was Born* (1972), which recounts Peter's travels in East Africa, his explorations of the country's past, and his search for the tribe that was still pursuing its ancient way of life. I was impressed by the narrative and had noticed that it was dedicated in memory of his wife, Deborah Love Matthiessen. The front of the book also listed Peter's nine other publications. Given all this, I interpreted George's comment to mean that Peter was his most elderly friend because his wife had passed away and he had written all these books. I imagined that he was well into his eighties. I thought, "I better get up to New York City so I can meet this man while he's still with us."

About a year later, in January 1973, I traveled north with my friend John Rowlett. George invited us to his home on East Seventy-Second Street. (The first floor and basement of that townhouse served as the headquarters of the *Paris Review* from 1973 to 2005.)

He wanted us to meet his then-wife, Freddy, and little girl, Medora, and have dinner with his oldest friend, Peter.

We arrived at George's apartment after a day of unsuccessfully looking for the Northern Saw-whet Owl, the smallest owl east of the Mississippi, in the conifers that lined the parkways just inland from Jones Beach State Park. This small brown owl has a cat-like face, bright yellow eyes, and white vertical stripes on its belly. These highly nocturnal birds are seldom seen.

George, John, and I were dressed in our rubber boots, heavy coats, and wool hats, with our binoculars hung around our necks. Upon stepping into the living room, I quickly recognized Les Line, the editor of *Audubon Magazine*, and his wife. A handsome young-ish man, with a long face and clear blue eyes, was sitting on the couch next to a woman. I wondered, "Who are these people?"

It turned out to be Peter Matthiessen and his future wife, Maria. What George had meant by his "oldest friend" was the person he had known the longest. The two had met in kindergarten at St. Bernard's School, a private, all-male elementary school on the Upper East Side, and had been close friends ever since. Peter and George founded the *Paris Review*, along with Harold Humes, in the city of its title in spring 1953, and Peter later enlisted George to become editor of the publication. He served in this role for fifty years. The literary magazine has published some of the most important writers of the last six decades, including Jack Kerouac, Philip Roth, Nadine Gordimer, William Styron, Adrienne Rich, and Samuel Beckett.

At that point in my life, I had a habit of carrying around random objects in my briefcase to show people. During this particular evening, I was sitting with Peter and Maria, and I said, "I want to show you the most remarkable photograph that I've ever taken." I reached into my briefcase and pulled out a very small print that was all green. Peter and Maria peered at the image and undoubtedly thought, "What is this? And what does this man think is so remarkable about this photograph?" I pointed to the image and said, "That is an unbroken, pristine tropical rain forest photographed from a plane in southern Mexico, and it is positively teeming with birds."

Peter and Maria stared at the photo and then stared blankly at me. Later, they told me that they weren't entirely sure what to make of me.

During dinner, George said to Peter, "Would you tell your story of the rediscovery of Heath Hen?" (I had a feeling that this request had been made on other occasions.) Peter proceeded to tell this extraordinary story. As marvelous a writer as he was, in some ways, he was an even better storyteller. Subsequently, Peter wrote this story and it appeared in the March 1977 issue of *Audubon Magazine.*

That evening, Peter recounted visiting a friend on Tuckernuck Island, off the west end of Nantucket, in April 1968. During his visit, Peter encountered some grouse doing a courtship display. It was awe-inspiring to witness this. Peter thought that the birds resembled prairie chickens, but he knew that there were no prairie chickens east of Illinois. He also knew that the Heath Hen—now regarded as a subspecies of the Greater Prairie Chicken—once occupied the scattered grasslands of the East Coast offshore islands. A Heath Hen sanctuary had been established in 1908 (when only forty-five Heath Hens remained) on Martha's Vineyard. Unfortunately, despite that effort, the species became extinct. The last bird was seen near the sanctuary on March 11, 1932. It occurred to Peter that the birds he saw on Tuckernuck might be a surviving population of Heath Hens.

He was astonished to spot these grouse on Tuckernuck. It was foggy and the birds were distant, so he couldn't see them very well. After his sighting, Peter made an appointment with Stewart Udall, who was serving as secretary of interior (1961–1969). When he told Udall about his sighting, the secretary became very excited and decided that further exploration and identification were needed. Udall felt that this unusual sighting could help him in approaching the owners of Tuckernuck about a property transfer to the government so that a national wildlife refuge could be established to protect these birds.

Peter had collected feathers from where he had seen the grouse dancing. In order to verify the identification, he took the feathers to the Smithsonian in Washington, DC, and showed them to John Aldrich, an ornithologist for the US Fish and Wildlife Service. Aldrich was also very excited about this possible rediscovery of the Heath Hen. He delivered the feathers to Roxie Laybourne. The leading feather expert, she could examine a feather and identify the bird. Over the years, Roxie was routinely given feather remnants from the engines of crashed airplanes in the hope that the identity of the perished bird might provide more information as to the cause of the accident. On that particular day, she inspected these feathers and was intrigued by their appearance and by the possibility that they could belong to the extinct Heath Hen.

When Peter told this story, he described a tense moment when Roxie picked up one of the feathers, twirled it between her fingers, and said, "There's something about this feather that bothers me. It's not quite right." She went on to examine feathers on specimens of the Greater Prairie Chicken, the Heath Hen, and the Sharp-tailed Grouse. After several hours of observation, Roxie discovered that the feather fit perfectly the pattern of one of the feathers of the Sharp-tailed Grouse. Upon further investigation, it was discovered that the Massachusetts Department of Wildlife had released Sharp-tailed Grouse on the island many years earlier—and everyone had forgotten about this event.

Later in the evening, Peter said, "Anyone who wants to continue this party out at my house in Sagaponack is welcome to come out." John Rowlett and I jumped at the chance to visit his home on six acres of woodland in Sagaponack on the South Fork.

The next day, we went birding. We drove out to the eastern tip of Montauk, which was a special place for Peter. For a number of years, he had earned his living as a fishing guide, taking people out from Montauk on his boat and later writing about this region and its fishing community in *Men's Lives: The Surfmen and Baymen of the South Fork* (1986).

A rock walk surrounds the base of the Montauk lighthouse, authorized by George Washington in 1792 and completed in 1796. The Atlantic surf crashes against the barnacle-covered boulders. On a clear day, it's possible to spot the southern shoreline of Connecticut and Fishers Island, where Peter's parents owned a home, as well as Block Island farther east. It is a spectacular spot for viewing seabirds such as gannets when they migrate south in the fall by the thousands.

On that day, gulls flew by, and a few fishing boats dotted the cold waters. As we stood there at the foot of the lighthouse, an enormous flock of eider and scoter collected on the rolling swells of the Atlantic. There must have been a thousand ducks. At various moments, a hundred or so birds at the rear flew over the entire flock in order to take the lead position. Such "tumbling" is common among certain birds, such as Red-winged Blackbirds and Brown-headed Cowbirds, when they are feeding on the short grass during the winter. Here, on the rough waters of the wintry Atlantic, it was an extraordinary sight—this enormous circular mass of ducks tumbling over the metallic blue-gray surface of the ocean.

The Common Eider, which breeds in Maine and farther north, gathers in the winter in these large flocks. They dive down to the sea floor in order to find shellfish, clams, and mussels. As their name suggests, they are the source of the eiderdown used in jackets, pillows, and other items; the down comes from their nests since the female eider plucks the feathers from her breast to line the nest so that the eggs and then the young are kept warm. There are four species of eider in the world, two of which in North America breed mostly in Alaska, northern Canada, and Greenland. Each species is strikingly marked with black-and-white plumage accented, depending on the species, by lime green, soft gray, or peach. My lifer eider occurred in summer 1961 on a field trip to Monomoy Island when I was attending a course in marine botany at the Marine Biology Laboratory in Woods Hole, Massachusetts. But I had never seen a large flock until that day on Montauk Point with Peter and John. I took particular delight in observing such an immense concentration of waterfowl since they are among my favorite birds.

A few years after our day in Montauk, I invited Peter to be the principal speaker at the Texas Ornithological Society meeting in Galveston in spring 1976. I had been elected president of the society in April 1975. During his talk, Peter told the Tuckernuck story of the Heath Hen. I had asked Peter if he would be willing to join John Rowlett and me for a ten-day tour following the convention to the forests of East Texas and then farther south down the coast to the Rio Grande Valley. He accepted my offer—and the tour filled up quickly with twenty participants. In order to have sufficient space, we rented a second bus. This was the first large VENT tour.

We spent one day in the Big Thicket National Preserve, north of Silsbee, with botanist and activist Geraldine Watson. She identified local flowers, such as the Bird's Foot Violet, a large blue violet with an orange center that grows in sandy areas. In a small bog, Geraldine pointed out pitcher plants and Sundew insectivorous plants, which capture insects. Then we visited a longleaf pine savanna in search of two special birds, the Red-cockaded Woodpecker and the Bachman's Sparrow.

The longleaf pine savanna is one of the most beautiful ecosystems in North America with towering pines evenly spaced, forming an expansive open canopy, with a rich understory of grasses. Originally, it stretched from southeastern Virginia to northern Florida and then westward to East Texas. Comprising about 90 million acres, it was once one of the largest ecosystems in the world. Some of these pines reached heights of one hundred feet and lived more than three hundred years. Sadly, now only scattered small patches of this ecosystem remain, less than 3 percent of its original size. A variety of land uses, such as logging and farming, and fire exclusion in the management practices of the area have dramatically reduced this type of forest.

We had only walked a short distance when we heard the clear, bell-like whistle followed by a trill. This was the song of the Bachman's Sparrow, one of the most beautiful songs of any sparrow. Soon we spotted this large sparrow perched on a dead branch, about forty feet up in a longleaf pine. As we watched, it threw its head back, pointed its bill skyward, and emitted its signature song. (When the bird is not engaged in its territorial song, it tends to be secretive, shy, and difficult to spot.)

Nearby, we visited a colony of Red-cockaded Woodpeckers. These small, black-and-white birds are one of the rarest woodpeckers in the world. They excavate cavities in the pine trees that suffer from red heart disease. This disease rots the centers of the trees, making the trunk soft. White sap oozes along the rim of the cavity and coats the part of the tree just below.

While we were looking at the woodpeckers, Geraldine drew our attention to a bearded pink orchid (*Calopogon barbatus*), a rarely seen plant. She had only seen this orchid in three other locations in Texas, and this sighting inspired her to take action to preserve this particular area. Over the years, Geraldine worked tirelessly to catalog the Big Thicket and its remarkable collection of distinct ecosystems, as well as all the plants within them, in order to make the case for preservation. She was a vocal advocate for the establishment of the preserve in 1974, which was not appreciated by many of the local people who opposed the Big Thicket National Preserve.

Later, we traveled to the Central Texas coast, where we hoped to see the Greater Prairie Chickens performing their courtship dance. My friend, Randy Green, told me that he knew a rancher who lived near Port Lavaca and had prairie chickens on his property, but Randy wasn't sure if he would allow us onto his land. As it happened, the man admired Peter's books, so he granted us access. There, out on a short-grass field, Greater Prairie Chickens danced. The males made their haunting, booming call as their ears lifted up and the orange sacs on either side of their heads inflated. Then, the birds rapidly stamped the ground.

The next day, we went out on a large boat with Captain Brownie Brown to look for the endangered Whooping Crane, the tallest bird in North America, which is white with black primaries and a bare red crown. We had wonderful views of a family of cranes foraging for blue crabs along the muddy shallows. We also saw many other birds, such as Willets, Great and Snowy Egrets, and Great Blue Herons. At one point, the cranes flew overhead, giving us the opportunity to see their black wingtips. On the way back to the dock, we crossed Copano Bay. As we were returning, it occurred to

John and me, as we sat on top of the boat, to ask Peter if he would be willing to co-lead a trip to Africa and become an associate of our new company. To our great satisfaction, Peter said yes to both of our requests.

In South Texas, we visited the Armstrong Ranch, hoping to observe the Ferruginous Pygmy-Owl. In the United States, this tiny owl is confined to the mesquite thickets and live oak groves of far South Texas and a small portion of southern Arizona. It is often active during the day and night and feeds on insects, spiders, and small birds. We knew that seeing the owl would be a highlight for many people on the tour. I played a tape of the owl's call, and it flew into a tree very near us. It was a lifer for Peter and all the tour's participants.

From the ranch, we continued on to the Lower Rio Grande Valley. We visited the Santa Ana National Wildlife Refuge and other major birding hot spots, looking for Green Jays, Great Kiskadees, Long-billed Thrashers, White-fronted Doves (now called White-tipped), Altamira Orioles, Audubon's Orioles, and other birds found nowhere in the United States except in this region.

At the time, Peter was still working on *The Snow Leopard*. He had a copy of the manuscript with him on the trip. Several clients on the tour asked me if Peter would be willing to give a reading one afternoon. When I asked, he characteristically said that he was reluctant to do so because he was concerned that participants would feel pressured to attend when they might want to rest. I assured Peter that people wanted to hear him read.

Everyone crowded into a motel room. Some sat on the floor, and some sat on the bed. Before reading, Peter set the stage—how the trip came about, what Nepal was like as you walked into the mountains, how you went farther back in time. It was like fine brushstrokes on a canvas. In just a few words, he placed us in the remote, ancient areas of northwest Nepal. His description was as vivid as his writing. Then, Peter read a portion of his manuscript. After the reading, there was a moment of silence as people absorbed the beauty of his writing. *The Snow Leopard* was published a few months later, and in 1979, it won the National Book Award in non-fiction. In 2008, Peter won the National Book Award again for his novel, *Shadow Country*, making him the only writer to win the prestigious award in both fiction and nonfiction.

In the tradition of Edgar Kincaid presenting bird names, I selected bird names for my intimate circle of friends. George Plimpton chose his own, deciding on Hadada (after the Hadada Ibis found in Sub-Saharan Africa) because when disturbed, this species emits an extremely loud and raucous call, defecates, and flies away. To George, this series of actions was the perfect metaphor for journalists: "We make a lot of noise and then make a mess, and leave." Roger Tory Peterson was named after the King Penguin because he loved Antarctica, and this species of penguin was his favorite bird. I gave Maria Matthiessen, who was born and raised in Tanzania, the name of Namaqua after the Namaqua Dove, a very beautiful small dove that occurs in Africa, and I gave Peter the name of Curlew because of his fondness for shorebirds. All of the curlews are large shorebirds with long legs, and Peter was a large, tall man. In describing his affinity for shorebirds, Peter wrote in *The Wind Birds: Shorebirds of North America* (1967): "The restlessness of shorebirds, their kinship with the distance and swift seasons, the wistful signal of their voices down the long coastlines of the world make them, for me, the most affecting of wild creatures."

In the closing paragraph of the same book, he wrote about the curlews in words that to me are some of the most beautiful thoughts that he ever expressed:

> The departure of curlew from a given place often occurs just prior to a storm, and in ancient days, in England, the curlew's cry, the plover's whistle boded no man any good. . . . Both birds were known as harbingers of death, and in the sense that they are birds of passage, that in the wild melodies of their calls, in the breath of vast distance and bare regions that attends them, we sense intimations of our own mortality, there is justice in the legend. Yet it is not the death sign that the curlews bring, but

only the memory of life, of a high beauty passing swiftly, as the curlew passes, leaving us in solitude on an empty beach, with summer gone, and a wind blowing.

Almost every year, I visited Peter and Maria in Sagaponack. I loved their house, an old remodeled farmhouse surrounded by woods. On one side of the house, a huge fin whale skull leaned against the wall on a pair of blocks. The rambling house brimmed with books and wonderful objects from Peter's travels. I often stayed in the room that had been his son's. That bedroom was located down a long hallway and on one wall was a series of framed awards, such as the National Book Award and an honor from the National Society of Arts and Letters, and poems and letters written by various friends. There was a memorable poem by Galway Kinnell about playing tennis with Peter. There was also a bookcase filled with books about nature and scientific explorations and travel, including *Haylukt's Travels, The Sea and the Jungle* (1912) by H. M. Tomlinson, and *Birds of Massachusetts and Other New England States* (1925) by Edward Howe Forbush.

Peter had converted an old stable into a zendo (or meditation hall), where, on certain mornings, his Zen students would gather for services. When I was staying there, I always participated in these morning sittings. Peter would emerge from his bedroom in his monk's robe and we would walk down to the zendo. The space was simple and bare, with several rows of black meditation cushions. Prior to the service, Peter would instruct me on what procedures I should follow.

One of my favorite things to do at Sagaponack was to go birding with Peter. Given his assiduousness in pursuing his writing, these outings were shorter and less frequent than I would have preferred. Nonetheless, our time together was always memorable. We visited many beautiful spots along the eastern end of Long Island, including Sagaponack Pond, which was just down the road from Peter's house, or the nearby beach, where we could look out onto the expansiveness of the Atlantic Ocean, or Peter's other favorite spots, such as Hither Hills, Montauk, and Mecox Bay.

There weren't nearly as many birds on Long Island as along my native Texas coast, but we always saw a nice variety of terns, gulls, and shorebirds. One fall when I stopped by on my way home from Africa, I went birding with Peter and his son Alex, and I spotted an adult California Gull at Mecox Bay. The species had never been recorded in New York State. Unfortunately, we did not obtain a photograph. As a result, the New York State Avian Records Committee did not accept our sighting. Given Peter's fondness for shorebirds, it was particularly satisfying to see special ones, such as the American Golden-Plover, which we sometimes spotted in the potato fields near Peter's house, or the Baird's Sandpiper, which was a rarely sighted bird on Long Island.

We also liked to hike along the rolling wooded trails of Hither Hills State Park. With 1,755 acres of woodlands, dunes, and beaches, the park offers a vast network of trails traversing the area and the rocky bluffs overlooking the Long Island Sound and across the water, the southern shore of Connecticut. On one particular walk in fall 2011, we arrived at a clearing that overlooked the blue waters of Block Island Sound. Gulls and terns rested on the boulders that extended from the sandy shoreline. We climbed to the top of a bluff and took in the beautiful panoramic view. Peter looked out toward Fisher's Island and Connecticut, and said, "This is my world."

Of all my travels with Peter, the trip that I treasure the most is the one that we made to Sweden in 2007. After Peter and I had completed a VENT-operated cruise around Sicily, we flew to Stockholm in late May to visit our friends, Lars and Ragnhild Jonsson. Regarded as one of the finest living bird artists, Lars is also a renowned ornithologist. His first exhibition of work was presented at the Swedish Museum of Natural History when he was only fifteen years old, and, in the seventies, his series of European bird guides established him both as an artist and a bird expert. Lars uses a telescope and brush to create a painting that captures a bird in its natural habitat in such a way that it appears alive. In his work, he takes in the subtle details—such as seasonal plumage, wind direction, individual variances within bird species—and accurately depicts them in beautiful paintings.

During our first day in Stockholm, Lars took us to the Thiel Gallery, an art museum on Djurgärden, one of the city's many islands and a former royal game preserve. The government-owned gallery showcases the paintings of Bruno Liljefors, one of the most renowned bird and nature artists, as well as paintings by other Scandinavian artists. (The final decision dinner for the judges of the Nobel Prize in Chemistry is held in this museum each year.) It was a marvelous experience to visit the museum with Lars, who, as a young artist, had admired Liljefors. Although Liljefors died in 1939, Lars came to regard the talented artist as his adopted father and mentor, and he hoped that his art could someday approach the genius of Liljefors.

Upon entering the museum, we beheld a sixteen-foot-long painting of a flock of forty life-size Common Eider flying over a Winslow Homer–type winter sea. This particular painting, *The Flight of Eiders* (1901), hangs on the wall next to the staircase. It is one of the most dramatic bird paintings that I've ever seen. We looked at the masterpiece for a long time, observing its exquisite beauty.

After Stockholm, we flew to Gotland, Sweden's largest island in the Baltic Sea. This island is a back-in-time place with narrow country lanes and small settlements with beautiful churches. In *Birds and Light: The Art of Lars Jonsson* (2002), the artist describes this island:

> The Gotland landscape, along with its grandeur, harbours a sense of intimacy: one can settle down anywhere and feel embraced by the close environment. These individual sections, or micro-landscapes, often remain undetected until one's eye fixes on a detail and the perspective is transformed. In my case, it is often the birds that open my eyes to these close environments.

On the island, we visited Visby, the only completely walled city remaining in Europe, and a museum dedicated to the artwork of

Lars. Peter and I stayed at the Jonssons' guesthouse some miles away from where they lived. One morning, we saw a White-tailed Eagle being mobbed by Hooded Crows right outside our bedrooms. Later, we went birding with Lars and spotted a number of migrating land birds and many shorebirds, including both Black-tailed and Bar-tailed Godwits in breeding plumage. These shorebirds are beautiful shades of cinnamon and rusty red. We also saw a group of male Ruffs. Some had acquired their spectacular breeding plumage. One evening, we observed a European Woodcock flying over the treetops in the late-evening light.

We traveled with Lars and Ragnhild to Stora Karlsöe, an island made up of a flat limestone plateau that is home to nesting Common and Black Guillemots and Razorbills. The island is also a nature reserve, the oldest after Yellowstone National Park. During the late spring, blooming flowers—blue veronicas, white daisies, yellow stonecrop, fragrant violet thyme, and thousands of purple terrestrial orchids—dot the rugged landscape.

Lars had made arrangements for us to stay at the historic lighthouse, where there were only two bedrooms. Lars and Ragnhild shared one room, and Peter and I were in another. Over the years, Peter and I had shared rooms in many places around the world, but this time, it didn't go well since I had developed the occasional affliction of snoring. I had not been asleep very long when there was a sharp clap above my head. It was Peter, clapping his hands to wake me up and let me know that I was keeping him up with my snoring. I managed to get back to sleep, but soon there was another clap.

I decided that the only solution was to get up and walk around in the dark, listening to the nocturnal sounds and watching the full moon descend into the Baltic Sea and then watch the sun rise. For hours, I wandered around. I put on a pair of headphones and listened to Beethoven, my favorite composer, as I walked, waiting for the dawn. This part of the island was covered with low bushes and dense clumps of grass. Despite this difficult night, it was a marvelous trip.

When we returned to Gotland, Peter and I slept in separate rooms, and my snoring was no longer an issue. I remember appreciating Peter's keen eye: Between our bedrooms, there was a painting of terns. I said, "I think those are Common Terns." Peter looked up at the painting and said, "Warbler, look how short the legs are. They're Arctic Terns." He was right.

7

The Triumph

Horned Guan
EL TRIUNFO, MEXICO

The first time I heard about El Triunfo was in fall 1969. Armand Yramategui told me that he was planning a trip there in March of the following year. He described the ten-thousand-hectare reserve as a wonderful cloud forest located on the steep slopes of a dramatic, extinct volcano, El Triunfo (The Triumph), in the southeastern corner of the state of Chiapas in Mexico. This reminded me of the pristine forest that a farmer described to Armand, Carl, and me nearly fifteen years earlier on our first trip to Mexico. I later learned that many conservationists considered El Triunfo to be the most spectacular cloud forest remaining in Mexico. The moisture from the cool trade winds of the Pacific Ocean cultivates the lush growth of ferns and enormous trees. The bark of those trees is often covered with mosses, orchids, and bromeliads.

A few months later, on January 27, 1970, Armand was leaving Houston so that he could observe a comet away from the artificial glow of the urban lights. He was driving along the Southwest Freeway, not far from where I was living in a one-room apartment near St. Anne's Catholic Church. His car got a flat tire, and some teenage boys stopped on the highway shoulder to help him. They drove

Armand to a nearby gas station, where the tire was repaired, and then drove him back to his car. It was then that one of teenagers pulled out a gun to rob Armand and shot him in the chest. He died from the wounds within a few hours. He would have celebrated his forty-seventh birthday in little more than a month.

The call telling me about Armand's death was one of the most painful phone calls that I've ever received. He played such a significant role in my development as a naturalist and a young man, and he was one of my most important mentors for about two decades. Like my other mentor, Joe Heiser, Armand had great enthusiasm for all aspects of the natural world. He was also a dedicated teacher, thus being a mentor came naturally to him. I loved him dearly.

The last time that I saw Armand was when he stopped by my apartment with his fiancée, Sharon Davis, to congratulate me on my successful efforts to help elect a more progressive school board. Armand was working then as the curator of the Baker Burke Planetarium at the Houston Museum of Natural Science, a dream job for him, and he was about to be married for the first time. It was obvious to me that Armand and Sharon were very much in love.

For several years before his death, Armand had waged a hard-fought, grassroots campaign to conserve a stretch of wilderness river, formerly called Middle Bayou, twenty-five miles southeast of downtown Houston. The city and developers wanted to transform the natural area into a storm sewer and subdivision development. Armand's tragic death inspired a regional and national coalition to work together to preserve this property. I participated in one of the meetings with some of the executives of Exxon, which owned the land above the bayou. In 1974, four years after Armand's death and a protracted fight by a passionate team of conservationists, the Armand Bayou Nature Center was established in his memory. (The Texas Parks & Wildlife Department decided against using his last name because they thought it was too difficult to pronounce.)

A few weeks before Armand's death, I traveled to Chiapas to visit my friend Phyllis Kazen, a graduate student at Harvard who was working on her dissertation research on a ranch outside San Cristóbal de las Casas. When I left San Cristóbal to take the bus back to Tuxtla Gutiérrez, the capital and the largest city of this region of Mexico, I noticed a man, well into his sixties, also waiting at the station for the same bus. I couldn't really tell if he was a Mexican or an American who had lived in Mexico for so long that he dressed and looked like a local. As chance would have it, the only seat available when I boarded the bus for the sixty-kilometer ride to Tuxtla happened to be next to that man. His name was Thomas Baillie MacDougall, and he was a self-taught botanist, naturalist, and collector. Later, I would learn that he was born in Scotland, and after fighting in the battles of the Sommes and of Arras during World War I, he moved to the United States. At the time I met him, MacDougall was working with his brother in a nursery business in the Bronx.

Inspired by the writings of the nineteenth-century naturalist W. H. Hudson, MacDougall was eager to explore a region that had been relatively unexplored by naturalists. In the mid-thirties, he began traveling to Mexico every winter and continued these annual visits until his death in Oaxaca in 1973. He spent the dry season (November to May) searching for flora and fauna in the two southernmost states, Oaxaca and Chiapas. He would travel extensively via bus into the hinterlands and then walk the backcountry trails, traveling light with one shirt, one pair of trousers, and a straw hat. He carried a wooden flower press, a leather satchel, and very little food, and he often slept outdoors or found *posada* (lodging) with a local family. In some ways, MacDougall reminded me of a tropical version of the great John Muir.

After getting acquainted on the bus, we decided to have dinner together that night in Tuxtla. Like me, he was lodging at a cheap hotel in the city. During dinner, our conversation revolved around his many adventures. MacDougall established his home base in the town of Tehuantepec along the Pacific side of the isthmus. From there, he roamed in all directions, exploring the high mountains and cloud forests. Throughout the years, as a way to support himself, he sent thousands of mammal and reptile specimens to the American Museum of Natural History and plants to the New York Botanical Garden and later to specialty growers in

California. During these immersive trips, MacDougall also taught himself about all aspects of the environment and culture: the birds, insects, archaeology, language, fiestas, and rituals of the distinct groups of people who lived there. During our long conversation, he told me that he was working on a history of Oaxaca—its people, regions, and natural history. As it turned out, he didn't get a chance to publish this book before his death a few years later.

At one point during our meal, I asked MacDougall if he had ever traveled to El Triunfo. He told me that he had taken a bus to Jaltenango; hitched a ride to Finca Prusia, a coffee plantation in the foothills of the Sierra Madre de Chiapas; and then hiked up the mountain into the valley of El Triunfo. He stayed with several peasant families, who were squatters. There were a number of guan feathers scattered around their homes. They had killed these guans, including the rare Horned Guan, for food.

The Horned Guan is a turkey-sized bird that is black above and white below, with a distinctive bare red spike rising from its forehead. It has a broad, black long tail with a white band in the middle. Horned Guans live in isolated groups in remote areas of the mist-shrouded forests and high peaks in Chiapas and Guatemala, often feeding in fruiting trees. A striking bird, with a low, humming call, the Horned Guan is classified as severely endangered, with perhaps only two thousand left in the world.

I wished that I could have spent more time with MacDougall because I could tell that he had lived a remarkable life. I later learned that over the years, he had even discovered new species of reptiles and plants, as well as finding archeological sites previously unknown.

On this same trip, at MacDougall's suggestion, I stopped by the Parque Zoologico de Chiapas in order to meet Dr. Miguel Álvarez del Toro, the director of the zoo and the associated zoological museum in Tuxtla. Don Miguel, as everyone called him, was a tall, dignified, soft-spoken Mexican biologist whose appearance and bearing reminded me of an academic that I might encounter at a university in Madrid. As I learned later, Don Miguel is considered one of the first Mexican conservationists. Eight different species of reptiles were named after him. In 1989, President George H. W. Bush presented him with the J. Paul Getty Award for Conservation Leadership. During our meeting, I asked Don Miguel about El Triunfo. He told me that he had traveled there with a local farmer named Rodrigo Argueta Lopez to search for the Horned Guan. If I went to El Triunfo, Don Miguel offered to arrange for this farmer to meet me and serve as my local guide.

Over the years, whenever I traveled to Tuxtla, I made a point of going to see Don Miguel. During one visit, he gave me a copy of his 1985 memoir, *Asi Era Chiapas!* (*So Was Chiapas!*). In this poignant narrative, Don Miguel describes many of the beautiful places that he saw over the years. Sadly, many of these places no longer exist in their natural states. They've been destroyed or radically changed by development.

It took me seven years to follow through on the advice that Don Miguel had given me. In January 1977, after co-leading a trip to Catemaco and Palenque in eastern Mexico, I decided to travel to Finca Prusia in hopes of making arrangements to take a tour group to El Triunfo several months later. I was on my way to breakfast after a night at the Hotel Bonampak in Tuxtla when I noticed a van with the World Wide Fund for Nature (WWF) insignia on its side. I deduced that the van probably belonged to the well-known Gertrude Blom, who was the widow of the equally famous Danish explorer and archaeologist, Franz Blom. I asked the dining-room waitstaff if they knew Señora Blom and one of the servers pointed to an elderly lady wearing numerous necklaces of silver and turquoise beads. Blue eyebrows were painted above her actual eyebrows. Even in her late sixties (she lived to be ninety-three), Mrs. Blom was famous for riding a horse into Selva Lacandona rain forest to visit the Lacandon people, who made their home there and were one of the last Mayan groups to be living according to their ancient rituals, traditions, and religion.

Mrs. Blom spent five decades chronicling the indigenous Mayan cultures of Chiapas—in particular, examining the contrasting cultures of the Lacandon Maya (along the border of Guatemala) and the Maya of the highlands of Chiapas. Her photographs of the Mayan culture are collected in the book titled *Bearing Witness* (1984) and provide an authentic glimpse into this vanished way of life. I had a chance to introduce myself to her; it was an honor to meet such a legendary woman.

After breakfast, I walked to the only place in Tuxtla that rented cars and rented a Volkswagen Bug from a rather hyperactive woman named Gabriela. Before I left her office, she opened her desk drawer and pulled out a sideview mirror. "If you want this," she said, "I will attach it to the car, but it will be stolen and you'll have to pay for it." I didn't take the mirror. I had only driven a short distance when it started to drizzle. The windshield wipers didn't work. So I returned the Volkswagen to Gabriela and was given another vehicle.

By the time I finally departed Tuxtla, it was two o'clock in the afternoon. I had asked a number of people how long the drive was from Tuxtla to Finca Prusia, and I was assured that it was approximately five hours, which seemed like enough time to arrive there by sunset. I drove south from Tuxtla across the dusty central plateau. Agricultural fields spread out on either side of the road. Groves of oak trees and other vegetation covered the hills and ridges. Small villages had recently been established with names like Revolución and Independencia. Most likely, these were *ejidos*, or communal farming areas. The concept of *ejidos* was a product of the Mexican Revolution of 1920 when large haciendas were given to peasant farmers, who farmed specific parcels of land. These portions could not be sold, but could be handed down to family heirs. From a naturalist's point of view, the landscape was rather bleak since all the native vegetation—except on the steep, oak tree-covered slopes—had been cleared for farming.

As I traveled farther south, I had to ford a number of rivers. Fortunately, even though the clearance of the car's carriage was low, I successfully made it across three rivers. Just as darkness was settling in, I arrived in Jaltenango, the last town before Finca Prusia. I drove on, and soon it was pitch-dark. The dirt road became increasingly worse, with deeper dips and ruts, and larger clouds of dust were being kicked up by the wheels of my rental car. As I drove past modest settlements with farmers and other indigenous people standing by the roadside, I began to wonder if it was safe to be driving by myself for hours in this remote area at night.

Finally, I saw a light in the distance. It was the first electric light that I had seen in about three hours. My spirits rose because I assumed that it must be a light at Finca Prusia. As I approached the main building, huge dogs ran toward my car and barked loudly. It was rather frightening, but then, thankfully, one of the staff emerged, the dogs settled down, and I was able to explain the purpose of my visit.

The people of Finca Prusia were kind and generous. I was shown to a simple bedroom with a toilet down the hallway. When I told my mother this story later, she asked, "How did you know that the people would take you in?" And I said, "I didn't, but they knew that there was nowhere else for me to stay."

That night, at Finca Prusia, I slept well. When I woke, it was still dark. As I remained in bed, I heard what I thought was heavy rainfall. Immediately, I thought about the rivers that I had traversed and wondered if the rising water would make it impossible for me to return to Tuxtla. Once the early-morning light emerged, I realized that the rain was the sound of water rushing through the chutes of the coffee-processing plant. After a breakfast of corn tortillas, scrambled eggs, and black beans, I walked around the living room. Several stag heads with antlers were mounted on the wall and under each was a plaque: STUTTGART, 1927. On the bookshelf, I noticed a copy of *Mein Kampf* (*My Struggle*) in Spanish. For a young man whose father was Jewish, I found this very eerie. I later learned that the owner of the *finca*, Hubertus Von Knoop, had fought in World War II as a member of the German army and had been incarcerated in a prison camp in Tennessee during the war.

I stepped out of the main building and spotted the trail that led up the mountain to El Triunfo. It was a narrow path that bordered a stream and then went uphill through the uniform rows of coffee plants before ascending into the mountains. It was thrilling to look up this trail and know that I would be walking on it in a few months with a tour group that I would co-lead with my friends John Rowlett and George Plimpton. This was the trail that Armand would've taken if he had not been killed on the side of the freeway. As I stood on the trailhead, a flock of White-crowned Parrots alighted in a nearby tree. In the distance, I could see the high ridges covered with pristine cloud forest. Soon I would be up there, looking for the Horned Guan.

Señor Ocampo, the plantation manager, was very accommodating. He said that he would provide mules to carry our gear and food up the mountain and that our group could spend the night at the *finca* prior to making the hike. I was grateful for this offer and looked forward to returning to this remote area.

In early March, we assembled in Tuxtla and then drove to Finca Prusia. The first morning, we ate breakfast at the *finca*. I'm not a coffee drinker, but those who drank coffee said that this was the best they'd ever had. It was brewed from beans grown and roasted there. The manager informed us that the highest-quality coffee beans were sent to Germany in burlap bags stamped with the black double eagle logo and the words "FINCA PRUSIA." The next grade was sold in Mexico and the lowest-quality coffee was shipped to the United States.

After breakfast, we began the ten-mile hike up the mountain. Our climb took most of the day. During the first part, we walked through the coffee fields of the *finca*. The bushes were laden with beans, some of which had turned red and would soon be picked, and shaded by Inga trees, a tropical tree that grows rapidly and is often used in coffee plantations to provide shade. Its white pom-pom-like flowers attract hummingbirds, including the tiny Black-crested Coquette and the Berylline Hummingbird.

After a couple of hours of walking, we reached the upper boundary of the *finca* land, which was denoted by a stone marker. As we continued farther up the trail, we entered old-growth forest. The branches of the trees met forty feet over our heads, providing us with welcome shade. We were walking on a trail that had been built almost one hundred years earlier to provide a way to transport the coffee from the *finca* over the mountains to Mapastepec, a small town in the Pacific lowlands located on a railroad line. From Mapastepec, the coffee could be shipped by rail north to Veracruz. It could then be transported by ship to Germany.

The trail included countless switchbacks, which made the steep ascent easier. The first forest that we entered was part of the upper tropical zone and contained a great diversity of trees. In this zone, the bird life consisted of many species, including Ivory-billed Woodcreepers and Tody Motmots, the smallest member of the motmot family and one of the most difficult to find. At various times, we heard the calls of these birds, including the long descending call of the Ivory-billed Woodcreeper, which is somewhat reminiscent of the Canyon Wren of the Southwest.

After a couple of hours of hiking, we noticed a change in the vegetation when we saw our first sweet gum (or *liquidambar* in Mexico), a tree that is characteristic of the American South. In Mexico, however, the sweet gum is only found above about three thousand feet. At the same time, we started to hear different birds—Rufous-and-white Wrens and Collared Trogons. Then, we heard our first Brown-backed Solitaire. This thrush's song is quite remarkable. The crescendo of accelerating, bell-like notes starts slowly and then accelerates into a cascade, with a tempo like that of a teakettle releasing steam. It is the voice of the forest and one of the loveliest and most evocative bird songs that I had ever heard.

One wonderful aspect about walking up this trail is noting the change in the vegetation and bird life as one passes from one zone to another. For example, at the beginning of the trail, one might spot a Clay-colored Thrush, a brown bird with cream-colored underparts and a yellowish bill that is widespread in the lowlands of Mexico and Central America. Higher up the trail, one might encounter a White-throated Robin, and, upon entering the lush cloud forest, hear the Black Robin for the first time. The Mountain Robin is found in the peaks that rise above the valley of El Triunfo.

A few hours before we reached the valley of El Triunfo, the forest changed abruptly as we entered the cloud forest. This area is often bathed in clouds and mist, especially during the May-to-October rainy season. As a result, the undergrowth here is the most luxuriant, and mosses and bromeliads cover the trunks of the trees. We also saw bunches of tubular orange-and-yellow flowers, with brilliant petals that, oddly enough, resembled candy corn. Hummingbirds, including the Green-throated Mountain-gem and the Violet Sabrewing, often visit these flowers for their sweet nectar. In the cloud forest, we heard the lovely song of the Gray-breasted Wood-Wren and spotted a Golden-browed Warbler, with its bright rufous crown and ear coverts and bright yellow underparts. Both the wood-wren and the warbler fed in the dense understory, making it difficult to see them.

During the late afternoon, as I descended from the crest, I reached a spot where, for the first time, I looked down on the valley of El Triunfo, which would become my favorite place in the world, other than the Upper Texas Coast. The floor of the small valley had been cleared more than twenty years before, but unbroken forest blanketed the slopes. Clouds rested atop the ridge across the valley, and the small stream that ran through it was lined with bright green bushes. As I stood there, I experienced the peace of this pristine forest.

At that time, there were no park guards or staff of any kind residing in the reserve. On a trip about ten years later, I was pleased to encounter a park guard for the first time, and now the park employs several guards to protect the trees and wildlife. In the mid-fifties, three families of squatters had cleared some of the forests for growing potatoes and beans.

That evening, we camped near the stream and prepared meals of freeze-dried food. Once we arrived, our guides, Don Rodrigo and his nephew, Fidel, met us. They had hiked up the mountain from the Pacific side. For three days, we explored several trails, including the Palo Gordo trail, which entered the forest from the west end of the clearing. That trail bordered a small stream before ascending a steep ridge. As we walked away from the clearing up the valley, we entered a magnificent forest. The towering trees reached more than a hundred feet, and their bark was covered with mosses, orchids, and other plants. Tree ferns, up to seventy feet tall, grew along the banks of the stream.

During the next three days, we observed a wonderful selection of birds; some of these species—including the Black-throated Jay and the Blue-throated Motmot—are only found in extreme southern Mexico, nearby Guatemala, El Salvador and Honduras. One of the most memorable aspects of El Triunfo was the daybreak chorus of birdsong. The two most abundant singers were the Black Robin and the Yellow Grosbeak.

On some mornings, we could hear the plaintive call of the Resplendent Quetzal, which many people consider the most beautiful bird in the world. Among the Mayan and Aztec people, the Resplendent Quetzal was regarded as sacred. In the only surviving Aztec codex, there is a list of the tribute that different regions of Mexico were required to send to the Aztec ruler annually. The region along the Pacific coast of Chiapas was called the Soconusco. Its tribute consisted of four hundred quetzal tail feathers that were used to fashion the spectacular headdresses worn by the Aztec rulers. The cap of the headdress is covered with the blue feathers of the Lovely Cotinga. We were fortunate: More than once, a male quetzal flew across the valley, emitting its loud flight call of *whaca, whaca, whaca.* Its long iridescent green "tail" undulated behind its body like a flowing ribbon. These long feathers are not technically tail feathers, but lower back feathers that extend several feet beyond the tail. During mating season, these feathers can grow up to three feet long.

One of the birds that we most wanted to see was the Horned Guan. Every day we split into two groups, and after two days, almost everyone had seen this distinctive bird, except George Plimpton and myself. I was upset that I had failed to see this special bird. On the last afternoon of our tour, I was walking with two tour participants on a trail that went alongside one of the pristine streams that traversed the forest. I had only walked a short distance when I heard the low humming call of a Horned Guan on the ridge above us. This call is like the heartbeat of the forest, a pulse that travels at low frequency. You don't hear it. You feel it. The call of the Horned Guan is almost ventriloquial, making it hard to locate. We decided that it was coming from the ridge to our left, so we crossed the stream and made our way up the steep slope through the forest. We lost the call as we got closer to the top of the ridge.

Since some of the people with me had not had a good look at a quetzal, I decided to play its flight call, hoping to lure one. At that point, we heard the low, pig-like grunting the Horned Guan makes when it is disturbed, followed by castanet-like clicks. We walked along the ridge toward the spot where we thought the guan was. The forest was very dense, making the visibility difficult. All of sudden, there was a window through the trees where we could see out across the valley, and there, on a horizontal branch, was a Horned Guan. I was transfixed. Here at last was the bird that I had longed to see—and it was right in front of me. Then, as suddenly as it appeared, the Horned Guan vanished.

At that moment, we heard an entirely different sound—a loud raucous call—issuing from the other side of the ridge. At first, I thought it might be another type of Horned Guan disturbance call. We walked along the ridge toward that sound. As we drew closer, we realized it was not the call of the guan but rather a call made by a mammal. Fleetingly, I wondered if it could be the sound produced by a dangerous animal, like a jaguar. As we walked along, I picked up a large stick. Then, we realized that the sound was coming from high in a tree. I dropped the stick. We spotted a group of spider monkeys. They were agitated. Their faces were contorted. Feces rained down. They shook the branches of the trees, hoping to drive us away.

Within the space of a half-hour, we had encountered two of the rarest animals in the world. Undisturbed primeval forest surrounded us. From the top of the ridge, we could see the next valley. It was filled with magnificent trees. This setting was like the Garden of Eden, a pristine world of its own—and we were in that world.

From the beginning of my travels to El Triunfo, I have found that coming to know local people is one of the most rewarding aspects of these trips. One morning, a young boy from one of the squatter families brought a single egg to our camp to give to one of our guests since he knew that we didn't have any fresh food. A couple of years later, these squatters were moved out of the valley because they were living and farming there illegally. One of the children, Ishmael Galvez, became a part of the ranger staff that guarded the park, and in later years, he served as our local guide when we brought groups to El Triunfo. He had a remarkable ability to locate the Horned Guan, and he knew the common and Latin name of every bird found at El Triunfo. When a Mexican graduate student, Felipe Gonzalez, came to the area to study the Horned Guan for his dissertation research, Ishmael provided invaluable help to him. He showed Felipe the places in the forest where a Horned Guan would excavate an area below a mass of tree roots to construct a dust bath. They observed Horned Guans taking dust baths and reported seeing a male lead a female to the bath, bathe, and then mate.

More than twenty years earlier, on my first trip to Mexico with Armand, we had heard from the local farmer about a magnificent forest in a distant valley. This inspired me to visit such a place and walk on a trail bordered by giant trees. I'm sure that Armand felt the same way. This trip to El Triunfo fulfilled that dream, but sadly, he was not with me. Still, each time I travel to this enchanting forest and take in all its natural beauty, I think of Armand.

This inaugural trip had been so successful and had made such an impression on John Rowlett and me that we decided to return the following year with another group. As we talked to people about the trip, it became clear that there was so much interest in this region that we could take two groups. Several months before our scheduled departure to El Triunfo, I was in Mexico leading another tour when I received a telegram from Bettina Von Knoop, the wife of the owner of the *finca*. I still have a copy of it: *No hay mulas. No hay paso.* The owners had decided that they would no longer provide mules to take our supplies up the mountain, and they did not want us to travel through the *finca*. I was stunned and very disappointed by this news. John and I decided that we would take the first group to a cloud forest in Guatemala, where there was a chance that we would see some of the same birds found in El

Triunfo. We knew that it would be an entirely different experience, but it was the only solution. That trip was successful, even though we didn't encounter any Horned Guans. But it wasn't El Triunfo.

Prior to this trip, we traveled to Tuxtla, where we had arranged to meet with Hubertus Von Knoop. He was a large German man, who was very polite and friendly. He told us that it was unsafe to go to El Triunfo because people were growing marijuana there. We wondered if that was the true reason for his decision or rather that he felt that supplying us with mules would interfere with the work of his *finca*. During this particular visit, he told us a number of interesting stories. One was about hunting ducks along the Pacific coast of Chiapas at dusk. He shot what he thought to be two Black-bellied Whistling Ducks, but they turned out to be among the last Scarlet Macaws seen in Chiapas. He had shot the rare birds by mistake. Another story was about the *finca*. He had bought it from the previous Mexican owners when he was released from the prisoner-of-war camp in Tennessee, and he moved there with his family. He mentioned that a German botanist, who had visited them at the plantation, had discovered a new species of begonia that he named after Hubertus's wife, Bettina.

The meeting was pleasant, but unsuccessful in terms of gaining access to El Triunfo via Finca Prusia. John and I then flew to Tapachula to meet the group that we would take to Guatemala. The day before they arrived, we rented a car and drove to Mapastepec on the Pan-American Highway. From Mapastepec, we went to Colonia Guadalupe Victoria, where Don Rodrigo lived. Since Hubertus was unwilling to provide us with mules, we hoped that Don Rodrigo could arrange for horses from the Pacific side to travel to El Triunfo. We drove through the night on the highway, which was filled with cars and trucks, until we reached our turnoff, the narrow dusty road to Colonia Guadalupe.

After a couple of miles, we stopped for a stretch. The soft, tropical night immediately enveloped us. The peace and quiet of the Mexican countryside surrounded us. We looked up at the stars and heard the lovely calls of the Pauraque, a night bird related to the Chuck-will's-widow of North America. We had entered a different world. We had gone back into old Mexico. All of a sudden, we saw a horseman coming toward us. Oddly enough, this man turned out to be Don Rodrigo's nephew, Ariel, who was riding through the night to Mapastepec. We asked him for directions to Don Rodrigo's house.

We continued along the road that started to climb into the low hills, becoming rutted and rocky and challenging to navigate in our small rental car. Then, we arrived at the village of Colonia Guadalupe and were directed to the tiny, modest house of Don Rodrigo, who was surprised to see us. A small man, he possessed a type of energy and soulfulness that set him apart. We met his wife, Joventina, and his children. Chairs were brought from the house into the small yard, and we sat there discussing the possibility of going to El Triunfo from his side of the mountain and whether he could assemble enough horses to carry our equipment. He assured us that this would be possible. We told Don Rodrigo that we would return in two weeks.

We decided to take the second tour to El Triunfo, climbing the mountain from the Pacific side. This group was mostly composed of the friends and family of Rose Styron, including her son, Tom, and one of her daughters, Polly. Among her friends were Cynthia Bumstead and the sculptor Jack Zajac and his wife. My friend Bob Warren, whom I had known since high school, joined us, too. We met the participants in Tapachula and drove to Don Rodrigo's house, where we spent the first night crammed together, occupying almost every inch of his tiny front yard with our tents. During the night, a pig ran through Rose Styron's tent. The next morning, we got up early and spent a long time packing and repacking in preparation for our hike. I'll never forget Don Rodrigo, standing on his front porch, holding a small bag about the size of a shopping bag and indicating that he was ready to go. It was quite a contrast to our excessive gear.

Eventually, we were ready to start the hike. The first day, we walked on a road along the Rio Novilleros that soon narrowed to a footpath. The valley became completely forested. We crossed the river three or four times, taking off our boots and wading across it. At one point, we spotted a King Vulture, eating the carcass of a dead animal while ten other King Vultures perched in a nearby tree. At other points, we saw Common Black Hawks flying along the river.

By mid-afternoon, we reached the tiny village of Tres de Mayo, where we bought warm soft drinks. This village of about one hundred people was connected to civilization only by the walking trail, and its inhabitants were quite surprised to see a collection of gringos passing through. Beyond the village, the trail once again entered the pristine tropical lowland forest. Late in the afternoon, Don Rodrigo pointed out a huge Spectacled Owl perched on a branch of a tree in a ravine. This beautiful owl with its buff underparts and its chocolate upperparts was a species that none of the group had ever seen. White streaks marked its eyebrows and lower cheeks, making its yellow eyes more vivid and bright.

In the late afternoon, we came to a small clearing where there was a concrete platform of about two hundred square feet that was used to dry coffee beans. The forested area around this platform had been cleared and planted with coffee bushes. This fifty-acre *finca* was named Paval, or "the place of the guans," since Crested Guans were found in this area. It was the only clearing that we had seen all day. We heard the screeching of parakeets and then watched as more than a hundred Orange-fronted Parakeets descended into the trees that bordered the clearing. The sun sank. We set up our tents on the concrete platform. We stared up at the forested hills, knowing that the next day we would be walking up the trail into these hills on our way to El Triunfo.

We bathed in the Rio Paval, a small river that ran just below our campsite, and the next morning, we started up the steep trail toward El Triunfo. Once again, we were immersed in tropical forests. The branches of giant fig trees intersected over our heads. This natural cathedral provided ample shade. Like the trail from Finca Prusia, this footpath consisted of multiple switchbacks, and although these made the climb easier, it was still strenuous.

By mid-morning, it had become hot. This hike had begun at a much lower elevation, and there was more distance to cover in order to reach El Triunfo. We continued hiking throughout the day until we reached the spot where a tiny spring provided much-needed drinking water. We learned from Don Rodrigo that this spot is called El Limon, since a lime tree had been planted near the spring. Our group had been strung out along the trail, and when we gathered at the spring, we realized that two participants—Rose Styron and her friend Cindy Bumstead—were not with us.

As it turned out, they had turned right at a fork in the trail, descending the mountain instead of continuing upward. Don Rodrigo and his nephew, Fidel, realized what must have happened. Fidel went back down the trail and located Rose and Cindy. By the time they joined us, it was almost dark and we could not make it to our next camping destination at Cañada Honda. As a result, we had to camp on the trail near El Limon.

Once it got dark, we heard a deep call, like a growl, coming from up the slope. I asked Don Rodrigo's nephew what it was, and he said it was the call of a frog. But Don Rodrigo said, no, it was the sound of an owl. I made a recording of the nocturnal call, but we weren't able to see the creature. It was only years later at Louisiana State University that I heard a recording of a Crested Owl and realized that Don Rodrigo had been correct in his identification. The Crested Owl is a spectacular bird that none of us had ever seen. And, as it turned out, my recording was one of the first recordings ever made of this species.

The next day, we continued to Cañada Honda, but since we were eager to reach El Triunfo, we didn't camp there. We went on up the mountain, mile after mile. Above Cañada Honda, the trail became much steeper. Switchbacks continued, but they were closer together. The forest changed dramatically—from the upper tropical zone with its many broad-leafed trees to the transitional zone, which was composed almost entirely of beautiful pine trees. On the branches of these pine trees were orchids and bright red and green bromeliads. At this time of year, most of the orchids were not blooming, but we managed to see a few magnificent blossoms.

Finally, we reached the crest of the Sierra Madre de Chiapas and descended into the valley, where we spent four nights camping.

Sadly, on the last part of the trail before the valley, we noticed the scattered feathers of a Horned Guan that a hunter had killed illegally. We spent three days in the El Triunfo valley, hiking the trails and hoping to find a Horned Guan. We were not successful.

The hike down the mountain to Colonia Guadalupe went as smoothly as possible. I was delighted to know that we could access El Triunfo from the Pacific side, even though it was a longer and more difficult hike, and that Don Rodrigo and his family could provide the horses and horsemen to carry our equipment up the mountain. This trip gave me the opportunity to see this side of the mountain, which is even wilder and more beautiful than the ascent from Finca Prusia.

I continued to make this trip from the Pacific side for a number of years until the establishment of the El Triunfo preserve and the eco-tourism staff of Tuxtla made it possible for us to return to the Finca Prusia route. Unfortunately, over the years, the valley on the Pacific side has changed dramatically with more and more clearings and farms. In addition, the road has been extended almost all the way to Paval. The experience that I had on that very first hike with King Vultures, Black Hawks, and hundreds of Orange-fronted Parakeets eventually became only a treasured memory. These are among the saddest moments for naturalists: When forests are cut, streams become polluted, and bird life diminished. My mentor Edgar Kincaid had seen this same change in other parts of Mexico and told me how sad it made him. Don Miguel also wrote about this loss of nature eloquently in his book, *Asi Era Chiapas!*

Some years ago, Inocente Argueta Sanchez, one of the farmers, wrote and asked me to advance his family and relatives three thousand dollars so they could have their homes connected to the electrical line being constructed in their valley. We sent them the money. The next time I saw Inocente, as I was about to leave for a hike, he looked me in the eye and said, "Don Victor, when the lights went on for the first time, we thought of you." These Mexican farmers have become a part of my extended family, and I treasure my decades-long experiences with them.

One of my most memorable trips was with my longtime friend, Kenn Kaufman. When Kenn and I arrived at the valley of El Triunfo with our tour group and set up our tents, the night was completely clear and filled with thousands of stars. Overhead, we saw Hale Bopp, the most brilliant comet in nearly twenty years, blazing across the sky, providing us with an incredible welcome. Kenn said to me, "There is no place in the world where I would like to be at this moment more than El Triunfo."

Sharing El Triunfo with Kenn was wonderful, but life is often a mixture of the wonderful and the sad. As we passed through Colonia Guadalupe Victoria, on our way to El Triunfo, we learned that my dear old friend, Don Rodrigo, was in the hospital, suffering from stomach cancer. When we came down the mountain, his relatives told us that he had come home from the hospital and was hoping to see me before we departed. After our traditional lunch at Ariel's house with our tour group, we stopped by Don Rodrigo's house. Small wooden chairs were brought into his front yard where he sat with me and Kenn as his wife and children and the members of the tour group stood nearby. He talked about his life and told me that the most important things in life are *amor*, *familia*, and *claridad*. Love, family, and directness, or clarity. Tears rolled down his wife's cheeks. It was hard to say goodbye because I knew that we would never see each other again.

After I returned home, I received the sad news that he had died a few weeks after we had seen him. It was Don Rodrigo who had first spotted a Horned Guan at El Triunfo as he was crossing the mountains from the interior of Chiapas to settle on the Pacific side with his family. It was his discovery of the Horned Guan that led Don Miguel to visit El Triunfo and to begin his ultimately successful effort to see that the area was preserved. Fortunately, on one of my trips, I asked Don Rodrigo to tell the story of his first trip over the mountain and his sighting of the Horned Guan. Sitting around the campfire, Don Rodrigo told this story, pausing every so often so that Andres Sada, one of our participants, could translate it into English for our group. As we listened to Don Rodrigo, we heard Fulvous Owls and Ring-tailed Cats calling in the distance.

My sister, Marilyn, age four, and me at two,
when I was also called "Bubba."

A friend of mine commented, "You looked like you just saw Jesus Christ." And I said, "Actually, it was a Rose-breasted Grosbeak." Photo: Reagan Bradshaw

I started Rockport Wildlife Tours as a way to use a Mercedes bus I had recently bought. Trips were offered near Rockport, Texas, departing on a large boat that took participants to view the wintering Whooping Cranes and other birds.

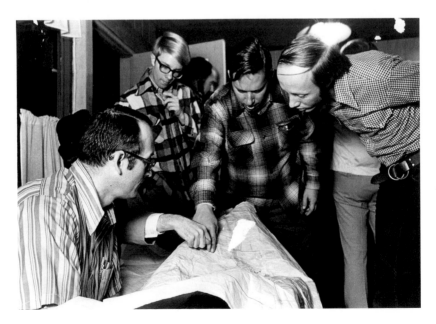

The Freeport Count was often among the top two or three in the United States in the total number of species sighted. During the late sixties and into the seventies, the competition for the highest count was among California, Florida, and Texas, where the night before the count area leaders met to finalize plans.

In 1978, I asked Roger Tory Peterson (center) if he would co-lead a trip to Mexico with John Rowlett and myself. He paused for some time as he considered my offer and all the other obligations on his schedule. Then, to my relief, he said yes.

My trips with Kurt Huffman, Peter English, and David Sugeno, were the inspiration for our summer camp program. Our first trip together to the tropics was to Rancho del Cielo. Many of the top young birders in the United States have attended one or more of our camps.

In 1978, Ted Parker and I visited a variety of areas in Peru, including Machu Picchu. At the end of our adventure, we traveled to the Explorer's Inn in a remote
location in the rain forest. Ted told me that someday there would be clearings
with cattle grazing almost all the way to the Explorer's Inn. At the time, I found
this hard to believe. Unfortunately, he was right.

Barry Lyon (pictured here with longtime VENT client Lorna Duncan), attended Camp Chiricahua, became a tour leader, and is now our chief operating officer.

George Plimpton during a trip to Bhutan in 1993, where we had a chance to observe the Black-necked Cranes. Photo: © William Mulligan

For a birder, seeing an Emperor Penguin is one of the most thrilling experiences. Peter Matthiessen wrote about one of our excursions onto the ice to see these wonderful penguins in *End of the Earth: Voyages to Antarctica*. Photo: © 2001 Greg W. Lasley

In 1995, shortly after George W. Bush was elected governor, I was asked to suggest spots where he, Laura, and their family could go on a birding excursion in South Texas. We went to the Rio Paisano owned by Frank and Mary Grace Horlock (also pictured here).

When I first traveled to El Triunfo, I was thirty-six years old. In late March 2016, I returned with my friend Ben Reynolds and was pleased to find the reserve was just as marvelous as when I first visited in 1977.

Warbler's Roost, Bolivar Peninsula

After Don Rodrigo died, I gave his family a copy of the recording as well as a small tape recorder. When I played it for them and they heard Don Rodrigo's voice, they started to cry. I'll never forget meeting Don Rodrigo at El Triunfo on our first trip and then returning with him the following year from the Pacific side. On that hike, we encountered a local man descending the mountain who said to Don Rodrigo, "*Donde va*?" ("Where are you headed?"). His response was "*al cielo*" ("to heaven").

When I first traveled to El Triunfo, I was thirty-six years old. I remember thinking on that trip that I hoped that I could still make it up the trail at seventy and that El Triunfo would still be pristine. In late March 2016, I returned to El Triunfo with my friend Ben Reynolds. I was pleased to find that the six-mile hike up from Finca Prusia was not a problem for me, even at seventy-five. I was gratified to find that El Triunfo was just as marvelous as it was when I first went there in 1977. In fact, the number of Horned Guans had increased since the reserve is now well protected.

On the last morning before we left, we encountered my old friend Ishmael Galvez who showed us a pair of Horned Guans. We watched them for an hour as they fed on fruit in a tree next to the trail just thirty feet above us. It was a magical experience and it was wonderful to be in *cielo* once again. I hope to return many more times.

8

Search for the Imperial Woodpecker

Montezuma Quail
TUTUACA, MEXICO

As a young birder growing up in Houston, Texas, I had heard about the American Ivory-billed Woodpecker, particularly about John James Audubon (1785–1851) seeing dozens of this huge wood-pecker along the banks of the Buffalo Bayou in the early nineteenth century. Audubon wrote of these encounters:

> I have always imagined, that in the plumage of the beautiful Ivory-billed Woodpecker, there is something very closely allied to the style of colouring of the great Vandyke. The broad extent of its dark glossy body and tail, the large and well-defined white markings and the brilliant yellow in its eye, have never failed to remind me of some of the boldest and noblest productions of that inimitable artist's pencil.

I knew the bird was virtually extinct. When I was eight years old, I read an article in the *Houston Chronicle* about the last remaining Ivory-billed Woodpecker that lived in Singer Tract, a stretch of vir-gin timber along the Tensas River in northeastern Louisiana. The property was named after the sewing machine company, which owned the land, and was the largest area of virgin bottomland forest remaining in the South. I remember wishing that somehow I could travel to the Singer Tract and see this magnificent bird before it went extinct. Unfortunately, that wasn't possible.

The American Ivory-billed Woodpecker was once found throughout the old-growth forests of the southeastern United States. Unlike the Pileated Woodpecker, the Ivory-bill was very specialized in its diet, feeding almost exclusively on the larvae of a wood-boring beetle that laid its eggs in large dead trees. According to James T. Tanner, a woodpecker expert with the University of Tennessee, each nesting pair of the American Ivory-billed Woodpecker needed 640 acres of forest (or one square mile) in which to breed. The cutting of the old-growth bottomland forest of the southeastern United States was one of the major factors in the decline of this species. By 1900, it had become very rare and continued to decline until the forties when one female in the Singer Tract was the only member of the species known to exist anywhere.

Roger Tory Peterson traveled there in 1941 with his first wife, hoping to see that last Ivory-bill. After looking for some time, Roger wanted to give up, but his wife, who was an avid birder, insisted that they keep looking. Evidently, an argument broke out between them about whether to stay or leave. While they were arguing, the Ivory-bill called nearby and they were able to see it.

Nancy Tanner, the widow of Dr. Tanner, describes seeing this female Ivory-bill perching at the top of a tall tree morning after morning. The woodpecker called repeatedly, hoping to attract a mate. In a film about the Ivory-billed Woodpecker, *Ghost Bird* (2009), Nancy says, "My only claim to fame is that I am the last person alive to have seen the last Ivory-bill."

In the late sixties, several reports of American Ivory-billed Woodpecker sightings not far from Houston circulated among the larger birding community. Controversy surrounded whether or not these sightings were authentic. Armand Yramategui went to look for this woodpecker and reported one near Evadale in the Neches River bottomlands, a stretch of forested wetlands sixty miles from Houston. His sighting inspired countless other birders and naturalists to search the Big Thicket in hopes of seeing the near-extinct woodpecker. Similar to the sighting reports in 2004 in the Big Woods of eastern Arkansas, no one ever obtained a photograph of that bird or the one that had been reported in East Texas.

Sighting the Imperial Woodpecker proved almost as challenging as locating the Ivory-billed Woodpecker. I first heard about the Imperial Woodpecker from Edgar Kincaid, who told me about his expedition in 1934 to northwestern Mexico with the famous botanist Hardy DeLeseur. In the Texas Ornithological Society newsletter, Edgar wrote that one morning they had gone over to the edge of a canyon to observe a large flock of Thick-billed Parrots. When they returned to their campsite, the Mexican workers told them that, while they were gone, an Imperial Woodpecker had perched in a tree near their campsite and then had flown away. It seemed unbelievable to Edgar that this huge bird could come and go so quickly, but evidently that was what happened. During the rest of their expedition, the group never spotted an Imperial Woodpecker.

In 1975, I learned that a man named Ben Tinker, a naturalist who had devoted his life to saving the wildlife of northwestern Mexico with support from the New York Zoological Society, had recently seen an Imperial Woodpecker. Shortly after hearing this report, John Rowlett and I were visiting George Plimpton and his wife, Freddy, in Manhattan. During our stay, I mentioned the recent reports of the Imperial Woodpeckers in Mexico. George was passionate about quests, so his immediate response was "Let's go and look for the Imperial."

I knew that Ben Tinker was a friend of Starker Leopold, the son of the legendary naturalist Aldo Leopold (1887–1948), who was perhaps best known for *A Sand County Almanac* (1949). Starker was also a great naturalist and author of *The Wildlife of Mexico: The Game Birds and Mammals* (1959). I called him at the University of California, Berkeley, where he taught, and I asked him how I could get in touch with Tinker, hoping to collect more specifics about his recent sightings of the Imperial Woodpecker. I then phoned Tinker with an invitation to accompany us on an expedition to search for this rare bird. Initially, he was quite agreeable, suggesting a possible route across the border to the small town of Madera, located in western Chihuahua. From there, we would travel by mule up the headwaters of the Yaqui River to a remote area called Estrellita.

Later, though, Tinker telephoned to say that he had to undergo cataract surgery and would not be able to go with us. I pressed him for further details on the exact coordinates where he had seen the famous woodpecker, but he was vague, saying, "Well, it's a vast country, Mr. Emanuel. It's all one vast mountain range." I mentioned that we had hired a bush pilot to assist in our search. "Well, if he knows the country," Tinker said, "he will know where the woodpecker is." I'll never know why he was unwilling to be more forthcoming. Nevertheless, I was determined to go ahead with this expedition in August, during the nesting season, when the birds would remain in one area and could possibly be observed.

Prior to our adventure, we convened in New York City for a trip to the American Museum of Natural History in order to see the specimens of the Imperial Woodpecker in the museum's collection. Dr. Lester Short, a museum ornithologist and a specialist on woodpeckers, ushered John, George, and me into the restricted research area with endless cabinets of bird skins. He presented us with a tray filled with a dozen or more of the American Ivory-billed Woodpecker and three skins of the Imperial. I was very impressed with the size of the Imperial Woodpecker. It appeared to be a fourth or a third bigger than the Ivory Bill, which was about the same size as a crow. The Imperial, in contrast, was similar in size to a raven. At one point, I held both woodpeckers side by side, and John took a photograph of me with the skins.

A few weeks later, after I had returned to Houston, I received a phone call from George. I could tell immediately that something was wrong from the tone of his voice. In his very polite way, George asked me if, by chance, I had taken the skin of the Imperial Woodpecker. The secretary of the museum director had called George to say that the bird skin was missing. I was stunned by this news. Neither John nor I had taken the woodpecker skin; in fact, I recalled returning the specimens to the tray and then departing the research area, led by Dr. Short. Fortunately, a few days later, this issue was resolved when the secretary called George again, saying that it was a paper on the bird, not the skin, that had gone missing and that the staff had managed to locate it.

Our August trip began in Tucson. On separate trips, Ike Russell, a bush pilot from Arizona, flew our group in a single-propeller, six-seat Cessna 180. John and I departed first with Ike, flying over the mountains of western Chihuahua and eastern Sonora. We landed at several places, looking for favorable habitats for the woodpecker. On each airstrip, Ike had to maneuver the plane low in order to scare cattle off the runway.

None of these areas looked like possible environments for the woodpecker, so we decided to continue south. En route, we flew over the magnificent Basaseachic Falls and landed on a rural airstrip nearby. Farther south, we reached Tutuaca, a small community of about one hundred people high in the mountains. We believed Tutuaca might be an optimal spot to look for the woodpecker. John and I set up camp there, and a few days later, George and Terry Moore, a photographer, joined us, and Ike returned to Tucson.

We became acquainted with several of the locals and heard stories about Imperial Woodpecker sightings (the locals' name for the bird was *pitoreal*). An older woman named Señora Salvador said that she had seen one only a month before. Antonio Marquez, the superintendent of the sawmill operations around Tutuaca, also claimed to have seen a *pitoreal*. George recounted Marquez's sightings in the article that he wrote for *Audubon Magazine* (November–December 1977) about our expedition:

> He told us that the year before he had seen two *pitoreals* in the top of dead pines on a ridge above a ranch called Cebadilla. He suspected they were a pair—a *matrimonio*. Before that it had been six years since he had last seen an Imperial Woodpecker. He took a comb out of his shirt pocket and whisked it through his hair. This last time he had watched the two *pitoreals* for a half-hour. They were working for insects in dead trees, but he never saw them alight on the same tree together.

And then Antonio mentioned that the woodcutters in the village Pitoreal—about fifty miles across the mountains—had seen six Imperial Woodpeckers during recent months.

We decided to set off into the mountains in an old logging truck to an area several hours west of the valley, where Antonio said the loggers were just cutting the forest. En route, I remember seeing the largest madrone trees that I had ever seen in my life. This beautiful species is an evergreen tree with white bark that peels easily and exposes a rusty layer underneath the curling white skin. Some of these trees stood as high as twenty feet tall. Most of the other trees were pines.

After a long drive, we stopped at Cebadilla, a small ranch nestled in a meadow at the edge of the forest where Antonio had seen the pair feeding in the dead pine trees. Pigs and chickens scattered on the dusty road. Aggressive mongrel dogs chased the chickens. A mountain stream sliced through the field. We hiked up into the mountains to a sawmill settlement named Pescados. Compared to the US lumber industry, Mexican lumber companies have developed a more sensible approach to their timber production. Rather than clear-cutting whole mountainsides, they only cut the larger trees and allow the rest of the forest to remain. In theory, this selective cutting should allow the Imperial Woodpecker to adapt to a relatively undisturbed environment.

We camped on a ridge a few miles from Pescados. Our campsite of two two-man tents overlooked the valley of rock and pine. After hiking for a good part of the first day, we returned to our campsite, built a fire, and fixed dinner. During August, the mornings were crisp and clear, but by the mid-afternoon, giant thunderheads rose out of the Pacific lowlands to the west. As the afternoon wore on, these thunderheads became darker and more ominous. While we ate, the first few drops of rain started to fall. We hurried and finished our dinner, so we could scramble into our tents before the deluge began. Shortly after dark, the heavens opened up. Thunder, lightning, and torrential rain took over the sky for several hours. Later in the night, the intense storm subsided and the stars emerged.

We woke up before sunrise, gazed up at the stars, and heard the pre-dawn songs of Purple Martins flying in the darkness over our campsite. The sun soon rose—and we began another day of searching for the Imperial Woodpecker. Every morning, John attempted to call up the woodpecker with his own imitation of what he thought sounded like the bird's call, cupping his hands together and producing a "mournful, quite nasal honk." (Unfortunately, no recordings of the call exist, and there is only one photograph in existence.)

While we were exploring this region, we walked a little ways down the mountain into the next valley where we happened to meet David Solis, a logging truck driver. He said that not only had he seen the woodpecker twelve days before, but had also shot one of the birds with a .22 rifle and had eaten the meat. Then, he flashed a broad grin, revealing a large gold tooth, and said that the woodpecker was *"un gran pedazo de carne"* (a big piece of meat). We stared in horror at him, but I couldn't bring myself to ask him how it had tasted.

As each day passed, it was becoming clear that we had arrived too late to see the great woodpecker. Our frustration reminded me of how the great ornithologist and naturalist Alexander Skutch must have felt as, year after year, he looked on his property in Costa Rica for the nest of the Nightingale Wren. He heard the wren and saw it, but was unable to find the nest, though he looked for it during thirty years of fieldwork. When I told that story during our trip, George said, "Thirty years looking for a nest—that must have driven him nuts." I responded, "At least he knew it was there!" I felt disappointed and dejected: Perhaps I would have not felt that way if we had been looking for a species that we knew existed, or for something like the nest of the Nightingale Wren. But with the Imperial, the sadder possibility was that the woods were truly devoid of these birds—and that we had arrived too late.

We continued to search in this area until it was time to return to Tutuaca. George had informed us before we commenced this adventure that he needed to return to Tucson to meet a deadline for an article that he was writing. One afternoon, we heard the rumbling engines of the logging trucks, but it was clear that they weren't going to drive as far as our campsite. I pulled out my handkerchief, trying to signal them, but the trucks drove on. Our food was running low. The night before we had only eaten a few hot dogs and a can of tomato sauce. The can was a bit swollen, and, foolishly, I poured it on the hot dogs, which caused us all to get sick. Here we were in a remote area of Mexico, not sure how we would get back to the valley where Ike was supposed to pick us up, and running low on food.

The next day, our luck changed. The logging trucks returned, and we managed to get a ride into the valley. While sitting in the bed of the truck, we spotted a few Montezuma Quail, a beautiful bird with a dark maroon chest and white spots covering its sides and back. Its face features distinctive markings of white and black. These quail moved across the floor of the oak forest, using their feet to dig for food. Since the truck didn't stop, we only got a quick look.

We returned to Tutuaca. Ike arrived on the appointed day to retrieve George. Unfortunately, the pilot was in a loquacious mood; rather than leaving, he sat down around the campfire, telling us stories and inquiring about our trip. It was getting warmer by the time he decided to leave. John and I stood at the end of the dirt airstrip and watched Ike maneuver the plane in order to prepare for takeoff. Because it was so warm, the plane gained altitude slowly. We were very concerned that he would not be able to gain enough height to clear the nearby trees. Later, George told me that after the plane's wheels almost seemed to tick the tops of the pines, there was a prolonged silence because Ike knew that they had experienced a very close call.

John and I stayed for a couple more days. We heard about another potential sighting, but again had no success. When it came time to leave, we found a man with an old green truck who agreed to drive us to the nearest town that offered bus service. We decided to name his truck "The Guaca" since it was green. Guaca is also the local name for the Thick-billed Parrot, a brilliant green bird that looks somewhat similar to a macaw because of its long tail. Sadly, this species is also declining because one of its favorite places to nest was a cavity created by the Imperial Woodpecker.

Several hours later, as we rode along a winding mountain road, we heard a loud sound under the truck. The drive shaft had tumbled onto the road, and the truck came to an abrupt stop. Amazingly, the man had an extra drive shaft, which he quickly installed, and we proceeded. We arrived at a small village and boarded the bus just as it was about to leave. John and I began our long journey home.

Even though we didn't find the Imperial Woodpecker, we had heard many stories about it and even met an individual who had eaten one. We had also seen some beautiful, remote country. I always hoped that I could return and continue the search, but that never happened. Over the years, I continued to hear rumors of sightings by Mexican biologists, but none of these resulted in hard evidence, such as a photograph. Sadly, by now, the Imperial Woodpecker—the largest woodpecker that ever existed—is almost certainly extinct.

9

My Travels with King Penguin

Bobolink

SABINE PASS, TEXAS

Like most young birders from my generation, I grew up knowing the name Roger Tory Peterson. Over the years, he became one of my heroes because he had created the first field guide for the birds of eastern North America, *A Field Guide to the Birds*. This book focused on the field marks that enabled the observer to identify any bird easily and thus represented a major leap forward for birding. It also contained plates with illustrations by Peterson; each plate included lines that highlighted the key marks to distinguish various birds from similar species. He had come up with this idea from reading the children's story, *Two Little Savages* (1903) by Ernest Thompson Seton, a classic semi-autobiographical tale about a young boy who discovers some mounted ducks at home. He makes sketches of the water birds and their feather patterns, creating something of a guide so that he could identify the live ducks in their natural habitat. The book also included hundreds of illustrations by Seton.

The field guide was published in 1934 when Peterson was only twenty-six years old. Initially, four New York publishers turned down the manuscript because it didn't contain the dry formalities and details of scientific ornithology. Houghton Mifflin agreed to print two thousand copies. The books went on sale at the Harvard Co-op and sold out in one day. Today, more than seven million copies of Peterson's guides have been sold, and the field guide series has been expanded to more than fifty titles.

This was the first field guide that I ever owned. On my eleventh birthday, my father gave me *Birds Over America* (1948), an in-depth account of birds and birding in North America. As an examination of environmental issues, it was very much ahead of its time. Later, I read *Wild America* (1956), the travel book that Roger co-authored with his friend James Fisher about their hundred-thousand-mile journey around North America. I loved it. I never dreamed that I would actually meet Roger Tory Peterson.

During summer 1961, I traveled to the East Coast for the first time. I was attending a course at the Marine Biological Laboratory in Woods Hole, Massachusetts. It was a very prestigious program. I was accepted because my professor at the University of Texas, Dr. Harold Bold, recommended me, and the faculty of the Woods Hole program had studied under him during their graduate studies. We collected seaweed and mounted it on large pieces of blotter paper. I loved the beauty of these things. (I still have this collection of seaweed.) At the same time, we were each to complete an individual project. I was given a sample of dirt that had been in the same bottle for fifty years. It included spores of algae. I placed the dirt in a Petri dish, and somehow the specimen became contaminated. People who did well in the course were asked to stay for a longer period. I was not asked to stay because I had failed to do this project in a careful manner. This underscored an aspect of my personality: I'm a good, persistent organizer, but I don't have a scientist's attention to data and detail.

This program introduced me to the Northeast. I had driven from Texas to Massachusetts in my small Triumph sedan. As I drove out onto Cape Cod, I beheld a world that contained a vastly different landscape from my native environs with different birds, plants, and habitats. On my way home to Texas, I decided to stop by Old Lyme, Connecticut, hoping to meet Roger Tory Peterson at his home on seventy acres. He had moved to the house in 1954. Old Lyme proved to be an ideal location for Roger, placing him between New York City, the headquarters of the National Audubon Society, and Boston, the home of Houghton Mifflin. (In a strange coincidence, the Petersons happened to be neighbors of a direct descendent of John James Audubon, Genie Copp.) Also, nearby was the Great Island Marsh, which provided a natural habitat to numerous pairs of nesting Ospreys and other wetland birds.

Unfortunately, Roger wasn't home that afternoon. I remember walking on a path by his house that was bordered on both sides by tall cedar trees. His studio with large windows was about a hundred yards up a hill from the main house. I thought about the great man who lived on this beautiful property and hoped that some day I would get to meet him.

During the fall of that same year, my dream came true: I met Roger briefly at the annual meeting of the National Audubon Society, which was held in early November in Corpus Christi, Texas. I attended the convention and co-led a field trip with Roger's old friend and wildlife photographer, Allan Cruickshank. Allan, who was also the organizer and compiler of the Christmas Bird Count in Cocoa Beach, Florida, wore his trademark red tam-o'-shanter. We birded the Aransas Wildlife Refuge, and I remember Allan spotting a Ladder-backed Woodpecker perched on a telephone pole. He stood among the group of forty participants and, in a loud voice, told everyone where the bird was and why it was a Ladder-backed Woodpecker. This provided me with a glimpse into what might make a good tour leader. Roger was speaking at this convention. After his talk, I got to meet him and shake his hand. He was a tall, pleasant man with a soft voice. Roger seemed rather shy and said only a few words to me.

In 1976, when I was serving as president of the Texas Ornithological Society (TOS), I came up with the idea of making Roger Tory Peterson an honorary life member. He would be the first non-Texan ever to be given this honor. I knew that Roger deserved it, in part, because he had written and illustrated *A Field Guide to the Birds of Texas* (1960), the first field guide to focus exclusively on

Texas bird life. In addition, I hoped that, if we made him an honorary member, he might accept our invitation to speak at our annual meeting. I wrote Roger a letter ten months before the date of the gathering, informing him of the organization's decision and inviting him to speak. In the same letter, I also asked him if he would consider leading a two-week tour of Texas with my then-partner John Rowlett and me after the meeting.

I received no reply. I continued to wait. I considered calling him, but decided that such a call would be too intrusive. Later, I learned that Roger answered all of his own mail and was often far behind in responding to the large volume of letters that he received. In November 1977, I was leaving my house to go to the Houston airport to fly to Amarillo for the fall meeting of TOS, where we would be making the final plans for our spring meeting. I had only driven about a half block when I spotted the postman walking toward my house. For some reason (I've never done this before or since), I got out of the car and asked the postman if he had any mail for me. I was astonished when he gave me an envelope with the return address of Roger Tory Peterson, Old Lyme, Connecticut. Holding my breath, I tore it open, and to my delight, I discovered that Roger had agreed to both my offers: He would speak at our annual meeting in McAllen and co-lead the Texas tour in April 1978.

I met Roger and his wife Virginia (Ginny) at the small airport in McAllen. He was dressed in a heavy suit, which was inappropriate for South Texas in early April. He had bushy hair, a long face, and a prominent nose. Roger told me that he had seen a flock of Black-bellied Whistling Ducks fly by as the plane was landing on the tarmac. These tropical ducks are some of the most colorful waterfowl with their chestnut bodies, black underparts, bright red bills, and bold white wing stripes. In those days, they were found nowhere else in the United States except the Lower Rio Grande Valley.

The TOS meeting was a success. Roger's presentation was wonderful. A few days later, we met our tour participants in Houston, and the next morning, we drove to Beaumont and checked into a motel. We spent the next day, birding amid the fields and woods of the Big Thicket National Preserve, where we saw many of the special birds of this region, including the Red-cockaded Woodpecker and Bachman's Sparrow.

Roger told me that he and Ginny had enjoyed hearing a Mockingbird singing all night outside their motel room. He said that he had left the door to their room open throughout the night, so that the song would travel more easily into the room. I remember thinking, "What about the mosquitoes? What about someone who might have ill intent?" This was but one example of Roger's total connection to and immersion in birds and nature.

For the next two weeks, we traveled down the coast of Texas, all the way from the Louisiana border to the Mexican border and then north to the Texas Hill Country. Nature obliged us in the most extraordinary ways. During the spring months in Texas, birders hope to witness a fallout, an event that occurs when land birds—such as warblers, orioles, tanagers, buntings, and grosbeaks—migrate north from southern Mexico and Central America. On this tour with Roger and Ginny, we observed not just one fallout, but three: one on the Upper Texas coast, one on the Central Texas coast, and one on South Padre Island. We also had wonderful wildflowers due to the abundant rains of the winter and early spring. All of this enchanted Roger and Ginny. They had only recently married (Ginny was Roger's third wife), and he was particularly eager to share the wonders of nature and the birds of Texas with her.

Another memorable sighting was a flock of fifty male Bobolinks that had landed near a weedy area right next to the Gulf of Mexico, near Sabine Pass. The male Bobolink is beautiful with its pitch-black breast, substantial amount of white on its upper side, and golden-yellow nape. I had never seen such a large flock in my life. An uncommon songbird in Texas, the Bobolink spends its winters in Argentina and migrates up the east coast of the United States to its breeding grounds throughout the north. During this sighting, the birds burst into a group singing, a Bobolink behavior that Roger had never witnessed.

This bird's song was the inspiration for William Cullen Bryant's "Robert of Lincoln," which is one of the poems featured in the Cornell Laboratory of Ornithology CD *Birdsongs and Literature*. The first stanza begins:

Merrily swinging on brier and weed,
Near to the nest of his little dame,
Over the mountain-side or mead,
Robert of Lincoln is telling his name:
Bob-o'-link, bob-o'-link,
Spink, spank, spink;
Snug and safe is that nest of ours,
Hidden among the summer flowers.
Chee, chee, chee.

During our few days in the Lower Rio Grande Valley, we saw almost all the birds of that region, including Red-billed Pigeons, Ferruginous Pygmy-Owls, White-tipped Doves, Buff-bellied Hummingbirds, and Ringed and Green Kingfishers. As we headed north, we realized that we had not yet seen a Verdin, a tiny bird that is now placed in its own family because it is so different from any other bird. We stopped along the side of a busy highway, hoping to spot a Verdin since the brushy habitat of mesquite looked right. To my surprise, Roger, who was sixty-nine at the time, heard the Verdin across the highway, despite all of the noise generated by the traffic. We were able to track down the bird and show it to the group. The male Verdin is gray with a yellow head, a sharp small bill, and a deep red spot on the corner of its wing. Roger was delighted that he had been responsible for our finding a Verdin.

Later, as we approached the Texas Hill Country, just south of Uvalde, we came upon a sizable flock of male Lark Buntings feeding on the ground in a short, grassy field. Like the Bobolink, the Lark Bunting is a strikingly beautiful black bird. In contrast to the Bobolink, it features large white patches on its wings. These Lark Buntings were also engaged in group singing. Again, it was something that none of us had ever witnessed.

About an hour later, as we drove north of Uvalde, we observed on the west side of the highway a large field that was solid purple with prairie verbena. Thousands of white prickly poppies were scattered among the purple verbena. And next to the highway was a solid band of yellow coreopsis. It was like an exquisite picture painted by nature. In one of the mesquite trees, there was a gorgeous Bullock's Oriole, a dazzlingly colorful, deep-orange bird with black markings on its crown, nape, throat, and upper back, and a broad white wing bar. This was an extraordinary scene to share with a great naturalist.

During the last few days of the tour, we traveled through the Texas Hill Country and saw such special birds as the Black-capped Vireo and the Golden-cheeked Warbler. One afternoon, we visited the Frio Bat Cave in Concan. We watched a multitude of Cave Swallows circling over the cave. After the sun set, these swallows started to enter the cave to roost. Shortly after the last Cave Swallow flew into the cave, the first bat emerged. Soon, several million Mexican Free-tailed Bats (a subspecies of the Brazilian Free-tailed Bat), the most abundant bat in the world, poured out of the cave. As they flew over us, we could hear their wing beats. They flew north and then turned south. Suddenly, a Red-tailed Hawk appeared. It plunged into the stream of bats and caught one. The bat flight lasted an entire hour. It was an amazing spectacle. We couldn't have asked for a better two weeks in Texas.

After that tour, I stayed in touch with Roger, hoping to see him again. I was visiting a friend in Connecticut about a year later and called Roger to see if I might visit him and Ginny in Old Lyme. They invited me for dinner. During our meal, I asked him if he would co-lead another trip to the Yucatán and Palenque, Mexico, with John Rowlett and myself. He paused for some time as he considered my offer and all the other obligations on his schedule. Then, to my relief, he said yes. At that point, VENT was a young company, still trying to get on its feet. Although we were operating a few tours, cash flow was precarious. Soon after I spoke with Roger, I announced in our little mimeographed newsletter that he was co-leading the trip with us to Mexico. It immediately filled up, and the deposits of the participants signing up for this tour were a significant boost to our cash flow.

Our staff made reservations in the Yucatán and Palenque. The excursion was to begin on Cozumel Island, where we reserved rooms in the newest luxury hotel. About a month before the trip, the travel agency in Mexico informed us that our rooms in this hotel had been canceled because another hotel that was being built hadn't finished on schedule. Guests who had booked rooms in that unfinished hotel had been given our rooms. Needless to say, I was very upset. With some trepidation, I called Roger to let him know. I told him the situation, wondering if he would react angrily and wonder himself about what kind of organization Victor Emanuel Nature Tours was that they couldn't even handle hotel reservations properly. Instead, Roger's response was "Victor, don't worry about it. If we can't get rooms, we can go looking for owls all night." Then, he surprised me even more by saying, "If you can't get enough rooms, Ginny and I will be willing to share a room with another couple." Roger's response demonstrated his sensitivity and kindness. Some people considered him not to be a very warm and friendly person. I later realized that this perception was due to his shyness.

We resolved the lodging dilemma and began the trip a month later. During that Mexico trip, I asked Roger if he would consider becoming an associate of our new company and allow us to use his name on our letterhead to help establish our credibility. I offered to pay him a $1,000 annual honorarium. Roger agreed immediately, but declined the payment, saying that since we were a new company, we couldn't afford to pay him $1,000. So, we placed his name on our letterhead and soon planned another trip with him; this time to Peru.

Despite Roger's extensive travels, he had spent very little time in the South American tropics. He was taken by all aspects of this exotic region—the colorful birds, the birdsong, and especially the butterflies. During our Peru tour of 1980, we visited a number of wonderful sites in the foothills of the Andes, the coast, and Amazonia. On this trip, we spent some time in Tingo Maria, where Roger tried to catch a morpho butterfly, a large species with iridescent blue wings. Morphos fly very fast, so Roger wasn't successful in capturing one. He even poured beer on his hand as a lure. A morpho rested on his hand momentarily, but flew away before he could catch it.

We stayed at the Explorer's Inn, a lodge that had recently been built in the rain forest of southeastern Peru. Roger had read somewhere that butterflies are attracted to a mash made of ripe bananas, other fruits, and beer. Roger placed this mash mixture in a shopping bag and proceeded to deposit dollops of it in various spots along the trail near the inn.

Some of us were looking for birds by Rio de la Torre, a beautiful rain forest tributary of the Tambopata River. In the willow thickets, we saw many small birds, including several species of flycatchers and seedeaters. At times, White-winged Piping Guans perched in the trees across the river and emitted high-pitched ascending calls.

Suddenly, we saw Roger running down the trail toward us with a large animal right behind him. At the inn, the owners kept a pet tapir, a hefty tropical animal almost the size of a young pony. It had slurped up the mash that Roger was putting out for the butterflies and then figured out that he was the source of that delicious mixture. Hoping to get more, the tapir started chasing Roger. He was clearly distraught that this large animal was right on his heels. This scene amused us all. Roger threw down the shopping bag and the tapir ate more of the mash and then jumped into the river and swam around. Roger was relieved and proceeded to photograph the swimming tapir.

King Penguins were Roger's favorite birds, so he chose that species as his bird name. He loved Antarctica above all of the other places where he had traveled, and over the years, he made many trips to this frozen continent. The intrepid King Penguins live in this hostile environment, diving anywhere from one hundred to one thousand feet into the ocean for food. They breed on the shores of subantarctic islands, such as South Georgia, in colonies composed of hundreds of thousands of individuals. Penguins embody a sort of child-like spirit as they totter and, at other times, flop headlong across the ice. Most birders will agree: There is nothing quite like a King Penguin.

"They are highly specialized birds dedicated to penguinism," he wrote in *Penguins* (1979), "a life molded by the cold impersonal sea, harsh climate, and the crowded colonies in which they reproduce. Few other sights in the bird world are as spectacular as a wall-to-wall carpet of Kings." *Penguins* was Roger's homage to his favorite family of birds through photographs, paintings, and words. He even painted penguins on the wall above his bathtub.

When I moved to Austin in 1978, I became good friends with three young birders—Peter English, Kurt Huffman, and David Sugeno. During their high school years, we made many trips together and became quite close. Not having any children of my own, I regarded these young guys almost like substitute children or nephews. As a result, when it came time for them to attend college, I made the decision to visit each one at their respective colleges every fall. David enrolled in Connecticut College in New London; Peter attended Williams College in Williamstown, Massachusetts; and Kurt went to Carleton College in Northfield, Minnesota. When I visited David and Peter, I was able to see some of my other friends who lived in that part of the country. I concocted a rather wonderful itinerary for this journey that I made every fall for several years: I flew into New York City and stayed with George and Freddy Plimpton on the Upper East Side. Then I rode the Hampton Jitney out to Bridgehampton and stayed with Peter and Maria Matthiessen. Then Peter or Maria drove me to Orient Point on the North Fork of Long Island, where I boarded the ferry bound for New London, where Roger and Ginny picked me up and took me to their home in Old Lyme. After my visit with David and the Petersons, I drove to Williamstown to see Peter and then returned to Texas. This trip gave me a chance to see a special group of friends during a beautiful time of year in the Northeast and deepened my relationships with all of them.

It was during one of these visits with Roger and Ginny that I had trouble sleeping and ended up wandering around the house. At one point, I found myself in the dining room, looking at Roger's paintings of wildflowers and the medals and honors that he had garnered over the years. The King of Sweden and Prince Bernhard of the Netherlands, among many others, had bestowed honors upon him. It suddenly struck me that Roger was virtually unrecognized by his own country. On my return flight to Austin, I wrote an impassioned letter to President Jimmy Carter, asking him to consider Roger for the Presidential Medal of Freedom.

The following May, when Roger and Ginny were a part of our birding tour to the Dry Tortugas, they pulled me aside to relay the news that Roger would be receiving the Medal of Freedom in June. I told them about the letter I had written to President Carter the previous fall, suggesting that he give Roger the Medal of Freedom. Roger and Ginny decided that my letter was the catalyst for this prestigious award and arranged for me to attend the awards ceremony.

The ceremony took place in the Rose Garden on June 9, 1980, and I was honored to be among those present to witness Roger receiving his medal. Other recipients of the Medal of Freedom that day included Ansel Adams, Lucia Chase, Archbishop Iakovos, Clarence Mitchell Jr., Admiral Hyman Rickover, Beverly Sills, Robert Penn Warren, Eudora Welty, Tennessee Williams, plus four that were bestowed posthumously to Rachel Carson, Hubert Humphrey, Lyndon Baines Johnson, and John Wayne. President Carter read in his citation that afternoon:

Roger Tory Peterson has achieved distinction as a consummate painter, writer, teacher and scientist. As an unabashed lover of birds and a distinguished ornithologist, he has furthered the study, appreciation and protection of birds the world over. And he has done more. He has impassioned thousands of Americans, and has awakened in millions across this land, a fondness for nature's other two-legged creatures.

Being at this ceremony and the luncheon in the East Room was one of the most memorable days of my life. Among Roger's other guests were Lars-Eric Lindblad, the first person to take tourists to Antarctica and one of the pioneers in eco-tourism, and Joe Hickey, one of Roger's birding buddies when they were teenagers in the Bronx Bird Club. Joe went on to study wildlife management with Aldo Leopold. After Leopold passed away from a heart attack in 1948, Joe assumed his position as the professor in wildlife management at the University of Wisconsin. I had heard a lot about Joe and Lars-Eric from Roger, so it was special to meet them on this momentous occasion.

After the luncheon ended, everyone who attended the ceremony was free to wander around the public areas of the White House. We saw Tennessee Williams talking to a group as a Marine band performed nearby. After awhile, we walked out of the building through the gates, realizing that, as the gate shut, this special time had ended and we could not return. We walked across Lafayette Square to the Hay-Adams Hotel, where Roger and Ginny were staying. We had a drink and savored the day together. Roger was clearly, deeply moved by what had happened and was delighted to share this event with some of his closest friends.

In summer 1991, Roger contacted me and said that he wanted to attend Camp Chiricahua, our youth summer birding camp in southwestern Arizona. Our camp was the first of its kind in the birding world, and Roger wanted to experience it firsthand. (See chapter 13 for more on VENT youth birding camps.) Of course, I was delighted with his decision. I decided not to let the campers know that Roger was coming, but instead surprise them when they arrived in Tucson. When I eventually introduced the young campers to the legendary man, one of them said to Roger, "I can't believe you're here."

Not surprisingly, the campers were in awe of him, and they interacted with Roger very little with the exception of a young man from Houston named Cullen Hanks who was new to birding. He had come to the camp at the urging of a friend of his father. Cullen had heard of Roger Tory Peterson, but knew little about him. More than any of the other campers, Cullen spent time with Roger, asking questions and looking at birds.

Another camper, Dan Chiarvalli, brought along his spotting scope and tripod. One morning, a Harris's Hawk was perched on a telephone pole, drawing a crowd of young birders. Dan quickly extended the legs of his tripod and carefully arranged the scope only to find that the bird had flown away. In exasperation, he said to Roger, "By the time I get ready, it's all over with." With the perspective of eighty-plus years, Roger responded, "That's the way life is."

One afternoon, we took some of the campers up the South Fork of Cave Creek Canyon to a small swimming hole. Roger was taking a nap, so he didn't go. As we were walking up the trail toward the swimming hole, a young man, Will Duncan (who would go on to become an expert in stream ecology), came running down the trail, informing us that he and his parents had just seen an Eared Trogon (now called the Eared Quetzal), a spectacular large Mexican species that had only been recently recorded in the United States. Most of its body is an iridescent green with a red belly. While we were standing on the trail amid the sycamores and Arizona pines, a flash of red and green signaled the presence of the rare Eared Trogon. The bird's guttural call further emphasized its presence despite remaining in the shadows of the trees.

When we returned to the camp, the boys and girls who had seen the rare bird were pounding the sides of the vans and yelling, "Trogon! Trogon! Trogon!" The campers who had stayed behind at the camp to play games were crestfallen when they learned they had failed to see this rare bird. One of the boys burst into tears. When I told Roger about the trogon, he was dismayed, too. He said, "Now, I may never see a Eared Trogon." And he didn't, because a few years later, he passed away.

The last time I saw Roger was when he traveled to Rockport, Texas, in early fall 1995 to participate in the dedication of a portion of the Great Texas Coastal Birding Trail that included a marker in memory of Roger's old friend, Connie Hagar. Considered the bird woman of Rockport in the fifties and sixties, Connie was born in 1886 in Corsicana, Texas, where she started a nature club and then became involved with banding birds as a part of a series of national biological studies. Later, in 1933, she and her husband, Jack, moved to Rockport where they owned a motel that became famous among birders.

The day of the ceremony was unusually hot, well into the upper nineties, and extremely humid. A large crowd had assembled in front of the speaking platform near the trail. I was sitting in the front, next to my friend, Greg Lasley. Roger was sitting on the platform in the broiling sun. I remember being worried about the heat. There was no shade over the speaker's platform; the only portable awning available in Rockport was being used at a funeral. When it came time for Roger to speak, he stood at the lectern and only spoke a minute or two before he collapsed. Greg and I rushed to his side and stayed with him until the EMS came and transported him to Coastal Bend Hospital in Aransas Pass. After a thorough examination, the doctors said that Roger was going to be okay; he had become dehydrated from not drinking enough water.

Later, Ginny told me that Roger was never the same after that incident. That winter, he suffered a mild stroke, but was still able to work on the fifth edition of *A Field Guide to the Birds* for a few hours each day. About six months later, I was leading a trip to Manú National Park in the rain forest of southeastern Peru when the very sad news reached me that Roger had died in his sleep.

Roger had an incredible impact on American birding. In many ways, he *started* birding by providing a field guide from which people could identify the birds that they spotted. He promoted birding whenever he could. He hardly ever turned down an invitation to speak at an important anniversary of a bird club. He supported my company. He was a dear friend and a mentor, almost like a second father.

One thing that struck me about Roger—which might be characteristic of individuals who come from modest backgrounds and become famous—was his lack of appreciation for himself. He often said, "I wish I could write like Peter Matthiessen and paint like Robert Bateman." Roger's writing was very good, and his painting was quite beautiful, too. I think the fact that he never attended college caused him to have a lower opinion of himself, particularly around the famous people he knew, such as Sir Peter Scott, the great English naturalist, painter, and son of Robert Falcon Scott, the British explorer who died on his way back from the South Pole. And then here was Roger, who was raised in a modest Swedish-American family and grew up in Jamestown, a small town in upstate New York, near Buffalo. (The other famous individual who hailed from this town was Lucille Ball.)

The Roger Tory Peterson Institute of Natural History was founded in 1984, twelve years prior to his passing, in Roger's hometown. The mission of the institute is the preservation of his "lifetime body of work and making it available to the world for educational purposes."

Roger had a greater effect on American birding and conservation than any man since Audubon.

10

The Mozart of Birding

White-cheeked Tody-Tyrant
TAMBOPATA NATURE RESERVE
MADRE DE DIOS, PERU

In April 1970, I met Ted Parker at the Shamrock Hilton in Houston on the same day that I met my very first client, Dean Gorham. Ted was a gangly, outgoing eighteen-year-old on his first birding trip to Texas as part of the Big Year in which he would set a new North American record—627—for the most species seen in one year. (In 1956, the previous record of 598 species had been set by a twenty-five-year-old Englishman named Stuart Keith.) Amazingly, Ted did this without visiting Alaska.

During that first brief exchange, I was immediately aware of Ted's intense appreciation for birds and nature, and I felt an instant kinship with him. At the time, Ted was still living with his parents in Lancaster, Pennsylvania. I would learn later that, as a young boy, he would go to the local fish market to obtain fish innards so that he could dissect them and study the snails that the fish had eaten. By age twelve, he was a member of the Lancaster County Bird Club. After breaking the Big Year record, Ted became a young birding phenom.

Ted's first visit to the deep tropics was with his close friend Mark Robbins to participate in the El Naranjo and Catemaco Christmas Count in 1973. Ben Feltner and I had started the El Naranjo Count the previous year. Our idea was that after the El Naranjo Count, everyone would drive to Catemaco to participate in the new count. The day before the Catemaco Count, we birded the University of Mexico biological research station, located on the lower slopes of Sierra de los Tuxtlas. Ted spotted a male Lovely Cotinga, a marvelous, brilliant blue-and-purple, robin-sized bird that none of us had ever seen before. Walking along the trails, he heard several White-throated Spadebills (now called Stub-tailed Spadebill), a tiny flycatcher that sits in the undergrowth very near the ground. This was another species that none of us had ever seen or heard.

On the count day, I discovered a Pheasant Cuckoo, a large brown tropical cuckoo almost the size of a Roadrunner. The next day, Ted, Mark, and a few others went with me to look for the cuckoo. We walked slowly up a trail that ascended a hill in the forest. Suddenly, I spotted the cuckoo, sitting on the ground, sunning itself. When we found it, Mark started yelling so loudly that I was tempted to give him the bird name of the Brown Jay, a large tropical jay that emits an explosive *pyow! pyow!* After the Catemaco Count, Ted and Mark visited Palenque, where they discovered more neotropical birds that they had never seen, including the elusive Scaled Antpitta.

Not surprisingly, Ted was more interested in fieldwork than in sitting in the classroom and listening to lectures. One of his professors, Dr. Stephen Russell, called Dr. George Lowery at Louisiana State University (LSU) Museum of Natural Science and said, "George, there is a man over here that you need to have work with your Peru program because he's an excellent researcher and ornithologist. School is not working out for him. He needs to be out in the field." Dr. Lowery agreed, Ted moved to Baton Rouge, and he began a remarkable career in South America—first in Peru and then other areas. Ted's trademark talents—his charisma, extraordinary ear for bird calls, and passion for fieldwork—soon made him the premier field ornithologist working in South America. By 1978, he had spent a considerable amount of time in Peru as a researcher for the Louisiana State University zoology department, working with my old friend, Dr. John O'Neill.

Early on, Ted became the center and driving force of a group of young ornithologists who were passionate about neotropical birds and saving their habitats. During this time, Ted and I kept in touch through letters, particularly when he started going on LSU expeditions to Peru. One such letter was addressed "to all my Neotropical Friends." This letter described a trip of several weeks that Ted made from Cuzco to Puerto Maldonado along a road that passed through largely undisturbed forest. It traversed from thirteen thousand feet to five hundred feet along the eastern slope of the Andes, passing through the most biologically diverse region of the world. Ted wrote of seeing curassows and jaguars, as well as a host of antbirds, some of which were identified only to genus. Here was a pioneer field ornithologist learning to identify many species without a field guide.

From his earliest days in Peru, Ted compulsively tape-recorded every species of bird he heard. Many hundreds of them had never been captured on tape before. Audio recording technology was advancing rapidly, and with support from the Cornell Lab of Ornithology, a McIlhenny heir to the Tabasco company fortune, and LSU, Ted was able to equip himself with cutting-edge recorders and microphones. He lugged a huge, reel-to-reel Nagra recorder around for many years, capturing most of his finest recordings with it. Ted made nearly eleven thousand wildlife recordings and could identify some four thousand different birds just by the sounds of their vocalizations. All of this required thousands of hours in the field, beginning every day long before sunrise. He hiked in the darkness and got into position to record the dawn chorus.

VENT was only a year old when John and Ted suggested that we offer a tour to Peru. It sounded like a good idea, so I quickly agreed to lead such a tour with Ted in July 1978. I vividly remember the flight to Peru, which I spent flipping through my copy of *The Birds of Venezuela*, which, at that time, was the only field guide to any

South American country. Studying the colorful plates, I saw many birds that I had never before seen. One that caught my eye was the White-browed Purpletuft, a plump small bird with a white breast bordered by gray streaks and silky purple tufts. During the tour, we saw that lovely bird perched in a vine tangle close to us in the beautiful afternoon sunlight near Tingo Maria.

We visited the coast of Peru, a montane forest, and Machu Picchu, the ruins of the lost city of the Incas. At the end of this twenty-day adventure, we traveled to the Explorer's Inn in a remote location in the Peruvian rain forest. I'll never forget the departure from Lima. Once our plane ascended over the fog, which is common along the coast at that time of year, the nut-brown wall of the western slope of the Andes came into view. After crossing these scenic snowy peaks and clear blue lakes, we landed briefly in Cuzco and then continued on to Puerto Maldonado, the capital of Madre de Dios, a Peruvian state that contains one of the largest areas of pristine rain forest in the entire Amazon basin. Shortly after departing from Cuzco, we flew over the last high ridge of the Andes and suddenly the landscape changed from brown and seared to lush and green as we looked at the eastern slope of the Andes. Ted told me that the very highest ridge of this slope was called Ceja de la Selva, or the eyebrow of the forest.

The first time that I flew over unbroken tropical forest was with John Rowlett in 1969 when we flew from Tenosique to Yaxchilan. (This was the flight on which I took the photograph that I pulled from my briefcase when I first met Peter Matthiessen at George's apartment.) The view from the plane on the way to Puerto Maldonado was even more thrilling because we flew over an unspoiled forest—no roads, clearings, villages, or fields—for almost an hour. All we saw was the forest. It looked as pristine as Ted had described in his letters. As the plane approached Puerto Maldonado, we observed a network of sinuous rivers sparsely dotted with a few small clearings and huts.

We landed on a dirt airstrip in Puerto Maldonado. As we waited for our luggage, I spotted a huge bird flying high above the Tambopata River. At first, I thought it might be a Harpy Eagle, one of the largest raptors in the world and one of the birds that I most wanted to see. Instead, it was a Horned Screamer, a species usually seen walking along the riverbanks. As their name indicates, these massive, chicken-billed birds tend to be quite vocal and sometimes can be heard dueting to make their call—*ha-moo-co*. With a spiny appendage affixed to the top of its head, the Horned Screamer warrants the title "unicorn of the avian world."

We transferred to a dock and loaded onto a large, dugout canoe for the three-hour trip up the Tambopata to the Explorer's Inn. During the first hour of our boat excursion, we saw a few clearings and houses along the river, but soon there was only an unbroken forest of tall trees bordering the riverbanks. One of these trees was a species of Erythrina, whose crowns were covered with brilliant red blossoms. At times, we spotted Scarlet Macaws feeding on the vivid flowers. Ceibas are the most magnificent trees along this stretch of river. They are described as emergents because they tower above the surrounding forest. As a result, these trees are often used for creating observation platforms near lodges. I remember scanning the high horizontal branches of the ceibas, hoping that I might see a perched Harpy Eagle.

During that first trip, Ted told me that someday there would be clearings with cattle grazing almost all the way to the Explorer's Inn. At the time, I found this hard to believe. To be honest, I didn't want to believe that something like that could ever happen to this rain forest. Unfortunately, he was right. Cattle and clearings are now prevalent along the lower Tambopata for many miles. Fortunately, in 1990, the Peruvian government created the Tambopata Reserve Zone, which preserves 769,000 acres in the Upper Tambopata and has almost 600 species of birds and 1,200 kinds of butterflies. It also contains a dozen different types of forest and some gorgeous oxbow lakes.

We arrived at the Explorer's Inn dock late in the afternoon. Established in 1976 by a small group of Peruvian businessmen, the inn maintains a network of trails, including several that lead to the nearby oxbow lakes. When it was first built, the Explorer's Inn was the only lodge in the Amazonian rain forest, except for one in northern Peru, downriver from the city of Iquitos. Ted had heard about the Explorer's Inn from Peter Alden (my early inspiration to get into the business of nature tourism), who had recently taken a group from the Massachusetts Audubon Society there and returned with glowing reports about the abundant bird and animal life.

The lodge consists of a main building and a series of thatched-roof bungalows. The rooms are elevated by ten-foot stilts off the ground. Before dinner, Ted and I walked down the main trail for about a half mile or so. It was almost dark in the forest, and most of the birds had retired for the night. Still, we heard the calls of White-throated Toucans, Spix's Guans, tinamous, and other sounds that were totally unfamiliar to me. About two hundred yards away from the clearing in front of the lodge, the trail led into an enormous bamboo grove. When we walked through this dense grove, it felt like we were walking through a tunnel. As we stood underneath its leafy canopy, I heard a bird call that I did not recognize.

I asked Ted, "What is that sound?" The bird issued a single, repeated *tink-ink-ink-ink*. Without hesitation, he replied, "That's a Fasciated Antshrike." I had heard this species before in Panama, but its call there was a soft, repeated rising whistle. I mentioned to Ted that it didn't sound like the one I had heard in Panama. He said that the call that I was describing was the call of the male—and we had just heard a female. Later, a pair of researchers, Nina Pierpont and John Fitzpatrick, who were studying birds in Manú National Park determined that there were two species involved. One type of antshrike was associated with bamboo. They described this bird, appropriately named the Bamboo Antshrike, as a new form of species to science. Other areas of the forest (away from the bamboo thicket) were home to the Fasciated Antshrike, similar to the one that I encountered in Panama.

The most wonderful aspect about the Explorer's Inn is the main trail that leads into the surrounding forest. The lodge owners had no idea that by cutting this path through the forest, they would create a trail that intersects so many habitats. Around the clearing in front of the lodge, the terrain features typical riparian vegetation of lowland Amazonia, including giant river cane and cecropia trees.

With large, star-shaped leaves similar to maple leaves, the cecropia is a tropical relative of the mulberry, and its fruit is attractive to birds and other animals. It is one of the first trees to appear on river islands and at the edge of clearings.

Beyond the clearing is an area of transitional forest with a number of low ridges and dips in the trail. This part is susceptible to flooding when the nearby river rises. Giant fig trees are prominent there, and when they are bearing fruit, they attract a great array of birds, including toucans, aracaris, trogons, and guans. After about two miles, the trail ascends a slight rise and emerges into terra firma forest, which never floods. In the terra firma, the landscape features towering trees and very little undergrowth. Each section of the trail offers a different mixture of plants, birds, insects, and other creatures. When you walk along this path, you never know what you will encounter.

Many people possess the mistaken notion that a tropical forest teems with birds. In fact, you can walk a considerable distance and not see a single bird. In tropical forests, many of the birds stay close to the ground, where it's difficult to see them in the dense understory. Others perch high in the trees, often obscured by foliage. What is wonderful about tropical forests is that suddenly a mixed flock of birds may appear—either in the undergrowth or high in the canopy of the trees. It is an electric moment. Such an experience is very exhilarating and at the same time, to some degree, frustrating because the flock usually moves so quickly that it is not possible to get a good look at more than a few birds of perhaps thirty or more species in the flock. Studies of mixed flocks at Manú National Park by my friend Dr. Charles Munn have shown that most of a flock consists of one pair of each species, and these birds spend their entire lives with the same flock.

At another point in the trail, if you're walking quietly, you might see a tinamou. A member of one of the most ancient families in the world, with fossils dating to about 10 million years ago, this ground-dwelling species is similar in size and shape to a grouse. Tinamous lay the most beautiful eggs in the world. The ceramic-like gloss of the egg is about fourteen times that of a chicken egg, and the natural color comes in a number of exquisite shades— including sky blue, lime green, and rich chocolate—that have an almost iridescent sheen. Unfortunately, tinamous also are the most delicious birds in the world to eat and tend to be vulnerable to predators—animals and humans alike—because they walk along the ground, picking up seeds and insects, and nest on the floor of the forest.

Along that same trail, you might encounter a curassow, a turkey-size black bird that also walks on the forest floor. (Curassows are in the same family as the guans.) On one occasion, I was birding with John Rowlett when we spotted two Razor-billed Curassows, which we flushed so they would fly up into a tree. As the birds sat on a high branch, John ran back to the rest of our group to let them know of our sighting. In the meantime, I waited, doing my best to keep the birds from coming down from the tree. While I waited, sweat bees started to cover my face. As their name indicates, these bugs are attracted to the salt in sweat. If you kill one, it emits a pheromone that draws more bees. Nonetheless, I waited diligently and stoically so that the rest of our group could see these impressive birds.

I remember a later excursion in 1979 to the Explorer's Inn when we split into two groups for a morning outing. I led one and Ted the other. When we returned for lunch, Ted gave me a devilish look and said, "We saw a bird that no one has ever seen before." Of course, I immediately insisted that he tell me more details. Ted explained that as he and his group were passing through the bamboo thicket at about noon, he heard a bird that sounded similar to a Flammulated Pygmy-Tyrant, a tiny drab-brownish flycatcher, but he recognized that the call was somewhat different. It's a testament to Ted's acuity that, at the end of a long hike when many in the tour group were doubtlessly talking about various things, he could hear this small bird. He looked in the direction of the call and, amazingly, he saw a black-and-white flycatcher with a rufous crown and white cheeks perched on a bamboo branch.

Even though Ted had never seen a picture of this bird or a specimen, he immediately knew that it was a White-cheeked

Tody-Tyrant. Emmet "Bob" Reid Blake netted this species in Peru in the fifties, but then it was never seen again. Blake worked mostly with the Field Museum of Natural History in Chicago. He published many books on flora and fauna, including the first book on the avifauna of Mexico, *Birds of Mexico: A Guide for Field Identification* (1953). In fact, this was the guide that I used on all of my birding trips to Mexico until Roger Tory Peterson's *Field Guide to Mexican Birds* was published in 1973. Blake's Mexico book contained only a few portraits of birds in color and a number of black-and-white sketches. The descriptions of each species were written in the style of an academic ornithologist, making it difficult to identify birds in the field. Ted had rediscovered a bird that was only known from one specimen, and he was the first person to see it in the wild. Fortunately, the rest of us were able to return to the bamboo thicket and also observe this very rare species.

A few years later, in 1983, Ted suggested that we run a birding workshop at the Explorer's Inn, so participants could study tropical birds. I thought this was a great idea, so I put together a team of several leaders, including Ted, John Rowlett, John O'Neill, and me. Ted recommended that we hold the workshop in late June, when the rainy season normally ends since there would be abundant bird song at that time. In the past, we had traveled to the Explorer's Inn in late August when the forest was so dry that the leaves on some of the bushes and trees were droopy and almost wilted.

Right away, fifty individuals signed up for the workshop. When we arrived in the afternoon at the Explorer's Inn, the weather was pleasant. It was sunny and mild. During the night, a heavy rain started to fall and continued into the morning. In my experience in the tropics, such rain lasts a few hours, or at the most, a day or two, but this, for some reason, was different. No weather reports were available, so we never knew what was happening, but we wondered if a tropical depression had settled over our area of the forest.

It rained for seven days and nights. It wasn't tremendously heavy, like a thunderstorm in the American Southwest, but it was constant. We would wake at five-thirty in the pitch-black morning, not hear the rain, and look forward to seeing the early-morning bird activity. Then, as we ate a simple breakfast in the lodge, the raindrops would start to hit the roof and it would rain throughout the day.

Despite the bad weather, we went birding all day, every day. We did, in fact, see a lot of species, but they all looked gray. Due to the rain clouds, there was no light to see the vibrant colors of these wonderful tropical birds. Nevertheless, we saw almost three hundred species. Ted and the other leaders were disappointed with the conditions on the trip, but they did the best they could to find birds to show the participants.

Perhaps the least enjoyable aspect of the Explorer's Inn was that, like many lodges, the owners kept tamed animals, including a squirrel monkey named after one of the owners, Max Gunther. This monkey had the unfortunate habit of getting under the table and waiting for an opportunity to snatch food. If, for example, you looked away and then glanced back at your strawberry jam, Max's hand might be in it. At this point, the waitstaff would chase the monkey around the dining room with a broom, hoping to shoo the critter out of the lodge. Instead, Max would climb to the rafters, leaping from one to the next, sometimes urinating as he did. The Explorer's Inn owners also kept a tamed tapir (the one that chased Roger Tory Peterson) and a Collared Peccary, or javelina, as pets. Sometimes when you were looking at a bird, the peccary would try to force itself between your legs. It was a strange experience.

During this first Explorer's Inn workshop, the low areas along the trail flooded; the water was more than two feet deep, higher than the almost knee-high rubber boots that some of us wore. The Tambopata River rose twenty or thirty feet and washed away the dock, which made it impossible to receive supplies, food, and filtered water from Puerto Maldonado. On the last day, the rain stopped and the sun came out. This was one of the most difficult trips of all my years of leading tours, but, remarkably, the participants on the tour took it in stride.

My favorite Ted Parker story is one that he told me in 1982 while we were on the train to Machu Picchu. He had traveled to Yanac,

Peru, in the Andes, to look for several bird species that had only been collected by his hero, M. A. (Melbourne Armstrong) Carriker (1879–1965), an American ornithologist and entomologist who covered his trip expenses by the sale of bird skins to the Carnegie Museum and mammal skins to the American Museum of Natural History. Carriker's energies were legendary: He contributed greatly toward our modern understanding of the neotropics and enlarged the tropical bird collections of several museums. Ted felt that Carriker's contributions to ornithology were not sufficiently recognized since, like Ted, he lacked academic credentials.

The birds that Ted hoped to find lived in one of his favorite habitats, the highest forests of the Andes, composed entirely of polylepis trees. When Ted arrived in Yanac, he met a man named Felix. Ted asked him if he would be his guide to look for the birds that Carriker once saw. As it turned out, Felix had been Carriker's guide years earlier on many of his treks through this region. Felix replied that he would be happy to take Ted to these same remote locations, but first he had to harvest his potatoes and tend to other matters. He suggested that Ted come back in a year. Ted did just that: He returned in a year's time and trekked with Felix into the Andes. At about fourteen thousand feet, they were overtaken by an immense snowstorm, almost whiteout conditions. Felix said, "Don't worry. I know a cave for shelter that I sometimes use for hunting. We can take refuge there."

Felix and Ted remained in this cave until the storm passed. Animal skins hung on the damp walls. Ted told me it was like stepping into the primitive dwelling of a prehistoric man. After a while, the storm stopped and the pair continued their hike. They saw a taruca, a north Andean deer that Ted had never before seen. Felix took Ted to one of the best polylepis forests, where they found all the birds that Carriker had discovered. Ted was delighted. As they were walking through the puna, a kind of high Andean grassland, Ted spotted an Andean Tinamou and pointed it out to Felix. Felix replied, "Yes, I saw that same bird in one of the dioramas in the Museum of Natural History in New York." This piece of information stunned Ted. He couldn't believe that Felix had been to New

York City. "You went to the American Museum of Natural History?" Ted asked. And Felix replied, "Yes, my brother has a gas station in Brooklyn."

On Tuesday, August 3, 1993, Ted Parker, age forty, departed with five colleagues and a pilot on a Cessna six-seat plane from Guayaquil. They flew at low altitude on a routine mission to survey the canopy of a rapidly diminishing cloud forest of southwestern Ecuador, some five hundred kilometers from Quito. The others on the plane included the premier tropical botanist Alwyn Gentry; Ted's fiancée, Jaqueline Goerck; one of Ecuador's leading conservationists, Eduardo Aspiazu; and two Ecuadorian biologists, Alfredo Luna and Carmen Bonifaz. During the late afternoon, their pilot became disoriented in the clouds and crashed into a remote mountaintop forest. They were still alive, trapped in the wreckage, but Alwyn, Ted, Eduardo, and the pilot died the next morning. Later, Russell Mittermeier, chairman of Conservation International (CI) in Washington, DC, the organization that the team was working for at the time of the flight, said that Ted Parker and Al Gentry "carried two-thirds of the unpublished knowledge of neotropical biodiversity in their heads."

At the time of his death, Ted's natural gifts for fieldwork were having their greatest impact through the innovative Rapid Assessment Program (RAP). He had conceived this idea during conversations with Nobel Prize–winning physicist Murray Gell-Mann during a trip to eastern Venezuela and proposed this model of conservation to CI. Ted felt that too much time was spent amassing data and not enough action was being taken. CI adopted Ted's proposal and established RAP, which provides a quick assessment of the biological value of an area and identifies species in need of conservation action. As a result, large areas of tropical forest were protected, such as the Alto Madidi National Park, which is about the size of New Jersey, in Bolivia.

More than ten thousand of Ted's recordings are now archived in the Macaulay Library at the Cornell Laboratory of Ornithology in Ithaca, New York. He contributed more than three thousand specimens to the LSU Museum of Natural Science, co-authored more than fifty papers, and was working with John O'Neill and Thomas Schulenberg on a field guide to the birds of Peru. That guide, published in 2007, was the fulfillment of an idea that John and Ted discussed around a campfire on an ornithological research expedition in Peru in 1974. Work proceeded in fits and starts until Ted's tragic and untimely death in 1993. In addition, Ted added at least a hundred species to the lists of birds known from Peru, Ecuador, Brazil, Belize, Bolivia, and elsewhere. Ted once said during an interview with National Public Radio, "Most of the experience for me has always been auditory. More than 50 percent of everything that's happening in a forest is through the sounds."

Peter Seligmann, the president of CI, asked me to be one of the speakers at the memorial service for Ted, which was held in the greenhouse of the United States Botanic Gardens, near the Capitol in Washington, DC. I was honored to give one of the eulogies for my dear friend who introduced me to the joys of birding in South America and who had done so much for conservation and ornithology. In my tribute to Ted, I spoke about his position among the lineage of great naturalists:

> Every so often the elements come together to produce an extraordinary naturalist. These are people who love and appreciate nature intensely and are keen observers. I think of Chapman, Fuertes, and Sutton. All these persons were also marvelous human beings, kind, generous, sensitive, and full of life. Ted Parker was from the same mold as these naturalists. He not only followed in their footsteps but also made quite a few of his own.
>
> Aldo Leopold wrote that there are some people who can live without wildness and some who cannot. Like these earlier great naturalists, Ted was a person who could not live without wild places. I remember him telling me about camping for weeks above the timberline in the Carpish Mountains, hearing the drumming sounds and *char-woo* calls of the Cordilleran Snipe's nighttime display, seeing in the moonlight over two hundred miles away the snow-covered Cordillera Blanca to the north. He saw so much, he knew so much.

For me, Ted's death felt as though a massive tree had fallen in a pristine ancient forest, leaving a gap that would never be filled. Ted and I co-led many tours together. He played a key role in the growth of my company. We had become close friends. His death left an enormous hole in my life that is still there.

11

New Territories

Black-and-white Owl
PANAMA

VENT's first trips in 1976 traveled throughout Texas, Arizona, and Mexico—areas close to home that we knew quite well. It didn't take long for us to realize that we needed to branch out with our tours and go farther afield. One of the key years of the company was 1977 because we offered excursions to El Triunfo, Kenya, Botswana, Costa Rica, and Peru. Most birders were interested in traveling to Costa Rica because of its remarkable research stations; in contrast, few birders knew anything about Panama and its wealth of wildlife and birds. My friend, Dr. Robert Ridgely, who wrote the first field guide to the birds of Panama, suggested we offer a tour there. A superb book, *The Birds of Panama* (1976) features lots of excellent illustrations and details about the region's rich bird life.

We scheduled our first trip for January 1978. Rose Ann Rowlett and I traveled to Panama in early December in order to do some scouting. We experienced a rocky beginning to the trip. The first night we stayed at an inexpensive hotel in Panama City. Relentless traffic noise and uncomfortable beds made it very challenging to sleep. We also had difficulty sleeping because that afternoon we had met up with some birders who told us about some of their exciting recent sightings—a jaguar and a Rufous-vented Ground Cuckoo—along the Pipeline Road.

The Pipeline Road is fifteen miles long. It was built parallel to a pipeline that was designed to carry oil from the Atlantic to the Pacific in the event that the Panama Canal was bombed or sabotaged. This dirt road starts very near the Panama Canal and steadily climbs into the foothills. It transects mostly tall tropical forests, which come almost to the edge of the road, and crosses a dozen wooden bridges over streams. Usually the only traffic on the road is the occasional researcher from the Smithsonian research station on Barro Colorado Island. In most areas, the forest had been cleared way back from the road. Both Rose Ann and I kept thinking about what we might see the next day along the Pipeline Road, making it hard to settle in for a night's sleep.

At three o'clock in the morning, we abandoned our efforts to sleep and drove our small rental car out the Galliard Highway that runs along the border of the Panama Canal on the east side and through the town of Gamboa before turning off onto the Pipeline Road. Given the early-morning hour, we drove the length of the road in the dark with hopes of seeing jaguars and owls, but we saw nothing. Then, at the end of the road, the car got a flat tire. After changing the tire, we stopped at one of the bridges and waded up the stream for a couple of hours, hoping to encounter unusual birds and possibly see a jaguar. Again, we struck out. The Louisiana Waterthrush—a North American bird that had flown to Panama for the winter—was the only bird we saw. Downcast, we returned to Panama City to get some rest.

Fortunately, the remainder of our trip went very well. When I travel, I don't usually come up with a list of "target" birds, but there were three birds in Ridgely's book that I hoped to see: the Black-and-white Owl, the Yellow-eared Toucanet, and Rufous-vented Ground Cuckoo. In Colón, which is at the northern end of the Panama Canal, we met Jaime Pujals, an army doctor who was an avid birder. He took us birding in the nearby Caribbean lowland forest. One evening, using a tape recorder, he called up a Black-and-white Owl. This bird was even more spectacular than I had imagined.

There is something about black-and-white birds that has always attracted me. Perhaps it is the simplicity of their plumage and its bold pattern. This particular large owl is mostly black above; its underparts are finely barred with black-and-white stripes. What was especially surprising to me was that when the spotlight was shined on the owl, its eyes flashed a brilliant red. Almost all owls have little or no eye shine, unlike most nightjars, nighthawks, and potoos. Most owls lack a tapetum lucidum, a tissue-like membrane in the eye that reflects light. Our successful scouting made me look forward to returning a month later with VENT's first tour.

In January 1978, John Rowlett and I returned to Panama leading our first tour. Unlike the scouting adventure, we experienced a very auspicious start. On the first day, we walked along a levee that led us into a wetland located near our hotel. I was a bit ahead of the group when I spotted a bright red bill sticking out of the aquatic vegetation. Moments later, the bird walked out into full view. To my astonishment, it was a Spotted Rail, accompanied by four little black chicks. They walked slowly behind the adult. The participants and John came up behind me, and we all watched this striking rail, which turned out to be the first documented record for the country and a bird that none of us had ever seen. This was the first of many birds that our tours would add to the Panama list over the years.

Our trip to Panama in 1978 was the beginning of eco-tourism there. Before then, such ventures were an unknown business activity in that country. There were no lodges for birders. There were no wildlife centers with hummingbird feeders—or any other bird feeders, for that matter. There were no local guides. On our first trip, we stayed at one of the best hotels in downtown Panama. The noise from the streets and the live music being played in the hotel into the early-morning hours made it very difficult to sleep. So we decided to stay at La Siesta Hotel, which was adjacent to the international airport and was run by a Swiss man and his Panamanian wife. The hotel included lovely grounds, comfortable accommodations, and good food. Best of all, there were several rich birding areas neighboring La Siesta. I saw many birds on the hotel grounds and nearby that I had never seen in my life, including the Mouse-colored Tyrannulet, the White-winged Becard, and the Scrub Greenlet. In addition, the Arosemenas, the owners of a nearby ranch that contained wetlands, allowed us to bird on their property anytime that we desired. When the United States invaded Panama in 1989, the US military bombed La Siesta Hotel because they thought the dictator Manuel Noriega was there. As a result, the place where I had spent so many happy days was reduced to a burned-out shell of a building.

On later tours, I had the pleasure of introducing two VENT leaders, David Wolf and Kevin Zimmer, to Panama. The trip with David was especially memorable. We arrived a couple of days before our group. As we walked along the same levee where I had seen the Spotted Rail, we saw a cuckoo with a chestnut-colored throat, light-buff upperparts, and a brown back sitting in a small tree. It was unlike any cuckoo that either one of us had ever seen, and it didn't resemble any of the cuckoo species illustrated in the field guide to the birds of Panama. I suggested to David that the bird might be a juvenile plumage of a Squirrel Cuckoo, but neither of us had ever seen a Squirrel Cuckoo that looked like this bird. David remarked that it was unlikely because a juvenile bird would more closely resemble the adult version. Puzzled by what we were seeing, we returned to our room at La Siesta and called John Rowlett in Charlottesville, Virginia, where he was attending graduate school at the time, and asked him to get out his field guide to the birds of Venezuela, the only book with illustrations of South American birds. It turned out that our bird was a Dwarf Cuckoo, a bird that had never before been recorded in Panama.

Over the years, tour leaders of our company got to know Panama very well. We led many successful trips to this small country, which today has a longer bird list—more than a thousand species—than any country of its size in the world. As we became more familiar with the country and its habitats, we were able to locate many of these species, including some of the very rare ones, such as the Black-crowned Antpitta, the Rufous-vented Ground Cuckoo, and the Plumbeous Hawk. Like Costa Rica, Panama is a great birding area because of its rich variety of habitats and the extensive regions that have remained preserved. The forest along both sides of the Panama Canal remains intact because if it was cut, huge volumes of soil would wash into the canal during the long rainy season.

In exploring the areas near Panama City, we journeyed up into the Cerro Azul and Cerro Jefe mountains, just east of the capital. These twin mountains rise from the lowlands of Central Panama to an elevation of two thousand feet and are home to a number of species of birds that are not found in the lowlands. The bare red-clay road up to the mountain was quite steep in some places. In order to take groups up to this elevation, we hired a local man with a truck with chains secured to the tires and wooden benches in the back. We drove our rental cars midway up and then transferred into his truck.

One of the most memorable sightings on this mountain occurred when we heard the loud double rap of a woodpecker. We made a recording and played it back and to our delight, a rare woodpecker with a brilliant red head and underparts flew into a nearby tree. The bird also had a black mask surrounded by white. It was a Crimson-bellied Woodpecker, the most beautiful woodpecker that I'd ever seen and a relative of the American Ivory-billed and the Imperial Woodpeckers.

In another outing along the Pipeline Road, John Rowlett and I had driven our group far off the road in rental station wagons. John had started back to the main road. As I proceeded to drive out behind him, I heard an unfamiliar call that I thought might be a type of woodpecker. I got out of the car, made a recording of it with my Sony 5000, the type of recorder I frequently carried with me in the field, and played it back. At that moment, a huge Ornate Hawk-Eagle flew in and perched on a large branch midway up a nearby tree. I was stunned to see this magnificent species. The Ornate Hawk-Eagle is the most strikingly plumaged of the three species of hawk-eagle. It is black above with white underparts barred with black. Its hind neck and upper breast are a rich tawny color. Its most distinct feature is its long black crest. John returned with his group, and everyone had an opportunity to see this marvelous bird that none of us had ever seen.

Every time we went to Panama, we longed to travel to Darién, the easternmost province that borders Colombia. The Pan-American Highway, which starts in Alaska and stretches all the way to southern Chile, has a gap in the Darién region. The highway ends at a town called Yaviza on the Tuira River and resumes in Colombia. For years, people talked about building a road through that region to connect the South American portion of the Pan-Am Highway with the northern region. Panama has resisted efforts to extend the road because it might lead to Colombian settlers moving into that part of Panama and bringing in cattle infected with hoof-and-mouth disease. Drug trafficking is also a concern. Not surprisingly, environmentalists are thrilled that the Darién Gap still exists; if a road was built through it, the deforestation along the existing road would spread throughout the region.

Through members of the Panama Audubon Society, Bob Ridgely and I heard about a young American named Gary Conn, who lived in Darién. We had lunch with him in Panama City. He and his wife had built a small simple lodge outside of El Real, one of the two places in the Darién province that offered air service from Panama City. He told us that if we came to Darién, we could stay at his lodge and then travel by river farther east to more remote areas. We were excited by this possibility and planned a trip for March 1980 that Bob and I would co-lead.

We also learned that there was a small airstrip at Cana on Cerro Pirre, a mountain that rises above the town of El Real. At fifty-four-hundred feet, it is the highest mountain in Darién. In the early 1900s, a Scottish company had established a gold-mining operation and even constructed a small railroad from the mine down to the river. Many years later, operations had ceased since the vein had been exhausted. However, a Spanish company had recently acquired the rights to try and re-open the mine and find more gold. For our trip, we flew by charter plane from Panama City to that remote airstrip on Cerro Pirre, where we planned to spend four days exploring. Then we would be transported by charter flight to El Real. We would stay in Gary Conn's lodge and travel up the river to Pucuro. As the plane approached the Cerro Pirre airstrip, two huge Great Green Macaws and four Scarlet Macaws flew from the nearby trees. As we looked out the windows of the plane, we had a clear view of these impressive birds.

Once we disembarked, we were all delighted by the abundance of birds around the airstrip and the mining camp. Just walking around the area that first afternoon, we saw almost a hundred species of birds. Many of these—such as the Black-tipped Cotinga and the Barred Puffbird—had never before been seen by the participants.

We camped near a primitive building at the mining camp, which was about two thousand feet above sea level and located on a small clearing. Behind the camp, the forested slopes of Cerro Pirre rose steeply. There was one toilet and a shower. We cooked our food over a small fire.

The first morning, we walked a trail that descended from Cana down to the Tuira River and saw some marvelous birds, including Great Jacamars, Dusky-backed Jacamars, Scarlet-browed Tanagers, Fulvous-vented Antpittas, and Double-banded Graytails. Best of all was the sighting of the spectacular and rarely seen Black-crowned Antpitta, which we observed as it hopped on the ground of the forest. This large antpitta is rusty above with a black crown and boldly scalloped white underparts.

We knew that there were other birds that we could see only if we climbed the steep trail toward Cerro Pirre's summit. Pedro Galindo, the first ornithologist to explore this region, had ascended this same trail several years earlier. We met his guide, Cristobal, who worked at the mining camp. He offered to take us up that trail. It was partly overgrown, but using his machete, Cristobal cleared the trail as we climbed.

During that initial hike, I flushed two male Great Curassows, a huge member of the guan family. The male Great Curassow is black with a bright yellow knob at the base of its bill. They flew up into a nearby tree and all of us could see these birds. It was a species that I had long wanted to see after reading *At a Bend in a Mexican River* (1972). In this book, George Miksch Sutton wrote about taking a trip up a mountain in northeastern Mexico, hoping to see a Great

Curassow. At that point, the only other Great Curassow I had seen was a dead one in the canoe of the caretaker of the ruins at Yaxchilan in Chiapas when John Rowlett and I had flown there in 1969. It was a thrill to finally be seeing this marvelous bird.

We continued up the mountain and had just reached the point on Cerro Pirre where the cloud forest began. This was the habitat of the birds that we most wanted to see. When it was time to turn back, we had only seen a few of these special birds, including the Pirre Hummingbird and a Pirre Warbler, both species that are found nowhere else in the world. We reluctantly started back down the mountain in order to reach Cana before dark. When we got off the trail, I was surprised to see that David Galinant, who had been at the end of the line, was not with us. Some of the people told me that after lunch he had turned back without telling us that he had intended to go down the mountain alone.

When I returned from our hike, I asked people who were camping near the airstrip if they had seen David. They told me that he had gone down the trail to try and obtain photos of the Black-crowned Antpitta. As daylight diminished, I became increasingly worried about David's whereabouts, realizing that he had not made it off the mountain and was somewhere in the forest—either lost or injured from a fall.

I asked Cristobal to look for David. He told me that there was no point in going up the mountain in the dark because he was confident that David had wandered off the trail partway down the mountain where the trail went through a grove of palm trees and became very indistinct. He believed that David had probably gone to the left and down that slope to a point where he heard the noise from the rapids of a stream appropriately named Escucha el Ruido (Listen to the Noise) that we had crossed on the day we walked partway down the mountain. Cristobal said that David would find the stream, decide to follow it until darkness fell, and then sleep in the forest, and that the next morning, he would find the trail and return to camp. Nonetheless, I persuaded Cristobal to hike up the mountain, looking for David. He returned with the news that he wasn't able to find him anywhere near the trail. I was, at this point, beside myself with concern, wondering if we would ever find him. Even from an airplane, the forest is so dense, it would be impossible to spot David.

That night, I was so upset that I couldn't sleep. The next morning, Cristobal started up the trail and one of his coworkers hiked down the trail. After a short time, we heard a shot. This was the agreed-upon signal that David had been found. About this time, one of the local women who stood near the clearing said to me, "Here comes the big one." To my great relief, I saw David slowly hiking up the trail.

It was exactly as Cristobal had predicted: David told us that he was following the stream, and when it got dark, he lay down in the forest and tried to sleep. He said that there were some mosquitoes, but there was also a Black-and-white Owl calling right over him. As soon as the sun rose, he started walking again, reached the trail, and returned to camp as quickly as possible.

12

The Big Day

Great-crested Flycatcher

WHITE MEMORIAL PARK

ANAHUAC, TEXAS

One of my first books about birding was *Birds Over America* (1948) by Roger Tory Peterson. I was especially intrigued by the third chapter, "The Big Day," where Roger described a Big Day in Massachusetts with the American ornithologist Ludlow Griscom. This chapter captures the excitement of one of birding's most challenging contests. In the last paragraph, Roger wrote these prophetic words: "No one would want to engage in one of these endurance tests every weekend, but once or twice a year it is great sport, a test of the skills acquired by months and years of bird-watching. We are waiting for the inevitable day when someone will try it by airplane or helicopter."

When I was in my twenties and thirties, I organized and participated in annual Big Days in the Houston area. The rules are quite simple: A single team travels together, attempting to count as many bird species as possible during a single calendar day (midnight to midnight). Birds must be conclusively identified by sight or sound. If one is in doubt of a bird's identity, it can't be counted.

Birds attracted by sounds reproduced using a tape recorder or a bird feeder may also be counted. All birds must be alive and wild. Injured birds may be also counted if they have not been caught. Any geographic area may be covered during the twenty-four-hour window of time. According to the American Birding Association (ABA), travel may be by any means, provided that the entire team stays within voice contact with one another during all travel.

On a Big Day, species are divided into three categories: *basic species* are birds that are fairly common in an area and can be found without any extra effort. Examples of these in South Texas include Killdeer, Common Nighthawk, Eastern Meadowlark, Purple Martin, and Great-tailed Grackle. *Essential species* represent uncommon species sighted along the Big Day route in only one or two locations. They require additional effort to spot. Finding these "essential" birds is the key to a successful Big Day. Finally, *bonus species* are rare birds that are not usually present on the Big Day route.

Of course, my team always hoped that all the necessary variables—the weather, the birds, and our luck—would align and that we would break the Upper Texas Coast Big Day record or, better yet, break the national record. These attempts were always engaging and entertaining, but we never broke the Upper Texas Coast record and never really came close to beating the national record. On the Texas coast, you need a norther with strong winds and rain in order to create a fallout. We always scheduled our Big Day weeks in advance and found south winds and few migrants when we reached the coast. John Rowlett and I even tried starting in Austin where we could add twenty or so birds not found in the Houston area, but the drive to the coast took too long and often the same south winds greeted our arrival.

It had been many years since I had participated in a Big Day when, in early 1981, Roger Tory Peterson asked me to join him for a Birdathon in Beaumont, Texas, on April 25. A Birdathon is a Big Day event designed for fund-raising purposes, with the monies going toward conservation efforts and bird protection. Donors pledge a sum of money for each bird located by a team member on a Big

Day. On our day, we donated our funds to the National Audubon Society. Our goal was to locate at least 184 species.

Later that year, Roger and I began to make plans for another Texas-based Birdathon in 1982. We decided that our group would include the two of us, John Rowlett, and Ted Parker. At the time, Roger was seventy-four, decades older than the rest of us. It was impressive that he wanted to participate again, given the amount of endurance and stamina required and the lack of sleep suffered during twenty-four hours of nonstop birding.

As we began to plan, I told Roger that the only strategy that might help us to break the national record of 231 was to combine the Upper Texas Coast with the Lower Rio Grande Valley as Jim Tucker, the energetic founder and executive director of the American Birding Association, had done. (Tucker had identified 229 in a single day on April 28, 1973.) This approach presented its own inherent set of challenges—namely, the distances involved and the time it would take to cover them. The Tucker team had started near Sheldon reservoir, just northeast of Houston, and ended their day with a half hour of daylight remaining at Santa Ana National Wildlife Refuge near McAllen. I wanted to begin at Santa Ana and drive to Falcon Dam sixty miles upriver, cover the rich Bolivar/High Island/Anahuac region, and then conclude in the Piney Woods near Anahuac, Texas. This proposed new route involved even greater distances than the Tucker team had covered—and since Tucker's record-breaking year in 1973, the speed limit had been lowered from seventy to fifty-five miles per hour.

Roger suggested an alternate plan: We begin at High Island at noon, bird the Upper Texas Coast area until dark, then drive all night to Falcon Dam and bird there until noon. This seemed like a solid and feasible plan. There was only one problem: It violated the rule of a Big Day being confined to a twenty-four-hour calendar day. In response, I suggested another strategy: Start in the Rio Grande Valley and then fly in a twin-engine Cessna from Falcon Dam to Bolivar where a car would pick us up. This would enable us to cover the three hundred and fifty miles from Falcon Dam to Bolivar in about two hours versus seven hours by car. This combination of areas would also allow us to see birds that reside only in the western United States and some Mexican species that occur in the Lower Rio Grande Valley, such as Green Jays, Scaled Quail, and Pyrrhuloxias, as well as eastern land birds, shorebirds, and marsh birds in areas along the Bolivar Peninsula and the Piney Woods farther north. I knew that a Big Day with the use of a plane would not be comparable to one using only ground transport, but I thought that it would be an adventure and that it offered the most effective way for breaking the US Big Day record of 231, which was set in California on April 29, 1978.

Our date was selected: April 28, 1982. The first challenge was reserving a charter plane and locating airstrips. From previous visits, I knew there was an airstrip at Falcon State Park, but I was unsure about finding an available strip near Bolivar. I called a motel in Port Bolivar, and the owner referred me to the local constable, who referred me to a shrimp boat operator who owned a three-thousand-foot grass airstrip near his house in Crystal Beach. When I called the shrimper, I discovered that he was in Florida. His mother said, "Sure, honey, you can use our strip." When I asked where it was located exactly, she replied, "Over on this side of the highway." After further questioning, I felt like I had some notion of where the strip might be.

The next challenge was the weather. I recalled all of those Big Days of my youth that began with such high hopes in the hours of darkness and the cool morning air only to flounder in the humidity of the warm weather of a typical late April day on the Texas coast, with south winds and few migrants. The weather could mean a plus or a minus of at least twenty species. One thing I knew for certain: There was no way we could break the record without optimal weather conditions.

The week before the Big Day, John Rowlett and I were co-leading a migration workshop at High Island. It seemed like too much to hope that we could have migrants both for the week-long workshop and the Big Day. Two days into the workshop, a strong cold front hit, with rain and north winds—everything we needed for a fallout of migrants. Just as we had hoped, we saw thousands of birds.

We knew that as soon as the winds changed to the south and clear skies returned that the migrants would leave. But by some freak of nature, the cold rainy weather persisted day after day. No one could remember such a cold and rainy week in late April on the Texas coast. Every day we saw more and more migrants. We witnessed fields filled with hundreds of Indigo Buntings. A dozen Scarlet Tanagers, Baltimore Orioles, Catbirds, and Rose-breasted Grosbeaks festooned the mulberry trees. The woods brimmed with migrant warblers, flitting from branch to branch in search of insects.

Each day we held our breath and crossed our fingers: Would this weather possibly hold until Tuesday? It seemed impossible. Finally, late Saturday afternoon, the skies cleared and were filled with bright stars. As soon as it got dark, we heard the chips and lisps of thousands of birds migrating overhead. It was exciting to hear all this avian traffic, but also upsetting. What birds would be left for our Birdathon?

On Sunday morning, John and I flew to Harlingen. An excited Ted waited for us at the airport. Our plan was to make a trial run of the South Texas route on Monday to see how many of the target birds we could find. Roger was due to arrive Monday afternoon, and the Big Day would commence at 12:01 midnight on Tuesday, April 28. On Monday morning, we greeted the dawn at Santa Margarita Ranch, located along the banks of the Rio Grande, near Falcon Dam. The birding was superb. Almost too good. Midway through the morning, Ted said, "I wish this was *the* day. There is no way that we can do this well tomorrow."

A lingering Orange-crowned Warbler was a bonus for us, as were several flocks of Yellow-headed Blackbirds. By ten o'clock in the morning, we had found virtually every species we had hoped to see in the Rio Grande Valley, including Brown Jays and even the scarce Northern Beardless-Tyrannulet (which Ted heard shortly before dawn). The only worrisome factor was the potential for ground fog. If we experienced fog on the Big Day, the plane, flying from McAllen, would run late in picking us up at Falcon Dam State Park, throwing the entire day off schedule. On Monday, during our trial run, the fog hadn't burned off until ten o'clock in the morning.

We returned to McAllen to meet Roger. When we reached his motel room, he was on the phone with CBS. They had decided to send along a film crew and reporter to cover the Big Day. Already we had attracted quite a press contingent with Howard Simons, the managing editor of the *Washington Post*, and Tom Ludley from the *Dallas Times-Herald*.

Later in the afternoon, we drove to the Santa Ana National Wildlife Refuge to ask permission to enter the refuge after dark. This 2,088-acre refuge was established in 1943, thanks to Ira Gabrielson, one of the first staff members of the US Fish and Wildlife Service. In addition to being a biologist, Gabrielson was an avid birder. He realized that the subtropical riparian woodlands in this area were the largest remaining tract of this unique habitat in the United States and home to more than two dozen species of birds found in the United States only in the Lower Rio Grande Valley. All other large parcels of land had been cut to plant citrus groves and cotton. The Fish and Wildlife Service relied solely on Duck Stamp funds for land acquisitions. Years later, Ira told me that when he first visited this tract, he spotted two Blue-winged Teals. That sighting was the basis for his recommendation that the government purchase this property, using Duck Stamp money. At the time of our visit, hundreds of Mississippi Kites were migrating over the refuge.

We tried to get some rest in the motel, but I don't think anyone slept very much. At eleven o'clock in the evening, we ate "breakfast" at an I-Hop in McAllen and then returned to the Santa Ana National Wildlife Refuge so that, at the stroke of twelve midnight, we could start counting birds. Our first bird was a Dickcissel, a sparrow-like species. We identified it by its short, buzz-like call as it flew over our group in the darkness at 12:01 a.m. The tiny bird had made its way from northern South America to Texas on its migration north. Arriving at Santa Ana, we walked along the entrance road to the manager's house and heard an Elf Owl, a Barn Owl, a Great Horned Owl, and a Common Pauraque. The Elf Owl was our first essential species.

In Santa Ana, there were two other essential species we needed to record: the Black-bellied Whistling Duck and the Least Grebe. We drove out onto the levee that parallels the northern boundary of the refuge. A flock of Black-bellied Whistling Ducks flew directly in front of us, filling the air with their high-pitched calls. We played a tape recording of the Least Grebe on our portable Sony recorder, and one immediately answered from a weedy ditch. Having located all the essentials we had hoped for at Santa Ana, we headed west.

Our next stop was a seasonal marsh northwest of Mission. Here, we tallied, by voice, a number of waterbirds and marsh birds, including a Virginia Rail, a species that we had not expected to encounter in the valley. After twenty minutes in the marsh, we headed northwest and upriver to the Falcon Dam. At several points, we detoured down dirt roads to the river just below the dam, hoping to hear a Ferruginous Pygmy-Owl, a neotropical species that barely makes it into the United States. At one stop, John and Roger thought that they had heard the owl, but it only called once, and our best tapes did not elicit a response. So we reluctantly decided not to add the species to our list.

The early-morning hours of darkness passed slowly. Once we greeted the dawn and its brightening light, the minutes raced by all day. The television crew went to sleep at every stop. There were only a few night birds that we had hoped to find, and we found all of them—including Lesser Nighthawks and Poorwills—except the Ferruginous Pygmy-Owl, which would have been a bonus bird.

We drove to the nearby Santa Margarita Ranch and walked to the Rio Grande. It was cloudy, and there was not a burst of birdsong in the early-morning light. We heard the Northern Beardless Tyrannulet, where we had located it the previous day and also heard the loud *pows* of a noisy flock of Brown Jays. Birds were not as numerous as we had hoped. We spent more than an hour walking along the river through groves of cottonwoods and willows. Water filled the depressions that had been left when the river was higher. Our best sightings were a Green Kingfisher that John and Roger observed flying upriver and a Groove-billed Ani that we heard across the river. I glimpsed a hawk diving into the brush on the opposite bank of the river. Its secretive behavior and shape suggested that it was a Hook-billed Kite, but with only a split-second look, I decided not to count it. By this time, it was becoming quite warm, and the morning clouds were beginning to burn off. We returned to the car and drove to Falcon State Park and the dam.

Here, we experienced better luck in locating the hoped-for essentials and even a few unexpected migrants, such as a Philadelphia Vireo and an Olive-sided Flycatcher. We arrived at the airstrip near Falcon Dam at ten o'clock in the morning, but the plane was not there. As a result, we decided to make a quick dash for the dam. This run turned out to be very productive: We added a Hooded Oriole, an Audubon's Oriole, and a Red-billed Pigeon—all birds that do not occur on the Upper Texas Coast—as well as an American Kestrel and a Baird's Sandpiper, which we did not expect to see on the coast.

We returned to the airstrip, boarded our plane, and departed at ten-thirty, heading for the Upper Coast. We were pleased with what we had accomplished so far. Our total list stood at only 107, but it included 50 species that either did not occur on the Upper Texas Coast or were not to be expected there in late April. During our flight, we hoped to observe some essentials from the air. We had our pilot detour and fly over King Ranch, but a solid layer of low clouds obscured our view and any potential sightings of a White-tailed Hawk or a Wild Turkey. The pilot circled over Corpus Christi Bay, where we hoped to see a Brown Pelican, but we saw none. We did add a Roseate Spoonbill and a Reddish Egret, but these were species that we could expect to see on the Upper Coast. During the two-hour flight, we ate, slept, and reviewed our list.

It was twelve-thirty in the afternoon when we reached the Bolivar Peninsula. We were eager to land and get back to birding. Unbeknown to us, the plane carrying the CBS television crew had gotten stuck on the small dirt airstrip. Local birders who were awaiting our arrival spent a half hour pushing the aircraft out of the mud. If they had failed in this attempt, we would have been forced to land in Galveston or Beaumont, and this detour would likely have made it impossible for us to break the record.

As it was, the runway was now shortened because of the difficulty that the other plane had encountered in landing. Our pilot landed perfectly on the airstrip. As we taxied to a stop, I spotted Baltimore Orioles in a small prickly ash tree—our first indication that the migrants were in the area. In addition, there was a slight north wind. Our spirits soared. If there was a fallout on the Upper Coast, we had an excellent chance to set a new national record.

Quickly we piled into a van driven by James Paulk, national director of the Birdathon, and headed for the Bolivar Flats. Along the route, I spotted a Red-headed Woodpecker on a fence post—a bonus bird for the coastal area. Bolivar Flats, a huge expanse of mud and sand between the North Jetty of the Galveston Ship Channel and the coast, is one of the best areas in the country for shorebirds and waders. That day, it teemed with hundreds of gulls, terns, and shorebirds. Our list grew quickly.

We found all the birds that we expected to spot, plus a few bonuses, such as an Eared Grebe in the surf and, best of all, a Black Scoter, a duck rarely seen on the Texas coast. We rested for a few minutes, reviewing the birds that we had seen at Bolivar and feeling good about our progress. The television crew used this break to corner Roger; they had been waiting to speak with him all morning. The interview took fifteen precious minutes, and then we were off toward High Island.

Our first stop was a small grove of trees and brush called Johnson's Woods. Right away we could tell that there was a fallout. Migrant birds were everywhere in the grass, bushes, and trees. Several species of thrush hopped in the crushed-shell road between the rows of oleander bushes. Catbirds, Indigo Buntings, orioles, and tanagers were especially abundant. Our excitement escalated. Each of us knew that a new US Big Day record was a real possibility. That said, there were not many warblers, but we searched diligently and found a solid number of species. After only a half hour, it was time to head north to High Island.

High Island described itself on billboards as the "bird capital of the United States." During the spring months, it certainly is. On this uplifted salt dome, amid the coastal marshes, enormous live oak trees provide refuge for the migratory birds that have just completed a seven-hundred-mile flight across the Gulf of Mexico. Even on a mediocre day, there are migrants, but this turned out to be a very good day for our team.

Once again, we took a short break. At the Louis B. Smith Bird Sanctuary (also called the Boy Scout Woods, or just Scout Woods), we added the Yellow-bellied Sapsucker, the Prothonotary Warbler, and the Lincoln's Sparrow. The Prothonotary was our two-hundredth bird that day. We were running out of possibilities among the migratory species, but it was hard to leave the bird-rich groves on such an extraordinary day.

We pulled into a roadside rest stop at High Island and looked for Bobolinks in a nearby field. I noticed a warbler searching for insects at the end of a live oak tree branch about thirty feet in front of the windshield. It was a male Blackpoll Warbler, a new species for our list and a bonus bird. Two other birds worked away on the same branch. Without even getting out of the car, we identified them: a Yellow-throated Vireo and a female Cerulean Warbler, both new species for the day. We had not expected to see these two birds because they are early migrants. While at Scout Woods, Roger ran into his old friend Lars Jonsson, the renowned Swedish bird artist. The two seldom had the chance to see each other, but Roger said, "I'm on a Big Day. I'll have to talk to you later."

We failed to see Bobolinks. Later, we learned that more than fifty had been observed along the route we had driven. We didn't see them, but Ted did spot a male Cape May Warbler in an isolated live oak tree. Conscious of the 95 percent rule, we surrounded the tree, hoping to see it as well. (On a Big Day, 95 percent of the birds tallied have to be seen or heard by every member of the team.) For a precious five minutes, we searched the tree, but never found the warbler.

At that point, we should have left High Island and traveled north to Anahauc and the Piney Woods. Instead, we drove to Smith Woods, another area of High Island, hoping to add a few more warblers to our list. We succeeded in finding a Bay-breasted Warbler, but did not locate the Blue-winged Warbler or Swainson's Warbler that other people had seen earlier in the day.

With the list tallying 207 species, we headed north over the Gulf Intracoastal Waterway. We realized that we were running out of time and would not be able to look for the Marsh Wrens or Swamp Sparrows, which we had spotted a few days earlier. We had tarried too long at High Island. It was now five-thirty. Ted insisted that we head straight for the Piney Woods. He was afraid that if we arrived there too late, many species would have finished singing and gone to roost. I had put much thought into the planned route, which included a stop in the rice fields for shorebirds, a half hour at Anahuac National Wildlife Refuge for marsh birds, and then the Piney Woods. But Ted argued that the Piney Woods had the potential to yield more species than any other area left on our agreed-upon route. With great reluctance, we decided to skip Anahuac Refuge. This meant sacrificing five to ten species, but Ted was right because it was a cloudy afternoon and soon it would be dark in the woods.

We made two very brief stops in the rice fields and added the American Golden-Plover, the Pectoral and the Stilt Sandpiper, the Gull-billed Tern, the Long-billed Dowitcher, and several Hudsonian Godwits, all essentials. Then, we sped north toward the all-important Piney Woods. As we passed the entrance road to Anahuac Refuge, I had a sinking feeling that we had blown our chance to break the record. How could we break it without those species that we could only see at Anahuac? Tension filled the car as we continued north.

Of all the critical habitats on our route, we had scouted the Piney Woods the least. As soon as we entered the woodlands, we paused on the road's shoulder to listen, but the highway traffic noise was so loud that we could hear very little. Frustrated, we got back in the car, drove a few more miles, and got out again with the same result. We added only one species—and time was growing short. I suggested that we drive directly to Lake Charlotte, an area I had scouted on April 11. But at that early date and on a cool afternoon, I had heard little birdsong. Today, we were placing all our hopes on what we might see or hear at Lake Charlotte. En route, we added a Red-shouldered Hawk, a Yellow-crowned Night-Heron, an Eastern Bluebird, a Brown-headed Nuthatch, and a Pine Warbler.

We arrived at Lake Charlotte at six-thirty in the evening. We all knew the next half hour would be critical. And that half hour exceeded our hopes. Louisiana Waterthrushes, Northern Parulas, Swainson's Warblers, and Yellow-throated Warblers were all singing. A pair of Wood Ducks and a small flock of Common Grackles flew overhead. An Anhinga and then Red-bellied, Pileated, and Downy Woodpeckers were tallied via their voices. A Northern Flicker called. New species came fast; we were adding all the birds we had hoped to find—and more. Already, we had added eighteen new species to our growing list.

At about seven o'clock in the evening, Roger asked me to play a tape of a Barred Owl. I did, and a pair responded in the distance. At this point, we thought we needed one more species to break the record. In our rush, however, a Common Crow had not been added to our tally, even though we had seen one en route. Later, we learned that those Barred Owls whooping in the cypress swamp were our record-breaking 232nd bird.

Thinking that we needed one more species, we continued to search for the Great-crested Flycatcher, but we failed to find this common Piney Woods bird. Finally, at 7:20 p.m. in White Memorial Park, we heard the loud, rising *wheeep* of a Great-crested Flycatcher. We cheered, knowing that we had set a new US Big Day record. (The CBS crew captured this moment on film.)

With light still left, there was a chance we could make it to Anahuac and spot a few of the marsh species we had sacrificed in our dash to the Piney Woods. It was dusk when we turned down the entrance road. In the dim twilight, we could barely make out a Purple Gallinule on a water hyacinth along the coastal irrigation canal. Then, when it was too dark to see, we heard the squeaky whistles of a flock of Fulvous Whistling Ducks taking flight from a rice field.

We now felt certain that we had 234 (actually, we had 235). We drove to Anahuac National Wildlife Refuge headquarters, all of us exhausted, and broke out a bottle of champagne and celebrated. It was eight o'clock. Our Big Day wouldn't be over for four more hours. We made a list of the species we could add by voice after dark: Marsh Wren, Sedge Wren, Least Bittern, Seaside Sparrow, Chuck-will's-widow. Two hundred and forty seemed possible.

"I doubt that we will add a single additional bird," Roger said.

He was right. We drove to Shoveler Pond. Fighting the swarms of mosquitoes, I played the tapes of the birds that we still needed, hoping to elicit a response. There was only a deafening frog chorus. None of the target species answered. It was now after nine-thirty. The sleepless night and long hours in the field began to take their toll on us. We decided to call it a day and headed for our motel at the Houston airport. We didn't even stop to listen for Chuck-will's-widows.

This was one of the most memorable days of birding in my life not only because we had set a new national record for the most birds ever seen in one day, but also because I got to do it with three close friends. On April 25, 2013, a team from the Cornell Lab of Ornithology recorded the amazing total of 294 species. (Three members of that team had attended our summer camps when they were teenagers.) That record still stands.

13

The Next Generation of Birders

Magnificent Hummingbird
CHIRICAHUA MOUNTAINS
CAVE CREEK CANYON, ARIZONA

In 1978, Rose Ann Rowlett was in charge of organizing a hawk watch in September outside of Corpus Christi. This hawk watch has evolved into one of the largest events of its kind in the country, with a wide array of hawks—Mississippi Kites, Broad-winged, Swainson's, Sharp-shinned, and Cooper's Hawks—flying over the region during the early fall months. Within the peak period of the hawk migration, thousands of raptors are counted as they travel from Canada to tropical destinations. Some, such as the Swainson's Hawk, migrate all the way to Argentina. In the 1978 watch, about thirty or so observers were stationed at different points along a twenty-mile, east-west stretch of land, spending the entire day at their designated post, counting the hawks that flew overhead, and identifying them.

Rose Ann assigned me to a spot called Fort Lipantitlán, a wooden-picket structure that was built around 1831 by the Mexican forces in anticipation of trouble with Anglo immigrants. The fort was named after a camp of Lipan Apaches in the vicinity. Nothing remains of this fort.

I arrived at eight o'clock in the morning. Hawks don't start flying until the thermals begin rising around nine or ten o'clock in the morning. Shortly thereafter, a car driven by David Braun arrived and three young birders—Kurt Huffman, David Sugeno, and Peter English—got out. I soon learned that these boys had met as students at St. Stephen's Episcopal School in Austin and discovered their mutual passion for birds. Kurt and David were thirteen years old, and Peter, twelve. We spent the day counting hawks. We didn't see many, but we had a good time together. These young birders, with their boundless enthusiasm for birds and nature, reminded me of the way I was at their age. During this hawk watch, I recognized that spending time and birding with these three young boys offered an opportunity to be a mentor, just as Armand, Joe, and Edgar had been mentors to me. Also like my own mentors, I didn't have children, so I had the extra time to spend with these boys.

After the hawk watch, I stayed in touch with Kurt, David, and Peter and took them to monthly Travis Audubon Society meetings. We also did some birding around Austin, particularly at the Hornsby Bend Sewage Treatment Plant and the South Austin Sewage Treatment Plant. One day, a few years later, the trio appeared at my house in the Travis Heights neighborhood to tell me the exciting news that they had discovered a Long-tailed Duck at the South Austin Treatment Plant. They took me to see this duck, a species that is very seldom observed around Austin. On another occasion, Kurt, Peter, and I drove to a spot south of Luling to observe a Northern Jacana, a tropical shorebird that is very rarely seen in the United States. Chestnut-colored with a black neck, head, and breast, and a yellow bill, the Northern Jacana has long, slender toes that allow it to walk on water hyacinths and lily pads.

I started to make a number of trips throughout the state of Texas with the boys. The first excursion was to the Lower Rio Grande Valley in order to participate in the Falcon Dam Christmas Count on December 27, 1981, which was organized by one of my mentors, Edgar Kincaid Jr. After the count, we spent a few more days birding this region, which is a part of the Tamaulipan biotic province. The uplands of this area are composed mostly of mesquite trees interspersed with prickly pear cacti. Along the Rio Grande, the riparian zone has larger trees, including cottonwoods, willows, and Texas ebony. In addition to the Falcon Dam Christmas Count, the boys often joined me on the annual Freeport Christmas Count.

We also visited the Santa Margarita Ranch, where Brown Jays had first been sighted in the United States in 1973. This large ranch is owned by an extended family of Mexican-Americans who raise cattle. Once the Brown Jays were discovered, birders started visiting the ranch to see this special species. I suggested that individuals pay five dollars to the owners in return for permission to wander around their ranch looking for the jays and other birds.

One afternoon, we pulled up to the collection of houses of Santa Margarita Ranch. Large dogs came out to greet us, and then the eldest member of the family appeared to collect the entrance fee. He spoke very little English. He told us that the family ancestors had received this land as a grant from Charles V, who was Holy Roman emperor when the Spanish occupied parts of the New World. When I visited there with the boys, we spotted a Hook-billed Kite perched on the horizontal limb of a large mesquite tree. This tropical hawk is very rare and one of the most difficult birds to observe in the United States. Later, we went to a cliff overlooking one of the wildest areas of the river. Part of the cliff is formed from the ancient beds of giant oysters more than six inches long. Because of these oyster beds, the Rio Grande below the cliff is shallower. This was where the Comanches crossed the river to conduct raids in Mexico. As a result, this spot came to be named Paso de los Indios. On the way home, in the spirit of Edgar Kincaid, the boys asked me to bestow bird names on them: I named Kurt the Kiskadee and Peter the Roadrunner, and David was later named the Antpitta.

A few years later, in August 1982, I took the teenagers on a trip to Mexico. We drove to San Benito with my friend Chuck Neil from Minnesota. There, we met Pete Moore, a lawyer who had spent significant time in northeastern Mexico and had invited us to go with him on a trip to Rancho del Cielito (Little Heaven), a property that was then owned by Juanita Colson. On our first afternoon there, parrots flew overhead, calling. The boys were beside themselves with excitement. Peter said, "This is neater than Europe, and I've been there."

We spent several days birding Juanita's property, where the boys saw many tropical birds that they had never before seen, including Squirrel Cuckoos, Blue-crowned Motmots, White-collared Seedeaters, Scrub and Yellow-throated Euphonias, Social and Boat-billed Flycatchers, Lineated Woodpeckers, and Ringed, Green, and Amazon Kingfishers. Then we traveled in Pete's four-wheel drive Land Cruiser up a rocky road into the Sierra de Tamaulipas to Rancho del Cielo, which was owned by Texas Southmost College (now the University of Texas, Brownsville). There, we hiked through a very different habitat with pine trees and oak trees that were covered with orchids and bromeliads. We marveled at the sight of a tiny Bumblebee Hummingbird with its brilliant iridescent reddish-violet gorget (or throat patch). This species is closely related to the Wine-throated Hummingbird, which I had seen at El Triunfo about ten years earlier. We also heard and saw the Singing Quail. A male and female of this species engage in a duet in which one sex sings part of the song and the other adds another part. Its loud rollicking call is one of the dominant sounds of the cloud forest. I could tell that these boys were becoming more and more fascinated with birds and nature, developing the same love for the tropics that I had experienced on my first trip to Mexico with Armand Yramategui twenty-five years earlier.

A few years later, we made another trip to Mexico over the boys' Christmas break. We drove to Roma, parked my car, shouldered our backpacks, and crossed the bridge on foot. We were planning to take a bus to Monterrey, so we could board the Regiomontana, Mexico's express train that departed Monterrey at six o'clock every evening, making only a few stops before arriving in Mexico City the following morning. But when we arrived at the border, the immigration official there denied our papers. Prior to the trip, I had obtained letters from the teenagers' parents that provided permission for the boys to travel with me into Mexico. These permissions had been signed and notarized, but the border official said that these papers needed to be taken to a Mexican consulate, presented to the appropriate officials, and stamped by their office before being accepted at the border. The nearest Mexican consulate was seventy miles away and was about to close its doors for the day. It appeared that our entire trip was about to fall apart.

I called the consulate and explained our dilemma to the consulate official. He had never heard of such a requirement and suggested that we travel to another border crossing. I took his suggestion and drove to Rio Grande City, which was about thirty miles away. Fortunately, my friend Juan Caro, who owned Caro's Restaurant there, agreed that I could leave my car in the parking lot behind the restaurant. He told me that his wife, Carmen, would drive us to the border for another attempt.

This time when I presented the papers for the boys, the border official said nothing about the documents needing to be stamped by a consulate, but informed me that he needed two copies—one to stay with the border office and the other to travel with us during our excursion. I asked Carmen to take the documents across the border to an office store where they could be copied and to return as quickly as possible. As the four of us waited, an old taxi motored across the bridge. I asked the driver if he could take us to Monterrey since we had already missed the bus. He named a price, and I agreed. When Carmen returned with the copies, we successfully received authorization to enter Mexico, piled into the rickety taxi with our luggage, and set out for Monterrey.

Near the start of our journey, the driver started to turn off the road that goes to Monterrey. I asked, "What are you doing?" He responded, "I need to tell my wife where I'm going." I said, "We don't have time for that. We need to get to Monterrey as quickly as possible to catch the train." Since the old taxi had very poor suspension, we couldn't go faster than fifty miles per hour. I was tense the entire journey, worrying that we would miss the train. When we arrived in Monterrey, it became obvious that the cab driver didn't know the location of the train station. Eventually, we found it, but the Regiomontana had already departed. At the ticket office, I asked if we could beat the train if we took a taxi to Saltillo, the next stop. The answer was yes—the train didn't travel very fast while it ascended to Saltillo, which is located at a higher elevation.

I approached another, newer taxi. The young driver agreed to take us to Saltillo in our effort to beat the train. Saltillo is only about sixty miles west of Monterrey. The winding, paved road climbs steeply into the mountains. Thanks to this driver, we arrived about twenty minutes before the train.

We were all thrilled to board the Regiomontana and occupy our rooms. Shortly after the train departed, we went to the dining car where we had a fine meal and relaxed, knowing that a trip that was about to fall apart had been salvaged. Our rooms adjoined each other; each room had a lower and upper bunk. The lower bunk afforded a view of the passing countryside and the stars. The train made only a few stops between Saltillo and Mexico City. At those stops, we didn't get off the train, but could look out the window and observe life from a distance and in a different way. Needless to say, this first leg of the adventure was very exciting for my young friends.

We disembarked in Mexico City at about eight in the morning, flew to Veracruz, rented a car, and drove about a hundred miles south to Catemaco. We stayed at a hotel located next to Lake Catemaco and visited the University of Mexico biological station on the lower slopes of Sierra de los Tuxtlas. The station's manager kept a pet margay, a jungle cat very similar to the ocelot, and we all got to hold this beautiful and rarely seen cat.

One night, we spotted a Northern Potoo (once called a Common Potoo) about a hundred yards out in a tall-grass field. The potoo is a large nocturnal bird, almost the size of an owl, with yellow irises that shine red when illuminated at night with a flashlight. This species is challenging to spot during the day, but can be observed more easily at night, perched on utility poles, fence posts, and low branches, and its distinctive red eye shine can be seen from a great distance.

We traveled by boat into the Sontecomapan Lagoon, which is bordered by mangroves. We were hoping to see a Sungrebe, a strange bird that is in a family that contains only two other species—the

African and Asian Finfoots. Brown above with a black-and-white-striped head and a long bill, Sungrebes resemble medium-size ducks. As they swim, they move their head back and forth. They have sacs under their wings in which they can carry their young. We were successful in seeing a Sungrebe, as well as a number of other birds in the mangroves, including the Common Black Hawk and Pygmy Kingfisher. Although the boys had been to Rancho del Cielo, this trip marked their first exposure to the deep tropics.

Throughout the years, I organized annual trips with these young men—some times with all three, and other trips, with just one. I attended their graduation ceremonies at St. Stephen's, and when they left Austin for college, I was worried that I would never see them again, that their studies and careers would take them some distance away. I decided to make an effort to visit these boys once they began college. Once when I visited Kurt at Carleton College in Minnesota, we traveled to Duluth and looked for owls with Kim Eckert, one of the VENT leaders. There, we spotted a Northern Hawk Owl, a species that I long had wanted to see. This large owl hunts rodents during the daytime and perches on tops of trees. With its long tail and swooping flight, it resembles a hawk. While we were driving down a road into a snow-blanketed forest, an ermine, an all-white weasel, dashed across the road.

These boys provided me contact with young people who shared my interest in birds and wildlife. They created a sense of a family. They became some of my best friends—and I've had the pleasure of watching them grow up and pursue their careers and start families. Each worked for my company at one time or another, leading occasional tours.

In early 1985, several of our leaders left to form a competing company. This split occurred after several years of attempting to negotiate a compromise over stock ownership. I had traveled to South Texas with my young friend David Sugeno to participate in the Falcon Dam Christmas Bird Count. We had a wonderful time and saw many of the special birds of the Rio Grande Valley. On the morning of January 1, we started to drive north to Austin. En route, we ran into the front edge of a very strong cold front, the type of weather system that Texans call a "blue norther." The temperature plummeted at least forty degrees that afternoon. When we arrived at my house in Travis Heights, it was dark and very cold. Upon approaching my front door, I was surprised to see a white envelope with my name on it stuck into the doorjamb. Inside was a letter from Rose Ann, Jan Pierson, and Bret Whitney, informing me that they were leaving VENT to start their own company. A few months later, John Rowlett resigned from our board of directors to join this new company. I was deeply saddened by this news even though it wasn't entirely unexpected. It was a very difficult time for me. It was like I had lost members of my own family, particularly since I had known John and Rose Ann for so many years and they were close friends of mine.

Later that year, I came up with a new idea. Given my experience with Kurt, David, and Peter, I had the thought that perhaps I could start a camp for young birders. I wanted to create an educational adventure for youngsters, so they could learn to identify birds, understand their life zones, and appreciate the environmental role that birds play in nature. In addition to being birders, the campers needed to learn what it meant to be an environmentalist, to be someone who cares about the world in which we live and tries not to harm it.

I found solace in this new endeavor because it was focused on serving the next generation of birders. It kept my mind off the emotional and financial challenges that I had recently experienced with VENT. With all our tours, we had begun to encounter intense competition from other bird tour companies. The young birders' camp was a totally noncompetitive, nonprofit venture. No such camps existed anywhere else in the United States. Local Audubon clubs, such as the Massachusetts Audubon Society and the Maryland Ornithological Society, had created young birder camps in their respective areas, but no organization had offered a camp on a national basis. Our camp therefore represented an entirely new idea and venture.

I selected the Chiricahua Mountains—about 150 miles southeast of Tucson—as the site for the first camp, which would be a two-week session for young birders, ages eleven to seventeen. Over the years, I had led trips there and had fallen in love with that beautiful region. The camp was scheduled for June 1986. I co-led the inaugural camp with Rick Bowers, a VENT leader who lived with his wife in Tucson. My young friends Peter English and David Sugeno agreed to serve as counselors for the camp. We promoted the camp through VENT's company newsletter.

I drove with Peter and David from Austin to Arizona, scouting the area before meeting the campers in Tucson. After meeting Rick in Tucson, we drove to the Chiricahua Mountains, where we had reserved cabins at the seven-acre Cave Creek Ranch located along Cave Creek with nearby views of the dramatic rhyolite cliffs of Cave Creek Canyon, one of the scenic highlights of this area. The diverse habitats near the ranch range from pine-oak woodlands and cottonwood-sycamore riparian areas to grassy meadows and the Chiricahua desert, thus attracting more than a hundred species of birds, including some of the southeast Arizona specialties, such as the Elegant Trogon, that occur nowhere else in the United States. The canyon is also the home of the Southwest Research Station of the American Museum of Natural History. Many years earlier, an acquaintance of David Rockefeller had visited a ranch in this area and had observed some very unusual beetles. As it turns out, Rockefeller was interested in beetles and decided to buy the ranch and establish a research station for the American Museum of Natural History in 1955.

Fortunately, the neighbors of the Cave Creek Ranch were Walter and Sally Spofford, who had bought the adjacent property after retiring to the area. Walter had been a doctor in Ithaca, New York, and Sally was one of the first employees of the Cornell Laboratory of Ornithology. Next to their house, they had set up a number of hummingbird and seed feeders that attracted a remarkable assemblage of birds. Their property was so close that the boys could walk there whenever they had free time and observe the birds at the feeders.

Since most of the campers had never traveled to southeastern Arizona, they had only seen one kind of hummingbird in their lifetimes. Thirteen of North America's eighteen species of hummingbirds occur in this area during the spring and summer. At the Spoffords' feeders, the boys often saw five or six species of hummingbirds, including the aptly named Magnificent Hummingbird, a large species with a black breast, a gleaming emerald throat, and a purple crown, and Anna's Hummingbird, a species that nests mainly in coastal California, but appears in Arizona in the late summer. An Anna's Hummingbird may need the nectar output of one thousand flowers to get the water and the calories it needs every day to survive. A human with the same energy needs would have to eat three hundred pounds of food and drink one-hundred-and-fifty gallons of water every day. Another large hummingbird that we saw was the Blue-throated, the largest of the species. Its heart beats 1,260 times per minute. When the boys returned to the ranch after being at the Spoffords for the first time, their faces beamed with excitement and joy.

Each morning started at five-thirty, so the campers got up with the birds. The birding on the grounds and surrounding the cabins was wonderful, and the boys spotted several species that they had never seen, such as Brown-crested Flycatchers, Bridled Titmice, and Canyon Towhees. To simplify our chores, we arranged to take all our evening meals during this part of the camp at the Southwest Research Station, which was about five miles up the canyon. We thought eating dinners at the station would give the campers a chance to meet scientists working there and perhaps talk to them about their work. Unfortunately, this did not happen. Instead, the campers filed into the dining room, went through the cafeteria line with their trays, sat together at a long table, ate their food quickly, and then went outside to look for birds. No one ever attempted to converse with the scientists or lingered over a meal.

On the last morning of the camp, after we returned to Tucson, there was a knock on the door of my room. When I opened it, there were all the campers, radiating with pride that they had been pioneers by participating in the first national birding camp. As I looked at these campers, I was filled with happiness because I could tell how much the camp had meant to them. By being a mentor to them, I had repaid my own mentors. This experience also brought home to me that a mentor who gives of himself to another person receives as much, or more, in return.

One of our VENT leaders in Washington State, Dr. Eugene Hunn, an outstanding naturalist and birder, suggested that we operate a second camp in summer 1987 in Washington that he would organize and lead. So, that following summer, we offered two camps—Camp Chiricahua and Camp Cascades. I co-led Chiricahua with Rick Bowers, and Gene led Camp Cascades with Peter English as his assistant.

Frank Graham's feature about our camp in the May 1988 issue of *Audubon Magazine* led to a life-changing event for a young man named Barry Lyon. Barry's father was a teacher and a lifelong naturalist and had taken his son on many trips to see birds and other wildlife. When Graham's story appeared, fifteen-year-old Barry read the article and told his father that he wanted to attend Camp Chiricahua. His father called the VENT office and was told that the camp was already full, but Camp Cascades still had available spots. His father signed Barry up for that camp. The following summer, he attended Camp Chiricahua and we met. Over the years, we kept in touch, and Barry eventually became a VENT tour leader. For the first few years, he led tours in various areas of the United States, including Texas, Point Pelee in Ontario, Hawaii, Florida, and other places. After a few years, he expanded his repertoire to include Belize, Guatemala, Panama, Newfoundland, Nova Scotia, Alaska, Hawaii, and Churchill in Manitoba. Later, he moved to Austin and worked in the VENT office as my assistant. Today, Barry works as our company's chief operating officer and is one of my closest friends. From the first time I met him, I was impressed with his interest and enthusiasm for all aspects of the natural world, his gentle manner, and his appreciation for birds, including common species.

Barry is not the only camper whose life has been shaped by participation in our camps. Many of the top young birders in the United States have attended one or more of our camps. Former campers have discovered new species to science. For example,

Dan Lane, who attended Louisiana State University and became an excellent bird artist, discovered a new species of barbet—the Scarlet-banded Barbet—in the mountains of Peru. Andrew Farnsworth, who attended our first birding camp, earned a PhD at Cornell and now works on the staff of the Cornell Lab of Ornithology, studying nocturnal migration. Dan Lebbin works for the American Bird Conservancy, one of the most important organizations working to preserve habitats of endangered birds.

In subsequent years, we offered young birder camps in Belize, Venezuela, and Costa Rica, in addition to the existing ones in the United States. From the outset, we decided to make the camps co-ed, but for the first couple of years, only boys signed up. The third year, we had two girls, and girls have enrolled at every camp since then. Now almost half the campers are female. We've always provided scholarships for young people whose families can't afford the full fee. We've done everything we can to keep the cost of the camp as reasonable as possible.

Running a camp is the most intense and hardest work that I do all year, but it also is the most satisfying. My greatest contribution in life is being a mentor. Like my mentors, I never married or had children of my own. Instead, I experienced this richness through sharing my passion for birds and nature with many young people. I believe that true reincarnation occurs when you share your philosophy with young people—or in the case of parents, with their children—and then that person may incorporate parts of this philosophy into his or her own spirit and hopefully, in turn, will pass it along to a young person.

I love the derivation of the word "mentor." When Odysseus was gone from Ithaca for twenty years, his son, Telemachus, was advised and raised by a friend of his father named Mentor. Later in Greece, when people witnessed an older person helping a younger individual who was not their child, they would say, "You are like Mentor. You are a mentor." It's one of my favorite words because of what mentors contribute.

Recently, the VENT offices received the following letter from a teenager who lives in Madison, Wisconsin:

My name is Ryan Treves, and I am 15 years old. I am fascinated with birds. For years, I have dreamt of seeing the bird-rich eco-systems of Arizona, yet it has been difficult for my family to find a way. When I heard about Camp Chiricahua, I was elated. This was my chance!

I started bird-watching when I was 5 and my parents' university sent our family to Uganda. Binoculars in hand, I accompanied my mom, dad, and older brother on trips with local guides to find some of my best memories. I was dazzled by rollers, hornbills, and sunbirds. I have since discovered equal beauty closer to home. One experience in particular touched me. When a Great Gray Owl strayed into my hometown in southern Wisconsin, I was lucky enough to spend hours observing this extraordinary bird. I remember watching the owl from a distance. It looked straight my way, then glided past, inches away. It happened fast, yet I will never forget the silent, graceful movement of that owl. More people showed up every day to see the Great Gray. While part of me wanted it all for myself, I also loved seeing so many people excited about an owl.

Now, I see birding as a beautiful way I can step away from a hectic school schedule and escape the superficiality of day-to-day life. I have recently enjoyed volunteering through the Madison Audubon Society as a way to connect with young kids and others in the community about something I value so highly. Through these opportunities I have seen that kids are the future of birds. Unfortunately, none of my peers share my passion. Camp Chiricahua is where all of this could come together—a place where I could share my passion with other birders my age and explore an entirely new ecosystem.

Sincerely,

Ryan

What makes these young birder camps so meaningful to me is that I'm giving these young kids an opportunity to have something that I never had—contact with other people their age who share their interest in birds and nature. Their enthusiasm augments the enthusiasm that I still have for all aspects of nature, but they express it in a way that only people their age would do—with high fives, by running at full speed when they find something unusual, by exalting over the memorable sightings of the day that night. It transports me back to my own childhood and helps me to experience again the excitement that I felt when I saw these birds for the very first time.

In many ways, my most interesting contact with young people was a nature walk I led for a group of blind children at Eisenhower Park northeast of Houston. Most of these kids had tunnel vision so they could make the hike unaided, but one slender white boy was totally blind. This boy proved the most adept at learning the songs of birds that I was identifying for the group. A short African-American boy named Ronnie took his hand and led the boy throughout the entire hike.

I had never led a group of kids with impaired vision, so I had to improvise. I picked leaves of plants that I knew had pungent odors when crushed and asked the kids to pass the leaves around and smell them. I also scooped up a handful of soil for them to smell. I played the recording of the call of a Pileated Woodpecker. One flew into a tree over our heads and drummed against it.

On the trip back to their school, I asked their teacher to stop the van. I told the kids that I wanted to pick some cattails so they could feel their fuzzy cigar-shaped heads. Ronnie said, "Get lots of them." When I returned to the van, the children eagerly passed around the soft heads of the cattails and touched them with delight and wonder.

14

End of the Earth

Emperor Penguin
CAPE WASHINGTON, ANTARCTICA

For years, I had heard about Antarctica many times from my mentor and friend, Roger Tory Peterson. He had traveled there many times with his friend Lars-Eric Lindblad, the Swedish-American explorer and entrepreneur who pioneered eco-tourism in this remote area of the world. In some ways, the idea of going to Antarctica wasn't high on my list because, like other naturalists, such as Frank M. Chapman who started the inaugural Christmas Bird Count in 1900, I had early on fallen in love with the tropics. Having grown up in a warm climate, I found the tropics more appealing than cold, frigid Antarctica.

So I was not on my company's first trip to Antarctica in January 1987. We reserved an allotment on a Society Expeditions ship called the *MS Explorer*, or, as it was nicknamed, the "Little Red Ship." This was the famous ship that Lindblad had used for his inaugural trip with the first group of tourists to Antarctica in 1969. We had enough participants that we were able to send a tour leader free of charge. (Typically, a cruise company will allow you to send one of your staff if you reserve a specific number of cabins and sell ten or more spaces.) When our leader, David Wolf, returned from the trip with glowing reports, I decided that I would be the VENT leader on our next excursion.

The second trip took place in November 1987. Again, we sold enough spaces to earn a free spot for me. Our company was also given a second free spot, so I invited my young friend Kurt Huffman, who was still a student at Carleton College. We boarded the ship in Rio de Janeiro and as we cruised out of the harbor into the open waters of the Atlantic, we soon encountered swells, not particularly rough, but the constant motion was something that neither of us had ever experienced. For the second time in my life, I became seasick, and so did Kurt. Fortunately, the nausea eased after about twenty-four hours, and we adjusted to the motion and began to enjoy numerous seabirds. We saw Atlantic Petrels, as well as Sooty and Yellow-nosed Albatrosses, the first albatrosses that Kurt and I had ever seen.

Our destination was South Georgia, a large, remote island in the South Atlantic that receives cold currents from Antarctica. As a result, its barren landscape is treeless and mostly covered with glaciers. For this trip, our primary nature/bird leader was Peter Harrison, a remarkable Englishman who had traveled around the world as a young man, painting seabirds. He wrote and illustrated *Seabirds: An Identification Guide* (1991), the first book that described all of the seabirds of the world. During our two-day voyage to South Georgia, Peter was out on deck, spotting and identifying seabirds for all of us. Every day, throughout the trip, he created a painting of one of the birds that we saw that day—and then he posted this painting on the bulletin board along with the list of species that we had seen during the day. At the tour's conclusion, these beautiful sketches were auctioned off to raise funds for a seabird study that Peter wanted to support.

As we neared South Georgia, we encountered a late-winter storm with high winds and heavy, persistent rain. A handful of passengers disembarked in Grytviken to visit the whalers' cemetery that includes the gravesite of Sir Ernest Shackleton, the famous British polar explorer who tried to lead a party across Antarctica. His fateful and final expedition is chronicled in the best-selling book, *Endurance: Shackleton's Incredible Voyage* (1959) by Alfred Lansing. Grytviken is also the location of the first whaling station ever established in the Antarctic. It was founded by Captain Carl Anton Larsen, who leased the site from Great Britain in 1905.

Initially, I didn't get off the ship because of the torrential rains, but later that afternoon, a group of us climbed up a cliff to observe a nesting Light-mantled Albatross on a rocky ledge. This seabird is exquisitely beautiful, with its soft sooty-brown plumage, silver mantle, and distinctive blue markings along its lower mandible. During this first trip, I came to love the Light-mantled Albatross above all other seabirds. I love the way it sails effortlessly on its narrow, long, pointed wings on the invisible air currents, issuing its haunting call. These birds are also known for their acrobatic ability, and courting pairs on breeding grounds will offer up a synchronized aerial display of formation flying.

The storm continued to intensify. The ship's captain said it was the worst storm that he had ever experienced in all his years at sea. Later, he told us that the staff had almost requested that all the passengers file into the main reception in case it became necessary to abandon ship. Needless to say, due to the heavy rains and strong winds, it was impossible to board the Zodiacs and land again on South Georgia. This was a great disappointment to Peter Harrison and many others on the tour. Peter grew very frustrated that he couldn't show his favorite place to the other passengers. After all, South Georgia is one of the few spots in the world where one can see thousands of King Penguins in nesting colonies that range in size from forty-thousand to more than five-hundred-thousand birds.

In desperation, Peter and Frank Todd, the great penguin expert from the San Diego Zoo, boarded a Zodiac and crossed the rough waters to a King Penguin colony, captured a King Penguin, and brought the large bird back to the ship so everyone could at least see it. This meant the bird could not count toward anyone's life list. (One of the rules is that you can only count as a lifer birds that are unrestrained and in the wild.) The penguin stabbed Peter in the hand with its powerful beak, and he was bleeding. After the brief show-and-tell, the bird was returned to the wild.

We proceeded farther south toward the Antarctic Peninsula, the northernmost region of mainland Antarctica. The peninsula itself extends for about eight hundred miles north with the Wendell Sea along its east side. Once we reached the peninsula, the weather improved considerably. The seas were still moderately rough, but nothing like what we had experienced at South Georgia. Our cruise director was a Scotsman named Angus Erskine, a former captain in the Royal Navy. He was very careful about where he would allow passengers to disembark. In fact, Peter Harrison became so frustrated with what he felt was Erskine's overly cautious approach that he contacted Society Expeditions and informed them that he would resign if Erskine didn't start making more landings.

The weather continued to improve, and we ended up making some spectacular landings, where we saw several large penguin colonies, including Adélie, Chinstrap, Gentoo, and Macaroni Penguins. We also saw Antarctic Fulmars, Blue Petrels, Cape Petrels, Black-browed Albatrosses, and hundreds of Antarctic Prions. One of the joys of being in Antarctic waters is to watch a tight flock of fifty or more Cape Petrels (Pintados) circling the boat. They have a lovely black-and-white plumage with a black head, checkered wings and back, and white underparts. For some reason, they are attracted to ships, perhaps hoping that the ship will stir up some food for them. Despite the bad weather in South Georgia, my first trip to Antarctica was marvelous.

A number of years later, my friend Robert Ridgely, an ornithologist who worked at the Academy of Natural Sciences in Philadelphia, told me that the academy had chartered a former Russian research vessel from a company called Marine Expeditions for a voyage to Antarctica. The 384-foot vessel, the *Akademik Ioffe*, was built in Finland in 1989 and based in Kalingrad on the Baltic Sea. Though not officially identified as an icebreaker, the reinforced steel hull was equipped to withstand impacts with thick ice and drifts. Bob told me that the trip went very well and, though the accommodations were somewhat spartan, they were more than adequate. The Marine Expeditions price for the charter was quite reasonable, so we decided to offer this excursion.

At this point in VENT history, we had never chartered a ship because of the significant financial risk involved. A charter contract states that you will pay the charter fee regardless of whether or not the trip is full. I asked Peter Matthiessen to be one of the trip leaders along with my close friend Greg Lasley, who at that time was a member of the Austin police force, an avid birder, and a devoted wildlife photographer. Brad Schram of California, a recognized expert on the birds of Southern California, also joined the trip as a fourth leader. Fortunately, the trip sold out quickly.

A few months before the tour, we learned that Marine Expeditions was not paying some of its bills to various fuel suppliers in South America and was, in fact, in significant financial trouble. This led to one of the worst days in my career as CEO of VENT: I arrived at the office one morning and our vice president, Shirley Anderson, met me outside the office in tears, informing me that Marine Expeditions had gone bankrupt. Fortunately, this turned out not to be true at that time, but a few months after our trip, the company did go bankrupt.

In January 1998, Peter Matthiessen, Rose Styron, and I traveled to Santiago, Chile, a few days before the tour. We stayed in a lovely small hotel on a quiet, sycamore tree-lined street, some distance away from the heart of Santiago. Since Peter's favorite birds are shorebirds, we decided to visit the El Yeso Reservoir, which is the major source of drinking water for the citizens of Santiago, and look for the legendary Diademed Sandpiper-Plover. This particularly beautiful shorebird has a distinctive plumage pattern: a chestnut-colored back and barred markings of white and black on its underparts. A row of white spots surround the crown of the bird, hence the name.

This small bird only nests in boggy areas of the Andes, well above tree line, from Central Peru to Central Chile and to spot one in Peru requires a drive up into the Andes to thirteen or fourteen thousand feet. Many people, including me, have difficulty acclimating to this elevation because of the lack of oxygen. However, farther south in Chile, the tree line occurs at a lower elevation, making it possible to see the Diademed Sandpiper-Plover at seven thousand feet.

A local guide took Peter, Rose, and me to this area. We walked across the alpine meadows to a stream. There, in this mountain stream, was a tiny island where a gorgeous sandpiper-plover was sitting on its eggs, surrounded by beautiful yellow flowers shaped like snapdragons, fern-like plants, and soft, green mosses. It was one of the most beautiful settings that I had ever seen for a bird nest.

A few days later, we met the rest of the group in Santiago. Robert Bateman, the famous Canadian wildlife artist, and his wife, Birgit, a German-born artist-photographer, were among the participants. After convening, the group traveled an hour by van to Los Farellones, a ski resort above Santiago, where we hoped to spot Andean Condors and other birds of the high country. During the first part of the drive, we traveled through a shrub zone, where we saw a Rufous-tailed Plantcutter.

Then the road ascended above the tree line where the landscape consisted entirely of short grass, which was brown at this time of year, with a scattering of large, gray rocks. Surprisingly, there were brilliant patches of California poppies, which had clearly been introduced into this area. One of the first special birds we saw was a Moustached Turca, a large tapaculo. A small family of South American birds, tapaculos always keep their tails cocked and pointed toward their heads. As a result, the undertail feathers are exposed. In Spanish, *tapaculo* means "cover your ass."

We saw other remarkable birds of the high country, including earthcreepers, yellow-finches, and hummingbirds. Even before we arrived at the tiny village, we spotted low-flying condors. Once we disembarked from the vans, we had magnificent looks at various condors as they crossed the ridge not far above our heads. The Andean Condor has one of the largest wingspans of any bird in the world. Its historic range was from Colombia to southern Chile. Sadly, its numbers are much reduced, and the species has disappeared from many areas where it once occurred. These declines are largely due to condors being captured, their heads and feathers used for native religious ceremonies and festivals. Fortunately, the majestic birds still exist in healthy numbers in Chile. Seeing a condor is one of the highlights of any trip to South America.

The next day, we flew from Santiago to Ushuaia, the southern-most city in the world. There we had an opportunity to visit the nearby Tierra del Fuego National Park. This park consists mainly of Nothofagus trees, which resemble beech trees, and small lakes. One of the birds that we hoped to spot was the magnificent Magellanic Woodpecker, a close relative of the extinct American Ivory-billed Woodpecker. Like the Ivory Bill, the male is an enormous black woodpecker—larger than a crow—with a crimson red head and crest that curves forward. In contrast, the female identifying marks include a black head and crest. We were not able to locate this splendid species on this trip, but, fortunately, we were successful on subsequent trips.

On January 20, 1998, our ship departed from Ushuaia, cruising east down the Beagle Channel. On our two-day journey to the Falkland Islands, we had many good looks at a variety of petrels, albatrosses, and other seabirds. The Falklands have a more temperate climate than some of the other areas that we would visit farther south, but the topography is virtually devoid of trees. The highlight of our excursion there was walking to the edge of a colony of Rockhopper Penguins. This small penguin has red eyes, a black head and upperparts, white underparts, and long golden plumes on the sides of its head. What is most remarkable about Rockhoppers is their ability to jump out of the sea and propel themselves anywhere from ten to twenty feet onto a rocky shelf. Once they land, the penguins start hopping up the face of the cliff, rock to rock, to reach their colony. While they are hopping, a wave will often crash right over them. When the wave recedes, the Rockhoppers, still erect, continue to hop as if nothing had happened.

In contrast to my first trip to Antarctica, the weather was extraordinary. We enjoyed calm seas throughout a majority of the cruise and made all the landings that we hoped to make, including one on Elephant Island. This is the island where Shackleton's men waited for almost a year for him to return and rescue them after their expedition ship had been beset in the ice.

On remote South Georgia (870 miles from the Falklands), we landed at numerous sites and saw several colonies of thousands upon thousands of King Penguins, one of the greatest sights in the natural world. By the end of January, some of the penguins were incubating their eggs. By this time, the young from the previous year of breeding were completely covered in long, wispy, brown feathers, making them look quite ridiculous. These juveniles—called "Oakum Boys," oakum being the fuzzy brown material similar in appearance to the bird's feathers—constantly squealed a high-pitched call, almost sounding like the chirping of a land bird. The young birds massed together in what are called "crèches" while their parents continue to feed them fish and krill. In the meantime, the nesting penguins sat atop a large single egg balanced on their feet, with a fold of skin from their stomach covering most of the egg. (Most penguins raise two chicks every three years.)

Nearby Snowy Sheathbills, a white chicken-like bird found only in Antarctica, patrolled the colony, hoping to find an exposed egg that they could peck and break open to feed on the yolk. At one point, we observed a sheathbill tear meat off a penguin carcass and carry pieces to its two downy young, looking like gray fluff balls, that sat nearby on a rocky ledge. Brown Skuas, a large, gull-like, dark brown seabird, soared overhead, hoping to find a vulnerable egg or a small chick to eat.

The landscape itself is largely made up of pristine glaciers and distant snow peaks. On this trip, we enjoyed sunny, blue-sky days, an anomaly in this part of the world where the shoreline and headlands are often swept with rain and fog. The island's highest point, Mount Paget, rose about two miles in the sky.

We disembarked on Prion Island and walked about three-hundred yards to a colony of Wandering Albatross. Each pair of albatross had constructed a huge nest of grass about three feet high. One member of the pair was sitting on the egg. When the mate returned to the nest, both birds started to produce loud calls and to throw their heads backward until their bills pointed skyward. They also outstretched their enormous wings. As we watched this remarkable display, we could see the snow-covered mountains and glaciers of South Georgia across the bay.

Peter Harrison's favorite spot in the world is Gold Harbor in South Georgia. During my first excursion, we hadn't been able to land there. But, upon landing on this subsequent trip, I quickly began to feel about Gold Harbor as Peter does. By now, the sun had fully come out and the clouds had lifted above the glacier and mountains. On the expansive beach of black basalt pebbles and boulders, a large assemblage of elephant seals lounged about, groaning in unruly rows. This species is the largest seal in the world and is capable of diving five thousand feet or more in search of food.

During our visit, the female elephant seals massed together, lying on top of each other, with others side by side, forming an enormous pile of creatures. During the breeding season, the dominant male patrols and protects his nearby harem. I watched as a male emerged from the sea and started inching his way toward another's harem. The dominant male reared back his head and emitted a bellow that was the deepest sound that I had ever heard in nature. The young male immediately retreated into the sea. Throughout the day, we could hear the deep bellows of the elephant seals.

Gold Harbor is the site of an enormous King Penguin colony. It consists largely of a flat plain that stretches to the base of the cliffs, which are covered in a long, golden-brown grass. From the cliffs, one can see tens of thousands of King Penguins. Some of us climbed up the three-hundred-foot cliff so we could get a closer look at the nests of the Light-mantled Albatrosses. Luck was with us: We found a nest and spent a considerable amount of time observing the young and adults while also overlooking the spectacular King Penguin colony. Even from the top of the cliff, we could hear the deep bellows of the elephant seals and the chattering noises of the penguins. To the right, we had an unbroken view of a huge glacier. At times, large chunks of ice from the glacier dropped into the water below.

Many years before this trip, I had read an article in *Audubon Magazine* about Antarctica. It included a photograph of the Snow Petrel, a small, all-white seabird with a jet-black beak and eyes. I was enchanted by this image and hoped that one day I would see a Snow Petrel. This wish was granted on this trip. We experienced spectacular views of these birds, particularly as we sailed up the Drygalski Fjord, just before departing South Georgia. This fjord is an ancient valley, less than a mile wide, shaped by glaciers and mountains, with black cliffs that rise more than a thousand feet over the water. The Snow Petrels sailed in front of these cliffs.

Our good fortune with the weather held as we crossed from South Georgia to the Antarctic Peninsula. On the peninsula, we enjoyed some of the most magnificent scenery in the world, as well as several huge colonies of Adélie and Chinstrap Penguins. The Antarctic Peninsula, even at the height of summer, is almost entirely white from the ice and snow. The only snow-free areas are the narrow black-rock beaches, with scattered bits and pieces of kelp, and a few of the nearby mountainous slopes. At times, white peaks surrounded us on all sides, stretching as far as we could see. One of the most famous areas of the Antarctic Peninsula is Lemaire Channel, a narrow waterway that cuts through a canyon for several miles. Black cliffs with swatches of snow border this spectacular channel.

While cruising through this passage, we spotted our first Antarctic Petrel, a species that we had hoped to see. This brown-and-white large petrel breeds even farther south. As a result, in the summer, it can be difficult to encounter in the Antarctic Peninsula. Fortunately, this petrel circled our ship, giving us an opportunity to observe its soft brown upperparts and brown-and-white wings. Shortly afterward, we came upon a pod of twelve orcas (killer whales). Most orcas are black and white, but in Antarctica, the white areas are yellowish because of diatoms, a kind of algae that grows on the whale's slippery skin. All the whales surfaced in a line at once and blew. At times, the large creatures swam right next to the boat. It was an incredible sight.

A woman who was studying the orcas and was a guest on the tour showed us some remarkable footage in which a group of orcas swim toward a flat chunk of ice upon which a seal is sleeping. By rapidly approaching the ice as a group, they create a wave so high that the ice tips up and the seal slides off. Rather than killing the seal, they surface under it and push the seal up into the air so high that it lands on the ice again. It turns out that this exercise is done to teach the young orcas how to hunt seals.

One evening, we visited one of the islands in Queen Wilhelmina Bay where the humpback whales were corralling fish by blowing streams of bubbles that caused the fish to gather in a dense ball. We stood on the bow of the ship, marveling at this singular sight. Every so often, a whale burst out from the middle of the circle, with its enormous mouth open, and attempted to collect as many fish as possible. This activity is called "lunge feeding."

On our return, we enjoyed remarkably calm seas as we crossed the famous seven-hundred-mile Drake Passage. This channel, named after the sixteenth-century adventurer, Sir Francis Drake, runs through the Roaring Forties, latitudes that are well known for high winds and tumultuous waters. As a result, the region has become a graveyard of ships. On this particular trip, the Drake was so calm that we called it the "Drake Lake." Thanks to this favorable weather, we were able to make a stop at Cape Horn. This pleased Peter as he had always wanted to visit this spot because many books mention the travails of ships rounding the Horn.

Just as we departed for Ushuaia, I was standing on one side of the boat when a flock of fifteen Baird's Sandpipers flew by. This long-winged, long-distance migrant nests on the expansive tundra not far from the Arctic Ocean and spends its winter in the very southern region of South America. Predominately buffy and golden with a distinctive white belly, it is one of the few shorebirds that has ever been reported in Antarctica, where one dead bird was found on an island in the Antarctic Peninsula after having flown the seven hundred miles across the Drake Passage. As I watched these shorebirds fly above the cresting waters, I wished that Peter was next to me, knowing how much he loved shorebirds. To my delight, I soon learned that he stood on the other side of the boat, and when the birds circled, he observed the same flock of sandpipers.

After we returned to Santiago, the group went with Greg Lasley to look for the Diademed Sandpiper-Plovers that Rose, Peter, and I had seen before the trip. Meanwhile, we three drove to Isla Negra, Pablo Neruda's seaside home, with Rose's friend, Isabel Letelier. Isabel's husband was Orlando Letelier, the foreign minister in the administration of Salvador Allende. After the coup led by General

Augusto Pinochet, she and her husband escaped Chile and went to Washington, DC, where her husband was assassinated by a car bomb. Once we arrived at Isla Negra, we toured Pablo Neruda's home, which faces the sea. Neruda liked to say that his house was like the country of Chile—long and narrow. It was filled with objects that he had collected: seashells, art, and even a stuffed horse that he had acquired when he was a little boy. After the tour, we had lunch in the Restaurant of the Poet. As we sat outdoors on a beautiful sunny afternoon, Isabel told us stories about her friendship with Pablo Neruda.

Robert Bateman told me that this had been one of the greatest trips of his life. This certainly was high praise coming from a man who traveled extensively throughout the world. I returned to my home in Austin, feeling on top of the world. My company had chartered an entire boat for the first time and operated one of its best trips. I walked into the front door of my house, and the phone rang. It was my nephew, Steve, calling to tell me that his mother, my sister, had recently been diagnosed with terminal lung cancer. One month later, she died at age sixty-two. Nothing better illustrates the vicissitudes of life—how you can go from being elated to being very sad in the blink of an eye.

This Antarctica charter had been so successful that I decided I would attempt an even more ambitious trip. We would charter half of a Russian icebreaker for a trip operated by Quark Expeditions and travel from Tasmania to the Ross Sea, the other side of Antarctica, where we could observe several colonies of Emperor Penguins. For this excursion, I asked Peter Matthiessen, Robert Bateman, and Greg Lasley to be leaders. I also wrote a letter to Sir David Attenborough, offering him a very large stipend in hopes that he would join us. I received a reply, thanking me for my generous offer, but informing me that he wanted to devote every possible minute of the rest of his life to filmmaking. I knew that there were many people who wanted to experience the other side of Antarctica and see an Emperor Penguin colony, so I was confident that we could sell all fifty spots.

The trip was scheduled for late November/early December 2001. Early on, it attracted about thirty participants, but then, unfortunately, the economy took a nosedive with the dot-com bust. When I returned from another trip in July, I was dismayed to discover that many people had canceled their reservations because of the downturn. In an attempt to fill more spots, we lowered the price and were able to add a few more participants. As it turned out, that trip proved one of the most memorable of my life, but it was also the costliest trip that my company ever operated. From a business perspective, it was a trying time as I anticipated the large loss that the company was going to incur.

Nevertheless, the tour proceeded as planned. We had a marvelous few days of birding in Tasmania with Dion Hobcroft, a young Australian who had just joined our company and turned out to be one of the best leaders that we have ever hired. After a couple of days at sea, our 423.5-foot ship, *Kaptain Khelbnikov*, a Russian polar icebreaker, entered the frozen waters of the Ross Sea and proceeded through the ice to the southern part of that sea, which is ice-free due to the prevailing winds.

During our excursion, we had seen a handful of Emperor Penguins as the ship proceeded south, but we were thrilled at the prospect of seeing a colony with young penguins still present. One afternoon, we approached Cape Washington, where a large Emperor Penguin colony is located. Anchored near the colony, the ship was rammed into the ice, so most of the vessel was surrounded by ice. As a result, we descended directly from the gangplank onto the ice and nearby land. (Normally, on Antarctica trips, land is reached via Zodiac.) This arrangement meant that we were free to come and go from the ship and walk over to the colony at any time of the day or night. Since it stayed light all night, we had almost twenty-four hours to experience our first Emperor Penguin colony close up.

As we approached, we spotted a group of young penguins. The birds were gray with black heads and conspicuous white face masks. They were already half to two-thirds the size of the adults and would soon be going to sea. For a birder or a nature enthusiast, seeing an Emperor Penguin is one of the most thrilling experiences. Peter wrote about one of our excursions onto the ice to see these wonderful penguins in *End of the Earth: Voyages to Antarctica* (2003):

> Along the snow path, we meet numbers of adult emperors, coming and going from the water. The adults have a portly walk, bowing and calling as they go; exhilarated by encounters with other emperors, they may slap flippers or bump chests like football players. The intense cold light illumines the white wing patches of the circling skuas and infuses the penguins' ivory breasts with a silken sheen.

After a memorable week touring the Ross Sea—the very area from which Roald Amundsen and Robert Falcon Scott had launched their separate attempts in 1911 to reach the South Pole—we headed north. We had visited two Emperor Penguin colonies and had enjoyed wonderful experiences with this magnificent bird, a treat that few people enjoy during their lifetime. One afternoon, the staff informed us that, while surveying with a helicopter (the ship had its own landing pad), they had spotted an Emperor Penguin colony that they had never before visited. We boarded Zodiacs and traveled up an ice canyon to a level area where the Emperor Penguins had a colony.

There we observed Emperor Penguins returning from feeding expeditions. As they approached the shore, penguins would burst out of the water like missiles being shot from a submarine, arch over the shore, and land on the ice. They then tobogganed toward the colony, using their feet to push through the snow. Later, the Zodiac was positioned a short distance from where Emperor Penguins were gathering at the edge of the ice after having walked from the colony. A long line of penguins stretched back toward the colony. The ones at the front stopped. Perhaps seeing our Zodiac made them hesitate, or maybe they were worried about the predatory Leopard Seals. We sat in the small boat, observing these dazzling creatures with the sun highlighting their beautiful colors of black, white, and gold. Suddenly, one plopped down on the ice and dove into the sea. Immediately, all the rest started doing the same thing.

Once we returned to the ship, we learned that there was an opportunity to be helicoptered to the top of an enormous flat iceberg, more than a hundred feet above the sea. There the crew had set up an ice bar and were serving drinks. It made for a spectacular setting with snow-capped mountains and numerous icebergs. We had a chance to walk over to a crevice and stare down into its blue depths. The sun dipped low on the horizon, but did not set. It simply reached a point where it did not sink any further, which created the illusion that time was standing still.

Once onboard again, we headed north to Campbell Island, one of the uninhabited, subantarctic islands, near New Zealand. En route, we passed through a terrific storm. Some passengers were thrown out of their beds, but, fortunately, no one suffered serious injuries. On Campbell Island, we saw a wonderful array of megaherbs, plants with huge leaves and flowers of varying shades of purple and yellow. We hiked up onto a windswept ridge, where Southern Royal Albatrosses nested right alongside the trail. We had seen this species during our cruise, but it was wonderful to see them sitting on their nests. The Royal and Wandering Albatross have one of the largest wingspans of any bird in the world, reaching lengths as great as twelve feet.

Our trip ended back in Hobart, Tasmania, where Peter did a reading in a local bookstore from his novel, *Killing Mr. Watson* (1990). About fifty people were in attendance. Peter read a section in dialect about the alligator hunters on the Chatham River of the Florida Everglades. (He was wonderful at imitating dialect. I wished I had taped that reading.) At the end, Peter and I performed a spontaneous skit on the stage, pretending to be a pair of Giant Petrels with our arms spread, like a petrel would spread its wings. We crouched over and butted our heads, just as we had seen these birds behaving while fighting over the fresh carcass of a seal. That had been a vivid scene with the birds' white heads splattered in blood from feasting on the dead seal. Our playful performance prompted many laughs among the audience—and thus provided a joyful conclusion to this remarkable adventure.

15

The Birds of Heaven

CRANES, ASIA, AND PETER

In January 1993, Peter Matthiessen and I decided that we would attempt to see all the cranes of Asia during a three-week excursion. Eight species of cranes breed in Asia: Demoiselle, Eurasian (or Common), Hooded, Sarus, Siberian, Red-crowned, White-naped, and Black-necked. This is more than on any other continent. We shared with George Archibald, the founder of the International Crane Foundation, a special feeling for cranes. As George wrote in the foreword to Paul Johnsgard's *Cranes of the World*: "Cranes have stalked the earth's wetlands for over 60 million years. Since time untold mankind has been inspired by their primordial calls, elaborate dances, impressive migrations, and graceful beauty."

For the first leg of the trip in northern India and Bhutan, we traveled with an intrepid group of thirteen individuals. These travelers included many of Peter's friends from the East Coast—Bill and Rose Styron, George Plimpton, Mary Wallace, Inga Morath, Barbara Hale, and Peter's wife, Maria. In addition, there was a group of six friends from Seattle who had traveled with my company several times. After the Bhutan segment, Peter and I traveled alone to eastern China and northern Japan.

India: Gujarat and Rajasthan
SARUS CRANE, DEMOISELLE CRANE, SIBERIAN CRANE

I flew eighteen hours from my home in Austin via Los Angeles to New Delhi, India. Weary from the hours of travel and jet lag, I arrived at my hotel, thinking a good night's sleep would be in order when a note was slipped under my door. It was a fax from my office. It read: "Victor, our agent in India says that he's having a problem getting a visa for the group for Bhutan because a number of people listed their occupation as 'writer' on their applications, and the Bhutanese government is worried that they might write something critical of their country. Our agent says each of these writers needs to write a letter to the Consulate of Bhutan in New Delhi, promising that they wouldn't write anything negative about Bhutan. If the writers do this, the Bhutanese *may* grant us visas." This certainly wasn't the best news to receive when I wanted to go to bed and recover from my international flight.

If we couldn't go to Bhutan, the entire excursion would be marred. It was the centerpiece of this trip. Located on the eastern end of the Himalayas and wedged between China and India, Bhutan is largely a mountain kingdom, where both the Buddhist culture and the natural landscape are very much intact. The agriculture consists of subsistence farming and animal husbandry. There are few people and few cities, and the country tightly controls the number of tourists admitted within its geographical boundaries. Bhutan is more pristine than any other area of Asia.

It was special to travel to Bhutan—and still is. The country and culture still embody a certain remote mystique. Starting in 1989, the king required citizens to wear native dress. This makes Bhutan different from almost any country in the world. Over the years, it has changed somewhat, but even to this day, you don't see people dressed in shorts and blue jeans except in the cities. Almost everyone—men and women alike—are dressed in traditional robes, which makes a visit to Bhutan feel like stepping back in time. The other destinations of the trip were significant, too, but going to

Bhutan was to be one of the high points of our adventure—as well as the only place where we could see Black-necked Cranes.

Another concern was that the Siberian Crane hadn't returned yet to Keoladeo National Park in Bharatpur, in Eastern Rajasthan, India, about two hours west of the Taj Mahal. The Siberian Crane was one of the birds that both Peter and I most wanted to show our group because it is one of the rarest cranes in the world. With each year, there were fewer birds in the Indian flock. Apparently, they were being killed as they flew over Pakistan, Afghanistan, and Iran. At the date of our arrival, no birds had been spotted yet, and the latest date that they had ever returned had already passed.

The Siberian Crane is also one of the most spectacular cranes in the world, a magnificent snow-white bird, similar in some ways to the size and elegant appearance of the Whooping Crane, the rarest crane in the world, which breeds in Wood Buffalo National Park in the northern part of Alberta, Canada, and winters along the Central Texas Coast. Most of the Siberian Cranes—a population of about two thousand—winter in Eastern China, but at that time, a few still wintered in Keoladeo National Park.

Every day, first thing in the morning, I spoke to our Indian agent, Raj Singh, an expert ornithologist from Delhi and the nephew of Kishan Singh, the maharaja of Bharatpur. I always asked the same questions: "Have we gotten our visas to Bhutan?" His answer: "No, we hope that they will eventually be granted." And then: "Have the Siberian Cranes returned?" Once again, Raj always responded, "No, they haven't been spotted yet."

In the meantime, our group continued on the India leg of its journey. At the time, there was a strike underway with Air India, so we flew in a TU-154, a Soviet plane on lease from Uzbekistan (the same type of aircraft that would crash during its landing in Delhi on January 19, 1993), to Ahmedabad, the largest city in Gujarat, the most southwestern state in India. From Ahmedabad, we drove west along flat delta country toward the border of Pakistan and into the Rann of Kutch, an extensive plain that includes a variety of ecosystems, from mangroves to desert. Overgrown mesquite shrubs encroached on many of the dusty roads and scratched the sides of our vehicles. Today this area still contains one of the largest wildlife sanctuaries in all of India.

We continued west to a desert camp in Zainabad set up by Dr. Shabeer Malek. His father was a Muslim *nawab* (the Hindu equivalent of a *rajah*). Dr. Malek always wore an ascot and maintained a small fleet of vehicles, similar to Land Rovers. Over the years, he had developed a passionate interest in birds and nature, so he decided to build this camp outside of the village of Zainabad. He erected about ten tents and thatched huts (rondavels) and called it the Desert Coursers Camp. (Coursers are birds about the size of a quail that hunt their insect prey by running close to the ground.) There were many birds to observe immediately around the camp. In fact, the very first morning, at sunrise, Peter was awakened by the calls of cranes. He spotted two large gray-silver Sarus Cranes—a species of crane that he had never before seen—flying over his tent.

Later, we observed Demoiselle Cranes. These elegant cranes were named by Queen Marie Antoinette of France because of the bird's graceful movements. From October to February, large flocks of Eurasian and Demoiselle Cranes gather in Zainabad, joining the Sarus Cranes. During the time of our visit in January, all three cranes were there. We saw flocks of both Demoiselle and Eurasian Cranes next to the small lakes, as well as several pairs of the magnificent Sarus Cranes. One day we went out for a drive to observe one of the area's main attractions—the Indian wild ass, one of the last three species of wild horse relatives left in the world. Currently, there is a surviving population of only several hundred. At the same time, five Sarus Cranes flew over the mixed herd of horses.

During this outing, we also observed the Desert Courser, for which our camp was named. At dawn, we often heard the resonant calls of the Southern Coucal (a bird that belongs to the cuckoo family) around the camp. Its distinctive call sounds like the hollow gurgle of water being poured out of a jug. Also within close proximity to our accommodations, several Indian Robins—a black version of the commonly sighted Oriental Magpie-Robin—fluttered in the thin, thorny branches of the nearby mesquite and scrub bushes. The male Indian Robin is glossy black with a white shoulder patch and rusty vent. It typically cocks its tail. In nearby areas, local people constructed bird-feeding spaces by cutting the branches of thorny shrubs and arranging them in a circle on the ground. They distribute grain in the middle of the circle. Many birds came to feed, including Ruffs and Reeves. We were told the people did this to gain religious merit.

After our stay with Dr. Malek, we continued on to Udaipur and Jaipur, both in the northern Indian state of Rajasthan, staying in wonderful old palaces and seeing birds, such as the Spotted Owlet, which is similar to the Little Owl of Athena that appears on ancient Greek coins. Throughout these travels and this sightseeing, I still asked Raj Singh every morning about the cranes and our visas. And, still he hadn't received favorable news on either front. At one point, the group of travelers from Seattle inquired if we could travel on without the writers. I asked Raj about that, and he said, "It's everyone—or no one—because it's a group visa."

We continued with our adventures in northern India and drove about two hours northwest of Jaipur to the village of Khichan. More than one hundred and fifty years ago, the hunting of Demoiselle Cranes was banned here by the ruler of Jodhpur. In the seventies, the people of the town decided to build an enclosure that was almost half the size of a football field. The townspeople chipped in money to purchase large quantities of grain. In the late afternoon, a local man scattered the grain, and more than five thousand Demoiselle Cranes gathered for the feeding.

When we arrived, the Demoiselle Cranes were resting in a wetland area east of the town. It wasn't yet time for the birds to be fed. We continued into the town and met Mr. Prakash Jain, who was in charge of organizing this cooperative activity for the wintering Demoiselle Cranes. (The birds consume more than fifteen thousand pounds every day throughout the season, and with community donations, this feeding has continued throughout the past forty years.) As we were having tea with him in his home, cranes noisily flew over the town on their way to be fed. We concluded our short visit and walked to the nearby enclosure. The cranes were gathered on the outside perimeter, waiting for their afternoon feeding of white millet seed. A man started to toss grain into the enclosure. Suddenly, one crane flew over the fence that surrounded the pen, alighted in the enclosed area, and began to feed. Then thousands of cranes crossed over as others spiraled down from the open sky until there were about five thousand cranes feeding inside the pen. It was an amazing spectacle. Toward dusk, the cranes began their flight toward the wetland areas east of the town to roost.

We drove back east and stayed in Jaipur before we traveled to Keoladeo National Park near Bharatpur. The sanctuary itself is a unique place. Around the turn of the century, the majarah of Bharatpur (not Raj's uncle, but an earlier majarah) came up with the idea of diking an area of several thousand acres of former rice fields in order to create a reserve for ducks. The majarah enjoyed hunting, and annual duck hunts were also organized in honor of visits by the British viceroys. During one shoot alone in 1938, Lord Linlithgow and a large shooting party killed 4,273 ducks. In 1985, the eleven-square-mile area was designated a World Heritage Site.

Today, the reserve is made up of broad dikes with paths that intersect the wetlands, creating a mosaic of rectangles amid the marshy lands. Bicycle-powered rickshaws carry visitors to observe the reserve's 230-some species. During our time at Keoladeo, the reserve was teeming with birds. The Siberian Crane had arrived a few days earlier. We were lucky to see five of them. These cranes were feeding in a wetland near the farthest part of the reserve. In the same wetland, there were more than one hundred Eurasian Cranes and a pair of Sarus Cranes. Seeing all three of these remarkable cranes in the same area was one of the highlights of our trip. We also saw a lot of other birds, including Painted Storks, Great Egrets, Eurasian Spoonbills, Sacred Ibis, Grey Herons, and many species of ducks, including the beautiful Garganey.

After this adventure, we traveled on to Agra and the Taj Mahal. My most vivid memory of the Taj Mahal was our morning visit to that world-famous attraction. We went to the site at dawn to witness the sunrise. The Yamuna River created a broad, shallow plain behind the imposing mausoleum. Along the river plain, a flock of fifty Small Pratincoles flew over the sandy islands. These graceful tern-like birds are beautiful with their soft gray backs contrasting with their pointed wings that have black-and-white feathers along the trailing edge. That morning as they flew through the brightening light, their wings were lit by the rising sun. It was the first time that I had ever seen this pratincole. Along the river, there were also the ubiquitous Red-wattled Lapwing and one elegant River Lapwing. Locals were planting melons on the sandy islands in the river. Our small group of birders was huddled together along the banks with the majestic Taj and the beautiful birds catching the changing light of dawn. It was so early and cold that no other tourists were out and about yet. During that moment, I felt a deep sense of pleasure and reverence for the ancient building and the scenes of nature playing out before our eyes.

Bhutan and Crane Valley

BLACK-NECKED CRANE

We finally got our visas. We flew back to Delhi and then on to Bhutan. We landed at an airport in the Paro Valley, about forty miles southwest of Thimphu, the capital and largest city of Bhutan. Located at about seven thousand feet, Paro is a town nestled in the only valley in Bhutan that is wide and long enough to accommodate an airstrip. That afternoon, we took a walk through the one-street town overlooking the rushing Pachu River. Penny Mulligan, one of the Seattle group, spotted an Ibisbill, a rarely seen mountain shorebird that has a long downward-curving bill. I had always wanted to see this bird, but it can be quite difficult to spot because its disruptive feather pattern of grays and blacks blends right in with the gray rocks of the river. This was our only opportunity to look for this special bird. We studied it through the scope as it probed for insects, larvae, and small fish among the boulders.

Also, during our time in Paro, we hiked up a hillside, across a valley from the Taktsang (Tiger's Nest) Monastery that is perched along the precarious face of the rocky mountainside in the upper valley. It is the home of Buddhist monks whose predecessors were historically responsible for bringing Buddhism to Bhutan. According to local legend, the Buddhist master Padmasambhava literally flew in on the back of a tigress and established the remote spot for the practice of Buddhism. (The monastery is also known for its thirteen caves, or "tiger lairs," that are used for meditation practices.) As we were looking across the valley at this beautiful monastery, festooned with long strings of colorful prayer flags snapping in the breeze, a large flock of Snow Pigeons—a species I had never before seen—circled the multistory structure. This pigeon of the High Himalayas resembles the Rock Pigeon that inhabits most cities around the world, but the Snow Pigeon has a snow-white collar and a black head. As he described in *The Snow Leopard*, Peter had seen flocks of Snow Pigeons on his trip to Nepal in 1973.

From Paro, we traveled southeast to Thimphu and then over the Dochu Pass (at 10,200 feet) to the hamlet of Dungdung Nesa. Before we crossed the pass, we experienced another rare sighting: Suddenly, a chunky bird with rounded, short wings flew just in front of us, and I knew immediately that it was a Wallcreeper, a bird that we had seen the day before while we were walking inside a dzong (temple) in Thimphu. That particular bird was creeping on the floor of the dzong. When this one flew across the road, we piled out of the bus to watch as it made its way along the dry bare slopes below the road and then flew a short distance, allowing us to see its brilliant crimson underwings.

A single muddy road descended into the Phobjikha Valley, our destination. As soon as we crossed the pass, the dry scrubby slopes were replaced by a pristine, lush broadleaf forest. There, we spotted two species of Forktails—the Black-backed Forktail and the Spotted Forktail. These birds feature a distinctive black-and-white plumage and a long tail and are found alongside streams. We also sighted a mixed species flock of birds moving through the treetops. There was a brilliant range of birds, including Barbets, Tits, Bulbuls, Yellow-naped Woodpeckers, Laughing Thrushes, Fantail Flycatchers, Sunbirds, and even a shy forest bird called the Long-tailed Cuckoo Dove. Then we spotted a pair of Yellow-throated Martens fighting up in a tree. In the distance, the snowcapped peaks of the Tibetan border serrated the horizon and stands of conifer trees dotted the steep hillsides.

The Phobjikha is one of the few glacial valleys in Bhutan. Most of the people are yak herders who live in modest farm dwellings nestled among the rugged landscape. The valley, at almost ten thousand feet, is enclosed by the Black Mountains on all sides. Also known as Crane Valley, the Phobjikha is the winter home to Black-necked Cranes that spend their winters in Bhutan and China and breed at about fourteen thousand feet in the high plateaus of Tibet. Peter and I had never seen this species of crane, and we were both eager to see the birds and share them with our group.

By the time we arrived in Crane Valley, the sun had set and darkness was steadily falling. In order to reach our lodgings, we used flashlights to illuminate our way down a rocky and narrow footpath through the forest before converging with the road that crossed over the Phobjikha River. Just beyond the bridge, we found our farmhouse. A local man had opened up his house for a fee, and we were given rooms. A potbellied stove stood in the middle of the living room. It turned out there were not enough beds and rooms for everyone. George and I volunteered to sleep in the living room on the floor. I was very happy to do that because I could be near the warm stove. It turned out to be advantageous, too, because we later heard that the people who slept in beds experienced the less-than-pleasant bites of fleas and other insects in their beds. We didn't encounter this problem. George and I had a good night's sleep.

The next morning, Peter and I were up before first light. Later, he told me that when he awakened, he had been delighted to hear the lulling singsong of Buddhist chants in Bhutanese. While other people were getting up and having some breakfast, Peter and I decided to go for a walk in hopes of seeing the flock of cranes before they scattered for the day. It was very cold, and patches of icy frost laced the path and the bare tree limbs. We walked down from the house, so we could have an unbroken view down into the valley. We spotted several hundred Black-necked Cranes at the foot of the snowy pasture. It was breathtaking. It was also very special for just the two of us to be out, with the sun coming up, the light reflecting on the snow and ice, and the cranes only a hundred yards away.

Lake Poyang, Southeastern China
SIBERIAN CRANE, HOODED CRANE, EURASIAN CRANE, WHITE-NAPED CRANE

Soon after the trip to Crane Valley, the tour ended. Everyone flew home from Bangkok except Peter and me because we had made plans to go on to Hong Kong. Before flying to mainland China, we traveled via a public commuter train to a wetland called Mai Po Nature Preserve, with Simba Chan, a Chinese birder and conservationist. We were hoping to see shorebirds, but the tide was out, so the shorebirds were resting on the distant mudflats. We did, however, manage to see the rare Black-faced Spoonbill, a species that Peter and I had never seen.

We then flew north to Nanchang, the ancient capital in the province of Jiangxi situated along the banks of the Gan River. Our friend George Archibald had recommended that we allow at least three days at Lake Poyang for locating the four different crane species—Siberian, Eurasian, Hooded, and White-naped. We were also warned that good sightings would likely be affected by the water levels and drought conditions. Our guide was Song Xiang Jin, the public relations officer of the Poyang Lake Migratory Bird Nature Reserve. On the drive from Nanchang, Peter and I sat for four hours in the back seat of a small vehicle driven by a chain-smoking driver through the most hammered countryside I had ever seen in my life. There was not a blade of grass. There was not a single bird. It had been decimated by human activity. It was winter, so there were no crops growing. There were no trees. We looked at the bleak landscape for hours as the radio blared loudly.

In the late afternoon, we arrived at Wu Town and the walled compound of the Poyang Lake Migratory Bird Nature Reserve. Poyang is the largest freshwater lake in China. Usually, during the winter months, more than 150 species of winter migrant birds converge here; the largest flocks are waterfowl, cranes, and storks. When we arrived, darkness had fallen and it was cold. Peter and I were escorted to the crane organization's headquarters, where there was an unadorned dormitory. We were led to our small room. There were two single beds covered by bedspreads embroidered with Red-crowned Cranes—symbols of good luck in Asia. But to my dismay, the blankets were very thin. The floor was concrete. Except for the lovely bedspreads, everything was rather cold and bleak. I already had a cold and an intestinal bug, so I wasn't feeling well. Our host informed us that dinner would be served in another building ten blocks away.

Peter and I walked through the town in the dark. Locals were celebrating the end of the Chinese New Year. It was the last day of the Year of the Monkey; the following day would mark the beginning of the Year of the Rooster. Clutches of people congregated on the streets, and a row of eight individuals masqueraded under massive light-green paper dragons. The illuminated creatures moved through the streets like giant caterpillars. We ate a very delicious dinner of white turnip soup, hot spicy buffalo, rice, bean curd, and bitter greens. Eventually Peter brought up the possibility of seeing the cranes with our host. Song Xiang Jin said, "No cranes." We were both shocked. Peter said, "No cranes?" And the man repeated, "Yes, no cranes. No water. No cranes." The area was suffering from a drought. It hadn't rained in almost four months.

Prior to departing on our trip, I had asked a Chinese friend in Austin to write down the Chinese word for cranes on a yellow index card. He wrote: NA ER YU HE, which translated to WHERE HAVE CRANE? I thought that maybe this man didn't understand what Peter was saying, so I showed him this card. But once again, Song Xiang Jin responded, "No cranes." We were dismayed that we had come this long way during a year when cranes could not be seen. We wondered why no one had informed us of this unfortunate situation.

As a sort of consolation, Song Xiang Jin mentioned that they had a video that we could view after dinner. Rather than consoling us, the thought of watching a video that we could have seen at home only upset us more. We walked to the Wu Town Theater. Several hundred people were watching a kung-fu movie. Many of the moviegoers appeared to be very old, and many were coughing. I already had a cold, and I remember worrying that a number of these people might have tuberculosis. I thought, "I'm going to get TB. I'm going to die. I'm not going to see the cranes." After the movie ended and the audience emptied out of the theater, we watched fourteen minutes of beautiful footage of the large assemblages of cranes that we would have seen during a year with favorable conditions. Then we walked through the streets amid the illuminated dragons and exploding fireworks, returned to our cold concrete room, and slept as well as we could. The following morning, I told Song Xiang Jin that we would only be staying for one more evening instead of the originally planned three days. Not feeling well, I was in no mood to spend time in this remote corner of China if we weren't going to see any cranes.

Peter and I set off on a small riverboat down the Xiu River. The only birds that we spotted initially were large flocks of geese. Farther on, we observed men using cormorants to catch fish, a traditional method once used in Japan, but now used commercially only in China. A metal ring is placed around the neck of a cormorant, so that when the bird catches the fish, it cannot swallow it. The fishermen release a cormorant on a line of string, so they could bring the bird in after it snatches a fish. Once in a while, the fishermen remove the ring and let the cormorant swallow the fish that it caught.

Eventually we climbed out of the boat onto the dry shoreline and walked across an expansive savanna of dead grass until we reached Plum West Lake. Peter lifted his binoculars and, in the far west corner of the lake, he spotted three white shapes that appeared too large to be more of the egrets that were wading in water several hundred feet away. Peter said, "Warbler, I think there are some Siberian Cranes across the way." I was skeptical, but I took a quick look through my binoculars. "Curlew, it's just a white piece of cloth and a horse," I said. "There are no cranes over there." I'm usually very positive, but I wasn't feeling well and was disappointed that there were no cranes. And here was Peter, trying to cheer me up. I decided to take a closer look with the telescope: They *were* Siberian Cranes! Peter *was* right. This was no video in the frigid Wu Town movie theater. The sight lifted our spirits enormously.

Although we had seen Siberian Cranes in India, we had wanted to see more. That afternoon, we were taken upriver to a small hamlet named Sha Hu, where Peter and I climbed to the top of a three-story building that overlooked Dahu Chi, a town across the river. On our way up the stairs, we spotted two Eurasian Cranes along the lakebed. Beyond this pairing of birds, we also spotted other cranes that appeared to be slightly darker and smaller—they turned out to be Hooded Cranes. I was very excited because I had never seen this species. Peter, who had seen Hooded Cranes, told me that there was likely to be a White-naped Crane among this assemblage. He suggested that we climb down from the rooftop and embark in the boat to the other side of the river so that we could get closer to the cranes.

Out in the field, we spotted nine Hooded and thirty-four Eurasian Cranes and there among them, a White-naped Crane. It was one of the most beautiful cranes that I had ever seen and a lifer for me. Thus, we ended up seeing all of the cranes of that region. Not in big numbers, but still we had seen the Siberian, Hooded, Eurasian, and White-naped Cranes. It was stunning: What had started out the night before as a disaster had ended up a successful visit, despite the drought. In all my years of birding, I had never experienced such a dramatic reversal.

Hokkaido, Japan
RED-CROWNED CRANE

Our next stop on the trip was the island of Hokkaido in northern Japan. It is one of the most popular pilgrimages among birders because it is the home of the Red-crowned Crane. Peter and I flew to Tokyo and then on to Hokkaido the following morning. As the plane ascended, we got an unbroken view of Mount Fuji through the airplane window. Mount Fuji is often shrouded in clouds, so we took this impressive sight as a good omen. When we landed in Kushiro, the capital of Hokkaido, we were met by Yulia Momose, a friend of George Archibald. Her husband, Dr. Kunikazu Momose, is a crane researcher. When George was a young man and studying cranes in Japan, he lived with the family of Dr. Shoichiro Satsuki, Yulia's father, and she became like an adopted sister to George.

Yulia first guided us to Tsurumidia (or Crane Lookout), a feeding station on the Watanabe Farm, where birders were engaged in the annual crane census. Heavy snow and ice blanketed the countryside. (Hokkaido receives more snow than any location at its same latitude on earth.) Right away, we spotted Whooper Swans. An array of tits and woodpeckers congregated around a nearby bird feeder. We didn't see any cranes at this birding station, but as we continued down the road, we observed a half-dozen cranes in the black water of the Hororo River.

At the next feeding station, near the Akan River, we spotted twenty-three cranes that had arrived for their daily feeding of *ugui*, a fish that is part of the carp family. The cranes danced in the field of snow. Peter wrote about this memorable sight in *The Birds of Heaven: Travels with Cranes* (2001): "They alight so daintily on long black legs that the toes seem to strain to touch the snow and even lift a little at the final second, as if flinching from the frozen surface." The farmers threw corn out for the cranes. We also saw the elegant birds roosting on a frozen riverbed.

On our final outing, we met an old farmer, Ichiro Sato, who lived near the Onbetsu confluence. He fed the cranes every afternoon at three-thirty during the winter season. As promised, eventually the white cranes soared overhead and down into the valley at the appointed time. The cranes fed on the maize, preened, and danced. More than twenty cranes, including five brown-headed juveniles, arrived for the daily feeding. Eventually the birds took flight toward the Muri River, which they followed until they reached the open stretch of the Onbetsu River.

Peter recounted the final moment of this scene beautifully in *The Birds of Heaven*:

Soon all that may be seen in the near-dusk are the last pairs of white wings flicking upward, the black plumes of the trailing edge like ancient oriental symbols, even to the sharp black blade in the middle of the wing that points straight forward like a compass needle. At first that strange mark seems to spoil the black-white symmetry of the great wings, but in fact it intensifies their beauty, like that twisted pine-tree silhouette on a high ridge over the Muri valley that redeems the dull perfection of the moon.

I love black-and-white birds, and the Red-crowned Cranes are among the most beautiful black-and-white birds. I don't know why such birds are particularly attractive to me—perhaps it's their simplicity that I love. Along with the last letter I wrote to Peter before he died, I included a set of postcards of Red-crowned Cranes that I had bought in Japan on our crane trip. The cards showed the cranes in flight and standing in the snowy fields just like we had seen them together so long ago.

16

Birding with the Bushes

Roadrunner and Green Jays
RIVIERA, TEXAS

In 1995, shortly after George Bush was elected governor of Texas, I received a phone call from my friend, Andy Sansom, who was executive director of the Texas Parks & Wildlife Department. He was seeking suggestions for spots where the governor, his wife, and their teenage daughters could go on a birding and nature excursion in South Texas. This trip was a part of a publicity effort by the governor to promote Texas as an eco-tourism destination. I suggested that they visit the Rio Paisano, a ten-thousand-acre ranch near Riviera. For several years, my company had been leading bird-watching tours to the Rio Paisano and the nearby King Ranch. Rio Paisano was owned by Frank and Mary Grace Horlock. The Horlocks were from Houston, where Frank had owned a beer distribution company. I thought the Horlocks might be friends with the governor's father and other members of the Bush family who live in Houston part-time.

Then I received a second phone call, asking if I would lead a bird walk for the Bush party at the Rio Paisano. Without hesitation, I agreed. I flew to Corpus Christi, rented a car, and drove out to the ranch.

The area surrounding the Rio Paisano is typical South Texas brush country, with mesquite, huisache, prickly pear, Texas ebony, and other thorny plants. This habitat is part of the Tamaulipan biotic province, which extends from south of San Antonio to southern Tamaulipas, Mexico, and is home to almost two dozen species of birds, including the Great Kiskadee, Long-billed Thrasher, Groove-billed Ani, Altamira Oriole, and Chachalaca. This region is the only place in the United States where these birds can be seen.

The bird walk was scheduled for ten o'clock on a July morning. Since South Texas has a hot and humid climate during the summer, I worried that it would not be a very successful outing. I later realized that the walk had been scheduled later in the morning (by birding standards) in hopes that the news media from nearby Corpus Christi would join the walk and provide some coverage of the trip. As it turned out, only one reporter joined us.

I met the governor, his wife, Laura, and Karen Hughes, his communication strategist, in front of the main house, a large stucco building with a Mediterranean Revival-style roof of overlapping red tiles. The Bush daughters did not join us because they chose to sleep in that morning. Immediately, we observed a few birds on the grounds, including White-winged Doves, Mockingbirds, and Cardinals. We started down a road that led into the thick brush. We had only walked a short distance when I spotted a Roadrunner about ten feet off the ground in a large mesquite tree. The bird was being mobbed by Green Jays. One of the most unusual birds in North America, the Roadrunner is a very strange, large cuckoo, with a long tail, powerful beak, and a prominent crest. The Green Jay, clad in shades of chartreuse, yellow, purple, and black, is one of the most beautiful birds in North America. Quite agitated, the jays called loudly with a harsh *shek-shek-shek*. Birds often mob another bird, such as an owl or a hawk, that might try to sneak up and attack them if they're alone or predate their nest, destroying their eggs and eating their offspring. By mobbing that species, they distract the predator and call attention to its threatening presence. On that hot July morning, we stood there for several minutes, observing this fascinating scene. The opportunity to observe any interesting bird behavior greatly enhances the experience of a bird walk. We were fortunate to encounter this memorable scene right at the beginning of our walk.

We continued along the dirt road and observed a few other birds as the heat of the day intensified. As a part of our excursion, we boarded an open vehicle: The governor sat next to me on the raised rear seat, and Laura sat next to the driver. We had only driven a short distance when she spotted a bobcat crossing the road. Later, we arrived at a small clearing with short green grass. A male Bronzed Cowbird was strutting around a female in the grassy patch. Clearly, he was courting her as his feathers were elevated, especially around the back of his neck. I knew what was likely to occur next, so I told the governor and Laura, "Watch that cowbird. In a few minutes, it's going to hover above the female, like a little helicopter, hoping that he will interest her in mating."

Within a minute or two, much to the amusement of our small group, this scene unfolded. Cowbirds are referred to as "brood parasites" because they lay their eggs in the nests of other birds. Typically, their eggs hatch before the host species' eggs and the young cowbird destroys or kicks out the eggs of the host species. The host birds unknowingly raise the young cowbirds at the expense of their own offspring. This scene was a wonderful finale to our short excursion. We returned to the ranch house for lunch, and the governor and his family continued on their tour visiting some of the wildlife refuges of South Texas, including Bentsen-Rio Grande Valley State Park. I returned to Austin, never expecting to see the Bushes again. About a week later, I received a handwritten note from the governor, telling me how much he enjoyed our bird walk. He said that I had made a birder out of him.

A couple of months later, my receptionist said that Laura Bush was on the line. Astonished, I picked up the call. Laura told me that she and the governor wanted to invite a friend and me as their guests to the gala dinner to be held the night before the inaugural Texas Book Festival. I immediately accepted and attended the festivities with my friend, Dr. Ruth Buskirk. One of the other guests at the

Bushes' table was Jenna Welch, Laura's mother. I connected with Jenna right away because, as it turned out, she was a birder, too.

Later, I learned how Jenna became a birder. She had been the den mother for Laura's Girl Scout troop. She decided that the girls should study birds in preparation for earning a bird merit badge. She contacted the Midland Public Library, hoping to find someone who could help out with this project. The librarians recommended my old friend, Frances Williams, who was considered the bird lady of Midland. Frances founded the Midland Naturalists and headed up her region's Christmas Bird Counts, in addition to leading many field trips to local ranches and regional state parks. Frances came to the Welch household and presented a slide show about the birds of Midland County. Jenna told me that she had been amazed to see photos of so many beautiful birds that were common where she lived. She had never seen or even been aware of these birds, including the Vermilion Flycatcher, the Scissor-tailed Flycatcher, the Painted Bunting, and many others.

After Frances's presentation, Jenna installed a bird feeder in her backyard. One winter, a Varied Thrush, a bird that breeds from Alaska to northern California, made an appearance at her feeder. Since this was the first sighting for Midland and one of the few records for Texas, many birders traveled to the Welch home to observe this rare bird. In turn, Jenna befriended many of these birders and became a lifelong birder herself.

A few months after the Texas Book Festival, Laura asked me if I would speak to her garden club in Austin. I agreed and gave a talk at the home of her longtime friend, Regan Gammon. My talk centered on the birds of Belize and especially on the wonderful Chan Chich Lodge. After my lecture, Laura and Regan told me that they wanted to come on one of my trips to Belize with their mothers. In February 1999, this happened. Regan, Laura, and their family members made up about half the group. As sometimes happens when we have a large group, we divided the participants into two subgroups: one was the Bush and Gammon families, and the other was composed of the other trip participants. In such cases, we often give these groups bird names. I can't remember what name we initially gave the Bush-Gammon group, but subsequently, they asked that their name be changed to the Laughing Falcons because they laughed so often.

When we returned to the Belize City airport, Laura went to check in herself and her mother. Jenna was sitting alone. I approached her to say goodbye. She looked me straight in the eye and said. "You made it special." At that moment, I understood where Laura had gotten the sweetness that is such a predominant characteristic of her personality.

Over the next few years, I saw the Bushes a handful of times. On one occasion, George Plimpton came to Austin to be part of the Texas Book Festival. Because of my friendship with George, I was invited to the Governor's Mansion for a reception the night before the book festival and the black-tie gala later that evening. This event took place just after the presidential election of November 2000 when the outcome was still undecided. During our time at the mansion, we encountered Dick Cheney, Condoleezza Rice, and other prominent members of the Bush team.

Not long after the festival, I received a phone call from Laura, inviting me to go with her and the governor to see a ranch near Crawford, Texas, that they were thinking of buying. I met the Bushes at the Governor's Mansion and drove to visit the ranch. One December day, several years after they bought the ranch and Governor Bush became president, Laura invited me to join them for an afternoon of birding and for dinner. I had invited a group of friends over that same evening to watch Bill Moyers interview my friend, Paul Woodruff, a professor of philosophy at the University of Texas. So, reluctantly, I told Laura that I couldn't make it out to the ranch. In response, she said, "Why don't you come the next day?" And I did.

During the afternoon, we drove around the ranch. The habitat looks much like the Texas Hill Country, with numerous cedar elms, junipers, and live oaks. There were several small beautiful canyons. A man-made lake had been built near the house and stocked with fish. During the drive, we spotted Cardinals, Lark and Chipping

Sparrows, Mockingbirds, and other species. We were headed back to the house when I saw a Harris's Sparrow, a very special bird that breeds only at the edge of the forest in the tundra in Central Canada. This striking sparrow was also one of the last species to have its nest discovered in North America in 1935.

While George Bush was president, I had little contact with his family other than annual Christmas cards. However, in 2003, I received an invitation to attend a Christmas party at the White House. I decided to go with my young friends, Peter English and his wife, Laura Jones. At events like this, where more than one hundred people are present, attendees have little interaction with the president. Instead, guests are given the opportunity to have a photo taken with him and his wife. When my turn came, I went into the designated room and stood with the president and Laura. To my surprise, Laura whispered to me, "I want you to lead a bird walk at the G8 meeting on Sea Island, Georgia, in early June next year." I told her that I would be delighted to do so and held my breath that I wasn't already committed to leading a tour at that time. Fortunately, I had no conflicts, and I was able to squeeze this outing between a trip to Ithaca, New York, to be presented the prestigious Arthur Allen Award from the Cornell Laboratory of Ornithology and a tour that I was leading throughout Alaska.

I traveled to Sea Island a day before the bird walk to scout the route with Stacia Hendricks, the chief naturalist at Sea Island Resort. After extensive security checks, I was given my credentials to enter Sea Island prior to the conference. During our initial scouting, I was dismayed to find a paucity of birds, especially that there were so few herons, egrets, and other waterbirds that are so abundant on my native Texas coast. The walk was designed for the wives of the G8 leaders who were attending the event, including Lyudmila Putin, Bernadette Chirac, and Cherie Blair. (The Canadian prime minister's wife, Sheila Ann Martin, had become ill and couldn't attend.)

The morning of the bird walk, the participants assembled at about nine o'clock. Laura had brought a pair of binoculars for each participant. Everyone rode in golf carts, making the "walk" more of a drive. Our route threaded through the golf course that bordered the Atlantic Ocean. We had only driven a short distance when we got a look at a Pine Warbler. This bird features gray upperparts and a bright yellow breast with gray streaking on the side. As its name suggests, this warbler resides in eastern pine forests. Unfortunately, only a few of the women managed to get fleeting glimpses of this small bird as it fed in the tops of the pine trees.

Nearby, we spotted a Gulf Fritillary butterfly laying eggs on the leaves of a purple passionflower. It made for an excellent natural history teaching moment: We were able to show the participants this orange-and-silver butterfly as well as its host plant and eggs. A little later, we observed a Snowy Egret, which gave me the opportunity to tell the group about the role that two women, Mrs. Augustus Hemenway and Miss Minna Hall, played in establishing the Massachusetts Audubon Society. The two also led the campaign to outlaw the killing of egrets to obtain the plumes for ladies' fashionable hats. At that time, the hat craze was in full swing—particularly among urban women, who preferred wearing hats piled high with feathers, flowers, furs, and other decorative accents. Laura enjoyed this story and how it illustrated the power of women in promoting beneficial change in society.

Although Mrs. Putin was dressed more for a cocktail party than a bird outing, she appeared to be one of the most interested—other than Laura—in what we were seeing and asked many questions through her interpreter. Mrs. Blair was also engaged and told me that a member of her husband's staff was an avid birder. Madame Chirac seemed the least interested in what we were seeing—almost to the point of boredom. She never lifted her binoculars; instead, her assistant carried the binoculars for her throughout the entire excursion.

Near the end of our hour-long excursion, I was sitting in the front of the golf cart next to Laura, and her longtime aide, Andi Ball, was sitting behind us. Prior to the start of our tour, I had been wired for the first time in my life, so anything that I uttered was transmitted to the earpieces of the participants in the other golf carts. Forgetting this fact for a moment, I started to say to Laura, "It seems like Mrs. Putin is more interested in what we're doing

American Avocet
Photo: © Greg W. Lasley

American Redstart
Photo: © Brian E. Small

Blackburnian Warbler
Photo: © Greg W. Lasley

Hooded Warbler
Photo: © Greg W. Lasley

Horned Guan
Photo: © Ted Eubanks

King Penguins
Photo: © Greg W. Lasley

Resplendent Quetzal
Photo: © Glenn Bartley

Roseate Spoonbill
Photo: © Greg W. Lasley

than . . ." A hand went over my mouth. It was Andi, preventing me from naming any of the other First Ladies.

Before the conclusion, we spotted a four-foot yellow rat snake crossing the golf cart path. We stepped out of the carts to admire the snake. I wondered if any of the women would be frightened to be this close to a large reptile, but no one seemed to be bothered. Shortly afterward, we spotted a large alligator in a small pond. Madame Chirac seemed interested in the alligator perhaps because its name is a French word. A Great Egret hunted for fish, walking along the shore of the lake, near the alligator. Stacia told us that alligators sometimes catch egrets, or herons, and eat them. She said that a large alligator could even grab the leg of a horse and drown it. When the walk ended, Mrs. Putin gave Stacia and me small elaborately painted lacquered boxes as gifts for our efforts.

My last excursion with the Bushes was in May 2003. Again, I received a phone call from Laura, inviting me and my friends, Peter English and Laura Jones, to travel to Camp David for a weekend of birding. We flew to Washington, DC, and then drove to Catoctin National Mountain Park and up the mountain to the entrance of Camp David, where we passed through security and were escorted to our accommodations.

That night, we were invited to join the president and Stephen Hadley, his national security advisor, for a game of bowling. Laura Jones proved quite an adept bowler. I didn't score quite as well, but still had a good time. The next morning, we met for the bird walk. Unfortunately, it was raining. Still, there were birds out that day. We had only walked a short distance when the president spotted a male Scarlet Tanager, one of the most beautiful birds in the world. The male Scarlet Tanager is an intense shade of scarlet with black wings and tail. Peter and I spotted an Eastern Towhee before the persistent rain put an end to our walk.

It was a privilege to spend time in such a historic place, where so many world leaders had been entertained by presidents and where significant events had occurred. While I was there, I called George Plimpton. During our conversation, he expressed envy that I was at Camp David. I also called Laura's mother, Jenna Welch.

I have always felt particularly close to Laura. Like her mother, she has a genuine interest in birds and nature and is a great conservationist. In 2011, she and her friend Regan formed a nonprofit organization named Texan by Nature. The mission of the organization is to champion stewardship and protect natural areas throughout Texas. In September 2016, at a fundraiser for Texan by Nature at the Bushes' ranch, one of the auction items was two canoe trips on the Trinity River—one in Dallas and one near Houston—with Laura and me. The Dallas trip was organized by my close friend Garrett Boone, who co-founded the Container Store and is committed to conserving the Trinity River bottoms. It was a pleasure to join Laura in this effort because it was something that we both believe in passionately.

17

Palace on Wheels

Rose-ringed Parakeet
RANTHAMBORE NATIONAL PARK
SAWAI MADHOPUR, INDIA

One of the most gratifying aspects of my job has been cultivating relationships with people in different countries throughout the world. Some of these individuals serve as our ground agents. I have learned that having a good ground agent is a critical component of running a successful trip in a foreign country. The best agent I've ever worked with is Raj Singh, an Indian gentleman who has owned a company called Exotic Journeys, Inc. since 1979. Raj is an expert ornithologist from Delhi and the author of *Bird and Wildlife Sanctuaries and National Parks of India, Nepal, and Bhutan* (1993). Over the years, he operated our India tours, and we became good friends.

Raj occasionally travels to the United States to visit his partner organizations, such as VENT and Stanford Alumni Trips. In 2000, Raj and I were having dinner when he said to me, "Victor, I see that your company has begun to charter ships in different parts of the world for your tours. Have you ever thought of chartering a train?" Raj explained to me his idea of chartering the Palace on Wheels, which, at that time, was India's premier luxury tourist train, and traveling to some of the best tiger reserves in the country. When

Raj proposed this idea, my immediate response was "Let's do it." I loved the idea because I love traveling on trains so much. When I'm on a train, it is as though I'm in a world of my own as I watch the landscape, and life, pass by. I'm removed from traffic and the clutter of roadside businesses, and often looking out at natural scenes. When I was at Harvard, I loved taking the train from Boston to New York. During part of the route, the train passed through wetlands, where I could spot ducks, geese, and swans.

The Palace on Wheels was created by Indian Railways in association with Rajasthan Tourism Development Corporation in order to promote tourism in this part of India. The train consists of personal coaches that were once used by the various rulers of the princely states of Rajasthan, Gujarat, Hyderabad, and by the viceroy of British India. Each air-conditioned car contains four staterooms with twin beds and a private bath and a small sitting room. Also, there are two dining cars, a bar and lounge car, and even a beauty parlor/spa car.

The train normally departed from New Delhi and then traveled to the cities of Jaipur, Jodhpur, Udaipur, and Agra. Raj explained to me that, if we planned far enough in advance, his company might be able to charter the entire train and arrange for an excursion to Central India, where we could visit Kanha, one of the largest tiger preserves. Kanha is home to an impressive population of tigers as well as leopards, wild dogs, langurs, and many bird species. A portion of the tour fee would be donated to the park to enhance the benefits of their staff and for use in buying equipment, such as night-vision binoculars.

Raj proceeded to make the necessary arrangements. Only someone like Raj could persuade the Ministry of Railways to allow us to charter its premier train and take it to an area of India where the train had never traveled. I contacted Peter Matthiessen, George Plimpton, Bob Fleming Jr., and Robert Bateman and asked them to be involved with this trip. To my delight, they all enthusiastically agreed. VENT publicized the tour, and the slots filled up with approximately eighty people. I was especially pleased that Bob Fleming agreed to be one of the leaders. He had grown up in India, where his father, Robert Fleming Sr., was connected with the Woodstock School in Mussoorie for twenty-five years and co-founded the United Mission to Nepal. Along with Lain Singh Bangdel, father and son wrote *Birds of Nepal* (1976), which was the first field guide to any Asian country. Bob possesses a remarkable knowledge of the history of India and its bird life.

The trip was to start on March 21, 2001. I arrived a day early at 4:30 a.m. in New Delhi. I was taken to the Hotel Oberoi, situated near the World Heritage site of Humayun's Tomb. I tried to get some sleep, but couldn't, so I asked the bellboys if there was a good spot for birding near the hotel. They directed me to the Delhi Golf Course, which was about three blocks away. Upon arriving at the clubhouse, I learned that the eighteen-hole course is Delhi's oldest and most prestigious golf club, with very restrictive membership and a waiting period of more than thirty years for prospective members. The sport of golf came to India with the British Raj, and when New Delhi was preparing to replace Calcutta as the country's capital in the late twenties, one of the first projects was to build a new golf course on a strip of land near the Barakhamba and the Lal Bagh tombs, close to the burial grounds of the fourteenth-century Islamic Lodi dynasty. Today, well-preserved sandstone tombs still dot the links.

When I arrived at the golf course, I was astounded to see an enormous billboard that read: BIRDS OF THE DELHI GOLF COURSE. Also, on the billboard there were a number of colorful illustrations of about fifty birds. Later, I would discover that the course also serves as a two-hundred-acre sanctuary for more than three hundred kinds of birds. Each hole is named after one of the famous feathered species (for example, the 445-yard, par-4 hole three is called the Red-vented Bulbul and the 208-yard, par-3 hole twelve, the Blue-cheeked Bee-eater). Other varieties of wildlife also abound: There are plenty of snakes—including the Common Cobra—mongooses, jackals, and sambars. Sambars, the largest species of deer in India, can weigh up to six hundred pounds, and they often leave deep hoof marks on the greens—not what you want to see when lining up a putt.

Soon after I arrived, I found a fruiting fig tree and saw a Rufous Treepie as well as Coppersmith and Brown-hooded barbets gorging on the fruit. In the golf course parking lot, some of the members' drivers cooked breakfast. I smelled cinnamon, cloves, coriander, and frying onions. As I stood there, I thought how magical it is to get on a plane, fly halfway around the world, see an entirely different group of birds, and experience a different culture.

While I walked along the edges, which were lined with indica trees and sticker bushes, I spotted Red-vented Bulbuls, Baya Weavers, flycatchers, finches, and other wonderful Indian birds. A large flock of lively peacocks gathered not far from the parking lot. While I walked around with my binoculars, a golf club employee approached me and said, "I can take you to see the little owl." He proceeded to direct me to a tree, where we observed a small Spotted Owlet perched on one of its branches. The combined screeching and caterwauling of this owl, as it frequently hunts moths and other insects near lampposts, is one of the most startling night sounds in many towns in northern India.

That night, we gathered at the hotel with the tour participants and leaders. Raj was very excited and proud that he was able to arrange this trip. No other tour company in India had been able to pull off a logistical feat like this unique excursion. Among the people at this gathering was the minister of tourism for India, who thanked us for coming and for creating this trip. E. L. Doctorow and his wife, Helen, Rose Styron, Maria Matthiessen, and the Swedish artist and illustrator Lars Jonsson and his wife, Ragnhild, were among the participants on the trip.

We boarded the train early the next morning and headed southeast. All day we traveled across Central India, with the steel wheels steadily clacking underneath our coaches. Farm laborers worked in the swaying wheat fields with scythes, harvesting and bundling the grain for threshing. People shared the nearby dusty roads with sluggish cows and oxen. Women clad in brightly colored saris carried large straw baskets atop their heads.

At one point, we passed through Gwalior. As a teenager, Raj had attended the Scindia School, an exclusive all-boys prep school in

Gwalior, founded in the 1890s for members of royal families. He explained to us that after he entered school in the fall, the gates were locked for several months until the students were given a break and returned home to their respective families. Later, we passed through Bhopal, the city where the toxic petrochemical disaster of 1984 killed thousands of people. Finally, we arrived in Gondia Junction, where we disembarked for the two-hundred-mile road trip through the state of Madhya Pradesh to Kanha National Park.

More than a thousand people were gathered at the station to greet us and see the famous, gleaming white train, the pride of the India Railway system, which had never come to their city. This event was comparable to the Concorde landing in a small town in Iowa. Soldiers with rifles held back the throngs. On a nearby track sat another train of out-of-date coaches, also operated by India Railways, packed with people who sat, stood, and hung out the windows. A live band performed military music. Various local dignitaries greeted us. Necklaces of fresh marigolds were hung around our necks as we disembarked the train. Each of us received a vermilion dot, or *tilaka*, placed in the center of the forehead. Journalists and photographers gathered to report on the train and our arrival for the local newspaper. A platform was erected for speechmaking by the local dignitaries. Unfortunately, there was no time for any of this. We had to depart right away to begin the long drive to Kanha.

Just before we boarded two large buses, we saw a large flock of Rose-colored Starlings. The drivers headed east toward the park. The bustling town gave way to a countryside of stony hills, shallow lakes, rice fields, and stretches of forests. It was easy to imagine where the tigers might have lived in these leafy landscapes during earlier times. Along the way, some of us spotted Sarus Cranes and Indian Rollers amid the passing landscape. Many Common Mynas frequented the edges of the road, and Fork-tailed Black Drongos perched on the telephone wires, occasionally sallying out after flying insects.

In the early evening we arrived in Kanha, an eight-hundred-square-mile national park in the Central Indian Highlands. Kanha is a beautiful tiger reserve with stands of Dipterocarp Sal along with a mixed forest of Terminalias, Indian Flame of the Forest, fig trees, and pale-barked Lagerstroemia, among others, all interspersed throughout the stretches of bamboo and swaths of golden grasslands. It was late March, the best time of year to attempt to see the orange-and-black-striped Bengal tigers since that is the height of the dry season when the undergrowth is less dense. It almost felt like autumn because the trees were shedding their leaves.

In those days, there were two ways to observe the tigers: One strategy was to drive the roads of the park in an open jeep with a park ranger, with hopes of seeing a tiger near or crossing the road. The other method involved climbing up a ladder onto a *howdah*, or a makeshift saddle of old blankets folded on a wooden frame, that sat atop the back of an elephant with a mahout driving. The elephant then takes you to a spot where a tiger has been located, resting on the forest floor. From atop the elephant, you can get a great view of the tiger. Recently, this practice was discontinued for concern that it might disturb the tigers. However, during our time at Kanha, everyone in our group got to observe tigers—both from the elephants and from the jeeps.

Doctorow wrote of one sighting in an article that was later published in the November 2001 issue of *Condé Nast Traveler*:

> Our tiger lies in the sun on a patch of dead leaves. He is in his brilliant array, regal, indifferent, his forelegs stretched out before him as he suffers himself to be gazed upon. Beside him, the remnants of a gaur. The elephant stands impassive. There is some mute understanding between them. The sun shines through the trees. And it comes over me how everything here is poised in beautiful equilibrium. Every creature in this preserve has everything it needs to live.

In February 1992, I had seen my first tiger with my dear friend Bob Fleming at Tiger Tops, a lodge located in the Himalayas of Nepal. At that time, the lodge staff baited tigers with a live buffalo calf or a young goat tied to posts in front of the blinds every evening. When a tiger came to the bait, the *shikari*, or a hunting guide, would appear in the dining room of the lodge and say, "The tiger has come to the blind and killed the goat. We will take you to see it." The guests then loaded into jeeps and drove through the darkness to the blind. There we were asked to take off our shoes and walk only in socks. Once we entered the blind, a powerful light was shone on a female tiger with her three cubs, feeding on the bloody goat, maybe thirty feet in front of us. She seemed very nervous, perhaps worrying that the male tiger would arrive, once he smelled the blood, and kill her cubs. I remember whispering to Bob, "Shere Khan at last," referring to the tiger in *The Jungle Book*. When I was a boy, my father had introduced me to Rudyard Kipling's classic, and I had grown to love the stories of Mowgli and Shere Khan.

The views of the Bengal tigers at Kanha were much more satisfying than the ones that I had witnessed at Tiger Tops in Nepal. Like many other naturalists, I have no problem feeding birds in order to attract them. But the idea of putting out an animal—live or dead—to attract a cat, such as a leopard or a tiger, diminishes the experience. It creates an artificial situation. Understandably, tiger-baiting is controversial. The naturalists of Tiger Tops justified it first for its value in attracting tigers, which can then be identified and studied, and second as a means of inspiring the fight to save the tiger from extinction. A few years later, however, this practice was discontinued.

Our good fortune in observing several tigers at Kanha was in sharp contrast to Peter Matthiessen's previous trip to the park, where he had spent an entire week with a private guide, going out every day on an elephant and never seeing a single tiger. In fact, he had never seen a tiger in the wild prior to our trip to Kanha. Needless to say, it was very satisfying for Peter—who had famously stalked the snow leopard unsuccessfully with field biologist George Schaller—to see a number of tigers with our group.

During our stay at Kanha, we also witnessed large herds of the chital, or spotted deer. This small, rust-colored deer is one of the favorite foods of the tigers. One of the park rangers' sighting tactics for tigers is to listen for the loud bark issued by the chital, which usually happens when a tiger or leopard is nearby. (This particular scene is described very well in the writings of Jim Corbett, the tracker-turned-naturalist who played a pivotal role in creating a national reserve for the endangered Bengal tiger.) Often, the herds of chital gather under trees where langurs, the pale gray, black-faced monkeys, swing from the branches, picking and eating fruit and nuts. Because these monkeys often climb near the leafy tree-tops, they spot the approaching tiger first and release a chorus of loud whoops and growls.

One afternoon, as we drove through the forest, we spotted a rooster-like bird on the side of the road. This was a Red Jungle-fowl, the ancestor of most domestic chickens. As soon as the bird saw our jeep approaching, it dashed into the forest. Our driver idled the jeep, and we heard the bird's distinctive *cock-a-doodle* call, the sound they make when they are hoping to attract a female or defend their territory. Colorful Indian Peafowl (peacocks) also scurried across the roads. Later, I was happy to learn, the lush sal and bamboo forests, grassy meadows, and ravines of Kanha had provided inspiration to Rudyard Kipling for his famous novel.

After two eventful days, we returned to Gondia, where we boarded the train and headed north to Ranthambore National Park, which is only 150 square miles but still ranks among one of the largest national parks in Northern India. It's in the Sawai Mad-hopur district of southeastern Rajasthan. Smaller than Kanha, the area of rugged terrain is considered one of the subcontinent's best tiger-sighting areas. (Unfortunately, there are many challenges in protecting the tigers here as the park is surrounded on all sides by villages with inhabitants who sometimes kill the tigers if the animals attack their cattle. Poachers also kill tigers for their bones, which are used in traditional medicine, particularly in China.) The thorn-scrub topography previously served as the private hunting grounds for the maharajas of Jaipur. The impressive park centers around the Ranthambore Fort, built about a thousand years ago atop a steep rock plateau. From different points in the reserve, the fort looms, providing a formidable contrast to the surrounding deciduous forest. There are other remnants of the past—from

Mughal cupolas to temples—scattered throughout the grounds. The park is also the site of the second largest banyan tree in India. Banyans are sacred to Hindus as, among other attributes, the tree symbolizes immortality. It is also much revered by Buddhists, who believe that, after achieving enlightenment under a peepal tree, Gautama Buddha moved over and sat under a banyan tree for seven days.

Five sizable lakes are scattered throughout the preserve, attracting a wonderful mix of waterbirds, including egrets, cranes, cormorants, and painted storks, with marsh crocodiles frequently resting on the nearby banks. Wild boars scavenge through the lakeside groves. Other memorable bird sightings included the Rose-ringed Parakeet and the Alexandrine Parakeet, which nests in the crumbling walls of the old palaces and forts. The Rose-ringed Parakeet is brilliant green, with a rose hind neck and a large red bill. The larger Alexandrine Parakeet has a maroon shoulder patch. At the entrance of Ranthambore, some individuals selling curios had scattered seeds on the nearby concrete platform and twenty or so parakeets gathered there. The raptors, particularly the Crested Serpent Eagle, were another highlight. This eagle hunts by sitting quietly on a branch and then pouncing on unsuspecting prey moving about the ground. Among other animals, snakes are often caught and eaten.

We also saw the Golden-fronted Leafbird, a bright green bird with an orange forehead about the size of a mockingbird. Another favorite bird from this region is the Scarlet Minivet, which is similar in size to a small oriole. Scarlet Minivets travel in flocks of six to ten birds around the forest. Some male minivets are brilliant red with black wings; the females are yellow and gray. You often see a single minivet in a tree about twenty feet above the ground and soon several others (both males and females) join it. They are active birds, making short sallies, trying to catch insects. After a while, the flock moves on, leaving a memory of bright colors and ceaseless activity.

A favorite food of tigers is the sambar, the huge gray deer that resembles an elk. One park ranger told me that two days before we arrived, he and some tourists were looking at birds along a lakeshore when a tiger emerged and proceeded to kill a sambar that was grazing on aquatic vegetation in the water. The tiger literally picked up the sambar and pulled it away before their very eyes. Although we didn't see anything that dramatic, we did see a young tiger sleeping on top of an ornate gate at the park's exit.

After Ranthambore, we traveled via the Palace on Wheels to Agra, where we stayed at the Amarvilas, a hotel with balconies overlooking the Taj Mahal. In the afternoon from our balcony, we saw a large flock of several hundred wagtails of numerous species feeding on the closely cropped lawn of the hotel. Every so often, a Shikra, a small accipiter, would appear and attempt to catch one of the wagtails. In terror, the birds would dive into the nearby bushes. While we were watching them, Lars Jonsson, the great Swedish bird artist, walked out into the garden and started sketching the wagtails. It was exciting to be there when these birds were migrating. It is typical to see only a few wagtails. To see several hundred was amazing.

We continued on to Jaipur. Early in the trip, Raj had explained to me that he had arranged a final dinner for us in a palace of the maharaja of Jaipur. Unfortunately, Raj had been informed a few days before we were scheduled to arrive that the princess of Thailand had decided to visit Jaipur with her family, and our dinner had been canceled so that the maharaja could entertain the princess and her entourage. Raj said to me, "Don't worry. I'll arrange another dinner at a private estate in the country." I had complete confidence that he would arrange something special.

In Jaipur, we boarded buses and drove to an imposing estate on the outskirts of the city. As we disembarked from the buses, an elephant decorated in elaborate glass beads and paint greeted us. On either side of the elephant stood horsemen holding colorful flags, pendants, and lances. As we entered the party, every man was given a red-cloth turban to wear and every woman was given a beautiful shawl. One side of the path was lined with colorful marigold blooms that spelled out WELCOME VICTOR EMANUEL NATURE TOURS. The main dining area was bordered by stalls, where locals sold curios, such as necklaces, shawls, and pottery. There was a sumptuous buffet—and when we sat down to eat, the dancing began. The lead dancer was renowned and often toured the world, performing some of the same dances that she performed for us that night. All this had been arranged by Raj at very short notice. George Plimpton said it was the most remarkable party that he had ever attended in his life. It made for a memorable conclusion to this unique adventure.

Beautiful Nuthatch

NAMDAPHA NATIONAL PARK
ARUNACHAL PRADESH, INDIA

After the Palace on Wheels tour, my friend Bob Fleming and I flew to Assam to co-lead a second adventure. My friends Steve and Britt Thal joined us, as well as Jim Rigali, Dick Lamster, and Maeve Sowles of Eugene, Oregon. We headed east to the state of Arunachal Pradesh. In Hindi, *Pradesh* means "state." Aruna is the god who commands the chariot of Surya, the sun god, so he is instrumental in bringing the sun at dawn, which first touches India in Arunachal. As a result, the far eastern region is called the "dawn state." As we drove, we passed through enormous tea plantations, and saw a sign stating that this was the western end of Burma (Ledo) Road. This road was built across the mountains of Burma to ferry supplies from India to China during World War II and involved a gargantuan effort by thousands of people. By the time it was completed, the war was almost over.

We finally reached the headquarters of Namdapha National Park where, unlike the first part of the trip, the rooms were simple. Due to the high humidity, the bare walls smelled musty. The next morning, we were paddled across the sizable Noa Dihing River on a flat-bottomed, wooden boat to a trail that led us into a wilder part of the park, where we hoped to see three species of large Asian forest hornbills: the Great Indian, the Rufous-necked, and the Wreathed. In addition, we were looking for the Great Slaty Woodpecker, the Grey Peacock-Pheasant, the Silver-breasted Broadbill, as well as various members of the Babbler family, including the Large Scimitar Babbler.

We hiked for about five miles to a clearing where tents had been set up for us. Even though this period fell during the South Asian dry season, the rains came early. We hadn't realized that this extreme eastern part of India has a Southeast Asia climate regime, and the seasonality here is different from that found at the same latitude just to the west, in Assam, Nepal, and beyond.

With the torrential downpours came the leeches. Prior to this trip, I had heard stories about the leeches of Southeast Asia, but never had visited an area when the bloodsuckers were active. (According to Dick Lamster, there were up to a million leeches per kilometer!) This turned out to be an entirely new and fascinating, but, at times, very unpleasant experience. We would stop on the trail, hoping to see birds, which were difficult to spot due to the rain. Then, looking in any direction, we saw leeches crawling in the leaf litter toward us. Prior to heading out on the trail, Bob Fleming had outfitted us with leech socks, which are tightly woven and came up to about our knees. The leeches can't bite through this dense fabric. He also armed us with spray cans of DEET insect repellent. Nevertheless, the worm-like creatures found a way of attaching to us, particularly if we walked through the bush. I saw a leech at the end of a twig, stretching its body to double or three times its normal length and waving up and down as it sensed my presence.

As I sometimes do in situations like this, I tried to develop a sense of humor. I came up with the idea of the Leech Dance: sense a leech, jump around, knock it off. I also said to the others, "If you see a leech on someone that they don't see—for example, crawling up their back—the nicest and kindest thing that you can do is to remove the leech." Literally, we watched each other's backs, hoping to spot leeches before they attached to our skin. We were mostly successful. A few of us got leeches. I got one in one of the worst places. Fortunately, leeches don't carry any diseases. They can easily be pulled off—and you can recover quickly from the bite.

Throughout our days in the park, we frequently heard the penetrating call of the Grey Peacock-Pheasant (the national bird of Myanmar). I used my portable tape recorder, slung over my shoulder, to play its call back. This ground-dwelling bird came very close to us, but we never saw it. Around our camp, we heard the Large Scimitar Babbler, so I taped the bird's voice and played it back. The elusive bird responded and circled our group, but stayed just out of sight, hiding behind screens of leaves and affording us only glimpses of a dark form darting across the opening.

At the end of a long morning hike, a few of us got a quick look at the Beautiful Nuthatch. This is the most prized bird of the eastern Himalayas, with markings of azure blue and black on its upperparts. On our way back to the campsite, we came around a small bend in the trail, and our sharp-eyed guides spotted a dark form sitting on a horizontal branch in a large, spreading fig tree. This male Hoolock Gibbon, a black primate with white eyebrows and extremely long arms, is the westernmost of the gibbons, or lesser apes, of Southeast Asia. We watched the animal for a short while, but as soon as the gibbon noticed us, it rapidly swung across the tree and out of sight. This hurried departure suggested to us that there was considerable poaching in this part of the park.

The leeches and the lack of birds were two frustrating results of the rain. A more immediate concern was the river that we had crossed: We knew that it was likely to be rising. If we didn't leave soon, we might not be able to cross back to the park's headquarters. One night, I was in my tent, listening to the relentless patter of rain and thinking, "We need to get out of here. The river is coming up." The next morning, our guides agreed. We broke camp. As we hiked toward the river, we kept meeting small streams filled with reddish silt flowing across the trail. As there was no thought of keeping our feet dry, we forded the streams in our shoes and then squished down the trail toward the river. Since we arrived at its banks one day early, there was no boat waiting for us. Fortunately, after a half hour, employees at the park headquarters spotted us and the boat traversed the rapids to retrieve our party.

Upon embarking, we were given instructions about how to save ourselves if the boat happened to capsize in the churning rapids as we crossed. I do not swim, so I was particularly worried. I sat between Steve and Britt, with the hopes that they would be able to save me if we tumbled into the river. The boatman informed us that, a few months earlier, the boat had capsized and some people had drowned. My anxiety grew. The captain angled the boat across the river as the strong currents pushed us downstream and we would hit the bank near the foot of the park headquarters. We made it across safely. We later learned that if we had waited an hour more, this would not have been the case. The porters, who had assisted us on our excursion, had to wait several days until the river lowered before they could cross back over to their families.

At the headquarters, I shared a room with Bob. Before we went to dinner, I mentioned my concern to him about getting out of the park since we had crossed several low-water bridges (similar to those we have in Central Texas). Bob said, "Don't worry, Victor, they have elephants to help us get out." The next morning, Steve, Britt, and I rode in a jeep toward a stream that had risen at least three feet. We stood there next to the vehicle in the pouring rain, with our umbrellas over our heads, waiting for the second jeep with Bob and the others. Shortly after they arrived, an old elephant, pink pigmentation decorating its forehead and coat, came down the stream with a mahout on its back. The elephant took one look at the situation and became very upset, swinging its trunk from side to side. The mahout hit the animal's head with an ankus in attempts to get it to follow his commands. The elephant was having none of it. After about fifteen minutes of this, the old elephant ran downstream, leaving us behind. Bob said that in all of his experience, he had never seen an elephant behave this way.

We continued standing there in the rain. Bob assured us that they would fetch another elephant. Sure enough, about an hour later, another elephant arrived with a mahout on its back. This elephant appeared to be younger and more compliant. Bob suggested that we wade across the stream even though the water was fairly high and rushing fast. He reasoned that if we locked arms and walked as a group, our chain could hold if one person slipped. It was a bit scary, but we managed to make it across the stream to higher land, where other vehicles awaited us. The jeep with our luggage attempted to cross the water, and, as expected, it stalled in the middle, with the high water reaching up into the engine. The mahout and staffers tied a rope to the axle, and the elephant grabbed the other end with its trunk and tried to pull the vehicle across the river. This did not work.

Eventually, they came up with a better idea: They wrapped the rope around the elephant's girth and then attached the rope to the jeep. The elephant walked out of the stream and pulled the vehicle across as if it was a small toy. Water poured out of the vehicle through the bottoms of the doors. Remarkably, once the water drained, we were able to start the jeep up and continue our trip. Given the difficulties we encountered, this was one of the most challenging trips that I ever led. But, as is often the case in life, difficult situations can be the most wonderful and unforgettable in their own way.

18

Birding on the Edge

Yellow-browed Warbler
ATTU
THE ALEUTIANS, ALASKA

As a young birder, I was not attracted to Alaska as a destination. Just as was the case with Antarctica, it was so distant from my home in Texas and I preferred warmer climates. But, after I traveled to Alaska in 1994 with Kevin Zimmer, who anchors VENT's Alaska program and is a great expert on the birds and wildlife of this northernmost state, I came to understand why Alaska is a dream destination for most avid US birders. It is the only place in North America where a number of special birds can be seen, including the Spectacled and Steller's Eiders, the Bristle-thighed Curlew, the Bar-tailed Godwit, the Bluethroat, the Western Yellow Wagtail, the Arctic Warbler, and a number of other noteworthy species. It also offers magnificent scenery and more opportunities for mammal viewing than any other region in North America.

I first heard of Attu, the westernmost island in the Aleutians, a chain of volcanic islands that separates the North Pacific and the Bering Sea, through Larry Balch's Attour trips that he started organizing and leading in 1979. (Balch, an avid birder, was a former American Birding Association president.) This large island is a 1,560-mile flight from Anchorage: It is actually much closer to Siberia, which is about two hundred miles away. On a map, the island sits to the east of the International Date Line, the arbitrary boundary that separates one day from the next, and takes a jagged jog west of Alaska. The date line follows this boundary so that Attu and the nearby islands, which belong to the United States, would be in the same time frame as the rest of the country.

Attu holds a monumental place in American history as the only territory of the United States that was occupied by a foreign army. On June 7, 1942, the Japanese invaded and occupied this remote island. As a part of this military effort, the Japanese removed the Attuans to Japan, and the island became the site of the Pacific's second bloodiest battle: About three thousand Japanese and American soldiers died during the two-week conflict in May 1943. Further, it was the only land battle where Americans and Japanese fought in Arctic conditions. The names of various locations on the island underscore the vicious battle of World War II—Murder Point, Massacre Bay, Terrible Mountain, and Devil Mountain. There is, however, also a Peaceful Valley. After the war, the native islanders were not allowed to return, and though groups of scientists and other scholars visited from time to time, the only people who live on the island are those individuals who work at the LORAN (short for "long range navigation") station of the United States Coast Guard.

Birders began traveling to Attu in spring 1973. They had learned that birds that migrate north in the spring and south in the fall along the eastern part of Asia might stray under certain weather conditions to this isolated island, making it an ideal location for birders looking for ways to expand their North American lists. Over the decades, thirty or forty species never seen in North America were sighted on Attu. First US records include such species as the Yellow Bittern, the Lesser White-fronted Goose, the Oriental Pratincole, the Great Spotted Woodpecker, the Lanceolated Warbler, the Narcissus Flycatcher, and the Pine Bunting. After Larry Balch established Attour, more than a thousand birders traveled to the island with Balch and his team over a period of twenty-two years. During their excursions, they stayed in deteriorating Quonset huts that remained from the American military campaign and endured challenging living conditions in hopes of spotting some of these Asian vagrants. Typically, Larry's groups stayed on Attu for two weeks, hoping for the right weather conditions; namely, a west wind that would cause some of these Asian migrants to deviate from their normal migratory path and put down on the island. Although bicycles could only be used on little more than six or seven miles because of rocky roads and trails, tour participants often used bikes because pedaling proved to be the most efficient way of reaching some of the best birding spots on the island. Some years, these tours were spectacularly successful; other years, not as many vagrants would be seen due to uncooperative weather conditions.

"Foul weather days were the best for birds, lost waifs far from home," wrote Roger Tory Peterson of his May 1982 excursion with Balch in the magazine *American Birds* (Spring 1990). "Blue sky days, fair weather days, were the poorest." During this particular tour, Roger added twenty-seven species to his North American list, although only seven species were new for his world list. Some avid birders traveled every spring to Attu, hoping to add more species to their North American lists. During the competition described in the 2004 novel *The Big Year: A Tale of Man, Nature, and Fowl Obsession* by Mark Obmascik (and 2011 feature film), all three participants traveled to Attu in hopes of increasing their tallies.

In late 1979, Reeve Aleutian Airways, the only operator with commercial flights to Attu's Casco Cove Airport from Anchorage, discontinued its scheduled flights. This was not surprising since Casco Cove is one of the most isolated and remote airports in the United States, and arriving and departing on this asphalt airstrip can be hazardous due to storms and high winds. (Winter squalls can generate powerful gusts in excess of a hundred knots.) Despite these conditions, Balch came up with the idea of chartering a Reeve Aleutian aircraft in order to continue his tours to the remote volcanic island. Some years, the weather conditions at Attu were so inclement that the plane couldn't land and had to divert to another island and wait until the weather improved. Balch's charters ended in October 2001 when the US Coast Guard decided that they would no longer allow any non-military planes to land on Attu. This was a significant loss—and disappointment—for many avid US birders.

In the travel business, I'm frequently approached by a number of people who want my company to use their services. Often I don't take the time to hear their sales pitches, but in spring 2004, I took a phone call from a representative from Cruise West. The organization was going to be giving a presentation of their operations in Alaska at a motel in South Austin not far from my home. I decided to attend the company's presentation—and I was impressed. A privately owned company, Cruise West had been in business for more than twenty years and specialized in trips along the coast of Alaska, using a fleet of ships that they owned. I told VENT's vice president Shirley Anderson about Cruise West, and she came up with the idea that we could charter one of their ships to take tour groups to Attu. She knew that I had been interested in such a venture, but had not been successful in locating the appropriate ship for this kind of intrepid excursion. Talking with the people at Cruise West, Shirley discovered that they had a ship named *The Spirit of Oceanus* that would be seaworthy for such a long and arduous voyage. The charter fee for this ship for a cruise to Attu was very expensive. According to the company's proposed twenty-five-day itinerary, participants would board the ship in Whittier, just south of Anchorage, and travel the length of the Aleutians, cruising across the Bering Strait to Petropavlovsk, a Russian city on the Kamchatka Peninsula.

Since we knew the return flights on Russian planes from Petropavlovsk to Alaska were below the standards that we desired for our travelers, Shirley found a US charter company that would send a first-class aircraft from Anchorage to Petropavlovsk to transport our group back to the States. This charter, too, was very pricey. The two charters would make this trip the most ambitious and financially challenging endeavor that VENT had ever offered. Because of this significant risk, I came up with the idea that we would advertise the trip and inform potential participants that if they made a one-thousand-dollar nonrefundable deposit, they would receive a one-thousand-dollar discount on the cruise. The tour itself sold for ten thousand dollars, which, at the time, was the most expensive trip that VENT had ever attempted to sell. I asked Larry Balch if he would be one of our leaders. Our team also included veteran VENT leaders Barry Zimmer, David Wolf, Steve Hilty, Jeri Langham, Pete Dunne, and Marshall Iliff as well as Attour veterans Thede Tobish, Steve Heinl, and Dave Sonneborn.

Fortunately, enough participants signed up and made the sizable deposit to make me feel comfortable signing the charter contracts for both the ship and the plane. Other cruise ships stopped at Attu during the summer months, if the weather conditions permitted, for a half-day of exploring while crossing from Alaska to Russia, but no tour companies had chartered a ship to deliver birders exclusively to Attu. The obvious advantage of chartering and filling a ship with birders was that we could stay a week at Attu. Also, we could make the trip in September when some of the Asian birds were migrating south and might stray to Attu. Lastly, another benefit of experiencing this remote island via ship was that, instead of staying in a leaky Quonset hut after a long day of trudging around the damp tundra of Attu, we could return to the lovely ship, a nice meal in the dining room, and our comfortable, warm rooms.

On September 13, 2008, we assembled in Anchorage. A great excitement percolated among the participants. Since the main objective of our trip was to bird Attu, we traveled nonstop, except to refuel at Dutch Harbor on Amaknak Island, for six days from Whittier to Attu. Often cruise ships traveling from Alaska to Russia stop at many of the Aleutian Islands to observe wildlife as well as to visit some of the old fishing villages.

Prior to the trip, I had received permission from the people at Cruise West to chum at certain times during the voyage. Chumming is a common practice on pelagic, or open ocean, trips. It involves throwing fish or other food items off the rear of the ship, hoping to attract a swarm of seabirds. Thede Tobish obtained a significant quantity of frozen fish in Anchorage that we brought with us on the ship. We purchased even more fish in Dutch Harbor. The chumming turned out to be wonderfully successful, attracting a diverse number of seabirds, including three species of albatross: the Black-browed, the Laysan, and best of all, the Short-tailed, one of the seabirds that American birders most want to see.

Short-tailed Albatrosses are large waterbirds that produce a considerable amount of good-quality feathers. It was once one of the most common albatrosses in the world, but the Japanese harvested it in enormous quantities from its breeding grounds on Torishima, an uninhabited volcanic island in the Philippine Sea, and used its feathers for the production of pillows, mattresses, and down quilts. By 1949, the species was believed to be almost extinct and no breeding colonies were known. Then in 1956, a colony of twelve nests was reported on Torishima, and the Japanese government established a reserve on this island. In 1988, eighty-nine eggs were laid. Still, the birds were vulnerable to disappearing completely, given the possibility of a volcanic eruption. Fortunately, after Short-tailed Albatrosses breed, they remain at sea for many years. Due to the protection of the Japanese government, this albatross species has slowly increased in numbers to approximately twenty-three-hundred birds.

The best place that American birders could hope to see the Short-tailed Albatross in US waters is in the Bering Sea. Even in these remote waters, it is hard to see this species because its numbers are so small. Thanks to our chumming efforts, our group was able to see several Short-tailed Albatrosses of different plumages (depending on the bird's age) following our ship. This was especially satisfying for me because of two previous frustrating encounters with this special species. On an earlier Bering Sea voyage, Dion Hobcroft, Barry Lyon, and I were eating lunch in the small dining room in the lower part of the ship when a huge, all-chocolate albatross with a pink bill flew past the window next to our table. We saw the bird for approximately five seconds as it passed by. We ran up to the deck, but were not able to locate it again. On another Bering Sea excursion that I co-led with Barry Zimmer, we spent countless hours on the deck, hoping to spot a Short-tailed Albatross. It seemed like every time that I would retreat to my cabin for a short rest or a cup of tea, a Short-tailed Albatross flew overhead.

Then, one night at dinner, the leader of a British group on the same ship burst into the dining room and exclaimed that he had spotted a Short-tailed Albatross flying by the ship. Hoping to attract it, I dashed to the buffet, grabbed a couple of filet mignon steaks from a buffet server, ran to the rear deck, tore the meat into small pieces, and threw them into the churning sea—to no avail. On that trip, the only view I had of a Short-tailed Albatross was one bird that was already almost out of sight. Needless to say, I was very pleased to get spectacular looks at this rare bird on our Cruise West charter to Attu. This was the first great event of our adventure.

We decided to bring a fifteen-foot birch tree and a twelve-foot spruce tree on to the boat. We secured these to the rear area in hopes that land birds that had been blown off-course would be attracted to the trees. While at sea, we were surprised at the number of passerines that circled our ship, and we were pleased when a Red-breasted Nuthatch and an Orange-crowned Warbler made use of the "Oceanus Memorial Forest," albeit briefly.

Farther west in the Aleutians, we came upon an enormous flock of Short-tailed Shearwaters feeding on fish, crustaceans, squid, and other marine creatures. It's hard to estimate the numbers in such a large group of birds, but we thought there might have been up to two million of these narrow-winged, dark gray birds. After breeding in southern Australia and Tasmania, Short-tailed Shearwaters migrate north and spend several months in the waters of the North Pacific. The birds forage mostly by diving and swimming under the sea—sometimes sixty-five feet below the water's surface. On this particular afternoon, these birds flew in short flights over this vast school of fish, diving and going briefly underwater, then emerging on the churning surface before diving again. The sea literally boiled over with shearwaters.

Sometimes Short-tailed Shearwaters forage with whales or dolphins. So, here among these two million teeming birds, twenty-eight Humpback Whales fed on the fish and krill. It was a remarkable, breathtaking scene: The huge whales emerged among the shearwaters to fill their large mouths with fish. We remained at this particular spot for about an hour so that we could witness this amazing assemblage of wildlife, and then we reluctantly continued our journey west to Attu.

During our voyage, we also saw the Whiskered Auklet, which is only found in North America in the Central Aleutians near Dutch Harbor. We had excellent views of this bird, a species that most birders on the ship had never before seen. This small slate-gray auklet sports a bright orange bill, three thin, white strips radiating along the sides of its face, startling white eyes, and two long black plumes that curl over its forehead, like a delicate headdress of sorts. Other noteworthy birds included Tufted Puffins, one of the most distinctive seabirds with its bold white "face mask," a bright red bill accenting its black body, and long, golden feathers curling over its head and neck. We also spotted Horned Puffins, which are similar to the Atlantic Puffins of the northeastern United States. In addition, we had the chance to see several species of whales, as well as Fork-tailed Petrels, Northern Fulmars, Mottled Petrels, and Pink-footed and Sooty Shearwaters.

After five days at sea, we arrived at Attu, the mecca of North American birding. The weather at Attu can be very unpleasant with rain, fog, and high winds. During this trip, however, we experienced wonderful conditions, with very little wind, moderate temperatures, and bright sunshine almost twenty-four hours a day. This kind of weather is not the most ideal condition for causing Asian vagrants to stray to Attu, but it made for beautiful hikes on the island. It is easier to find Asian vagrants in the spring because there is so little vegetation after the cold, snowy winter. Overall, visibility is better when shrubs are bare, and the other plants and weeds are withered and beaten down by the winter ice and snow. During our visit, the grasses, sedges, and other vegetation were at least knee-high. As a result, birds were more difficult to find.

Our first explorations ashore on Alexai Point produced a Gray-tailed Tattler, a Common Snipe, a Sky Lark, and other birds. Almost every day brought a new surprise, including a Red-necked Stint, a Spotted Redshank, a Wood Sandpiper, stunning juvenile

Sharp-tailed Sandpipers, and Snowy Owls. Every morning followed a similar routine: We disembarked the ship in Zodiacs, usually landing in three or four different spots along Massacre Bay. Some participants landed at the base of the peninsula that ends near Alexai Beach, some near the Coast Guard station, and others near South Beach, just south of Murder Point. We all carried radios so that if anyone found a rare bird, the others could be transported to the site as swiftly as possible.

The most exciting bird that we found turned up in the most unusual way. Larry Balch was leading a group to a spot where other participants had seen White Wagtails the previous day. A small, striking black-and-white bird, the White Wagtail is found regularly in North America only in northwest Alaska. It is somewhat more common on the outer islands. The bird has a long tail and walks along the ground, looking for insects among the rocks and vegetation. As the group approached the area where the wagtails had been observed, Larry noticed that a couple of women were lagging behind the group. One was new to birding, and the other one came on the trip because her husband was a birder. He motioned to them and called out that they should join the group. "We're trying to find these White Wagtails," he said. "We need to stay together."

When the women caught up with Larry and the others, the new birder said to Larry, "Would the Baikal Teal be a good bird?" Birders often use the word "good" as a way of asking if a bird would be unusual. Larry arched his eyebrows and said skeptically to her, "I've never seen one in all my thirty trips to Attu." She responded, "Well, we saw a female in a little pond down near the beach." Larry arched his eyebrows again and looked at her in disbelief. She then said, "I took a photograph of it." The woman had photographed the bird, using her small digital camera, and she showed the picture to Larry. With the brilliant sunlight, it was hard to make out the details of the digital image. Larry asked, "Can you enlarge it?" She responded, "This is a new camera. I don't know how to use it." Another tour participant took the camera and improved the quality, image, and size. Larry scrutinized the image more closely and then abruptly said, "Let's get back to that pond!"

The entire group followed Larry to the exact spot where the women had seen the bird they had identified as the female Baikal Teal. When they arrived at the pond adjacent to the maintenance building of the Coast Guard, there were no birds. The pond was only a quarter acre in size and contained a small island that was carpeted with dense brown reeds. One of the women who had seen the duck said, "Maybe it walked into the reeds on the other side of the pond." Larry said, "Well if the bird was a rail, it might have gone into the reeds, but a duck wouldn't do that." No sooner had Larry made this comment than the duck waddled out of the reeds and into perfect view in front of the rapt group of birders. Larry took one look and realized that the women were right: This was a female Baikal Teal, a bird that he had never seen in all of his previous trips to Attu—or, in fact, anywhere. "Freeze!" Larry shouted.

Baikal Teal breed only in Eastern Asia and, sadly, their numbers have become much reduced. The male is a spectacular small duck. His head features a beautiful collage of iridescent yellow and green feathers. A little larger than the Green-winged Teal, the male Baikal Teal has three long white stripes on its side, as well as a white bar on the side of its breast and near the base of its tail. It's one of the species that I had studied in bird books and dreamed about seeing.

I was out on Alexai Point with Barry Zimmer when we received the radio message from Larry about the Baikal Teal. Zodiacs were sent from the ship to pick up the various groups of birders and take them to the viewing spot at the pond. Our group had the most distance to travel and was the last to arrive. When we walked up forty-five minutes later, fifty birders, frozen like statues on the edge of the pond, were admiring this rare duck. We all had wonderful views. At that point in the trip, it was the highlight of our adventure.

Over the next few days, a number of other unusual birds were spotted during our daily excursions. Some of us made the four-mile hike up from Massacre Bay to the summit of Engineer Hill. This is the site of the peace memorial, built after the war by the Japanese in memory of the thousands of Japanese and American soldiers who died in the historic battle. The inscription at the base of the eighteen-foot, multi-pointed titanium sculpture reads (in both Japanese and English): "In memory of all those who sacrificed their lives in the islands and seas of the North Pacific during World War II and in dedication to world peace."

Later, Larry came up with the idea of inviting all the men at the Coast Guard station to a Christmas party, even though it was September. It was a lovely party with drinks and food, and two trip members, Don Wilkinson and Dick Spight, performed a memorable rendition of "Old Man River." Many of the participants said that the chance to celebrate Christmas with a group of homesick Coast Guard men was one of the most beautiful moments in their lives.

As we were about to depart Attu, I came up with yet another idea: Since we chartered the ship—and we could go wherever we wanted—perhaps we could cruise west and stop in an area of Attu that no birders had ever visited. In the past, birders had been confined to where they could walk or bicycle in and around Massacre Bay since they arrived by an airplane or a cruise ship that could only spend a few hours on Attu. I asked the ship's captain if we could continue on to the westernmost bay of Attu called Etienne Bay. Unfortunately, the captain replied that he didn't have the nautical charts for this specific area of the island because he didn't know ahead of time that we would be traveling there. About an hour later, the captain informed me that after searching through the drawers of the navigation room that they were able to locate the appropriate charts and that we, in fact, could travel to this part of the island.

The next evening, we arrived at Etienne Bay. All of the leaders disembarked, and we did a bit of scouting to figure out where we could take people the following day. The next morning, we birded the area right next to the shoreline. I asked one of our leaders, Barry Zimmer, to hike inland alongside a tiny stream—and see how far he could go and to let us know if he saw any unusual birds.

Midway through the morning, we received an electrifying radio message from Barry. "I have spotted a warbler!" We all knew this bird was almost certainly a species that we had not seen on our trip and was probably one of the Asian vagrants that we were hoping to encounter. The entire group trudged inland along the ridges of the slopes that were covered with a dense growth of artemisia. Eventually, we saw Barry standing above a stream that was only fifteen feet below, and we hiked over to join him.

Within this vegetation bordering the stream, Barry had spotted a small warbler, which was identified as a Yellow-browed Warbler, one of the smaller Old World species. This bird is distinctive for its golden "eyebrow" above both eyes and its bright olive-green body and pale upperparts. This sighting turned out to be the third record for North America. Most of the time, the warbler was hidden in the vegetation where it searched for insects, but occasionally it emerged from the foliage, allowing us to have a quick look. Most of the participants were able to view this rare warbler. Needless to say, no one—including Larry Balch and the other Attu veteran leaders—had ever seen this bird. When I put together the trip, I never dreamed that we would encounter these two species—the Baikal Teal and Yellow-browed Warbler—that none of the veteran Attu leaders had seen in North America.

After our hike along Etienne Bay, we reboarded the ship and voyaged west toward Petropavlovsk, Russia. As we cruised, our chumming efforts attracted even more Short-tailed Albatrosses, including a fully mature bird. This albatross, with its snow-white plumage, a golden head, and large pink bill circled the ship several times. Later, Marshall Iliff spotted a large dark seabird that turned out to be a Solander's Petrel, one of the northernmost records for this uncommon species that only breeds on Lord Howe Island off Australia and has an estimated population of only twenty thousand pairs.

On September 24, we arrived in Petropavlovsk, transferred to the airport, boarded our flight, and returned to Anchorage. Earlier in the trip, I was having dinner with my old friend Pete Dunne and his wife, Linda. Pete is one of the pioneers of North American birding and the former director of the Cape May Bird Observatory. We had been close friends for many years. Pete said to me, "Victor, no one else and no other company could have pulled off a trip like this."

19

Voyage on the *Sea Cloud*

Raptor Migration
ÇAMLICA HILL, ISTANBUL

My father didn't teach me to ride a bike or play baseball when I was a young boy. Perhaps this was because he had never ridden a bike or competed in any sports, despite being the manager of the baseball team in his hometown of Nordheim, Texas, and later the sports editor at the *Houston Post*. Instead, I inherited other things from my father: One of his greatest gifts to me was his passionate interest in history, literature, current events, and other intellectual endeavors. Like many people, my father was fascinated by the history and culture of ancient Greece and Rome. As a result, during my teenage years, I began to hear stories about Troy and the glory of fifth century BC Athens. Before long, I was reading *The Iliad* and *The Odyssey* on my own.

In 2003, I was invited to a dinner party hosted by my friends, Berthold Hass and his wife, Emily Tracy-Hass. That evening, when I walked in the front door, the first person I met was Paul Woodruff. As one often does in social situations, I asked him, "What do you do?" Paul replied, "I teach Greek philosophy." And I said, "I just reread Thucydides's *History of the Peloponnesian War* last week." We continued to talk about philosophy and the Greeks throughout the evening.

I had never connected with another person as quickly as I did with Paul. For me, it was exciting to meet an individual who was so knowledgeable about ancient Greece and its great philosophers. I know that, for Paul, the connection was just as swift because Thucydides is his favorite writer, and he had written several books about the Athenian historian. On that same evening, I also met Paul's wife, Lucia, who at the time was a violinist with the Austin Symphony. Since I love classical music above all other forms of music, I also made fast friends with Lucia.

After that dinner, the Woodruffs and I stayed in touch. I started to think, "How can I get to Greece with Paul and Lucia?" Then, the idea came to me: Barry Lyon and I could co-lead a tour to Greece with Paul. I envisioned a cruise—a first for VENT—from Athens to Istanbul on the legendary 360-foot *Sea Cloud*, the famous four-masted ship that was built for E. F. Hutton and Marjorie Merriweather Post in 1931 in Kiel, Germany, and is regarded as one of the most beautiful ships ever built. The luxury vessel carries thirty sails and accommodates up to fifty-eight guests in its twenty-eight cabins. We had chartered the *Sea Cloud* in December 1999 for a memorable voyage in the Lesser Antilles.

In September 2006, I flew to Athens to meet Paul, Lucia, and Barry, and our tour group of fifty-five guests. I'll never forget the moment as the plane descended toward Athens and I saw the mountains that hemmed the basin of the ancient city: Mount Aegaleo to the west, Mount Parnitha to the north, Mount Penteli to the northeast, and Mount Hymettus to the east. I remember thinking, "These are the same mountains that Plato, Socrates, and Pericles, and Thucydides saw more than two thousand years ago." It reminded me of my first walks on the paths of Harvard in fall 1963 when I thought about the thinkers and writers—Thoreau, Emerson, T. S. Eliot, and others—who had traversed those same paths.

This tour was VENT's first excursion designed to include lectures about the culture and history of ancient Greece, as well as tour some of the monumental ruins and see some of the birds that reside in this part of the world. My anticipation for the trip was heightened by the fact that there were many new birds that we hoped to see there: the European Bee-eater, the Sardinian Warbler, the Woodchat Shrike, and the Black-headed Bunting, among many others. Also, I was looking forward to witnessing the famous raptor migration over Çamlıca Hill in Istanbul; I had heard it was possible to view hundreds of hawks, eagles, and storks during a single outing.

On the first day, we visited the Acropolis, the most famous landmark of Greece, as soon as it opened in the morning. The Acropolis is a rocky hill that rises five hundred feet above sea level and offers commanding views in all directions. The most important building on the Acropolis is the Parthenon, considered by many to be the most beautiful structure in the world. The Acropolis was also a wonderful place for our first birding outing: We had superb views of Alpine and Common Swifts flying over the city, as well as Blue Rock Thrushes, Eurasian Kestrels, and Willow Warblers moving amid the brushy slopes.

Later, we visited the Agora, the public assembly and marketplace of ancient Athens. The Agora was the location where Socrates drank the hemlock after his trial on the charges of corrupting the youth of Athens. On the ancient olive tree–filled grounds, we saw House Martins, Eurasian Collared-Doves, Eurasian Jays, Hoopoes, Eurasian Blackbirds, Blue Tits, Great Tits, and Sardinian Warblers. A dramatic moment occurred when we were walking around the Temple of Hephaestus, one of the largest and best preserved of the ancient Greek temples, which was built to honor Hephaestus, god of metalworking, and Athena, daughter of Zeus. Suddenly, an owl flew out of the temple and perched in one of the nearby olive trees. It was a Little Owl, the Owl of Athena, a small, brown-gray, thickset owl with white spots almost over its entire body. After we enjoyed a wonderful study of this tiny owl, we sat on the ground and had a reading of portions of Pericles's Funeral Oration, a famous speech from Thucydides's *History of the Peloponnesian War*.

Later that afternoon, in Piraeus, the port of Athens, we boarded the *Sea Cloud*. As we left the harbor, I thought about the Peloponnesian War and the Athenian ships that departed from this very same port more than two thousand years ago to travel to Sicily on that ill-fated campaign. As soon as we departed the harbor, we spotted Cory's Shearwaters flying over the waves along with the Yellow-legged and Black-headed Gulls that followed our ship. Shearwaters display a very distinctive flight pattern. After a few flaps to gain a bit of altitude, they set their wings and sail downward toward the sea, almost touching the surface before they arc up again to repeat this exercise. The Cory's Shearwater and the Yellow-legged Gull often forage these waters away from their nesting colonies in other coastal areas of the Mediterranean.

On the first day at sea, after eating breakfast and witnessing the raising of the sails, we assembled on the lido deck toward the rear of the ship. We took in the magnificent blue Aegean in all directions. Our route followed closely the same route that the ancient Greeks traveled from Greece to Troy in order to fight the mythic Trojan War. That morning, Paul invited our tour guests to participate in a selected reading of *Antigone*, using Paul's own translation of the dramatic text. It is one of his favorite Greek plays. Barry and I also participated in this reading, taking the parts of Haemon and King Creon, respectively. This seemed rather fitting, given our age difference, to read scenes between a father and a rebellious son. The reading was a great success and immersed all of us in the world of ancient Greece. This experience also had a way of bringing the group together.

While we were at sea, some of us spotted an Eleonora's Falcon, a rare species that breeds only in the islands of the Mediterranean and winters in Madagascar. A sooty-colored falcon with sharply pointed wings, a slim body, and rusty upperparts, the species is named after Eleonora d'Arborea, who, as regent for the judge of Arborea, passed a law in order to protect this falcon. It was the very first piece of legislation ever passed to protect a bird. This beautiful falcon breeds in late August when it can prey on land birds migrating from Europe to Africa.

As we sailed to Troy, we spent a day on Samos, a beautiful island on the eastern side of the Aegean Sea, less than a mile from the jagged coast of Turkey. This small island includes considerable stretches of pine and oak forest and is home to the outstanding Archaeological Museum, which showcases the German excavations of Heraion, considered one of the most important museum collections in Greece. Some of the group accompanied Barry and me to a wooded valley, where we encountered a group of migrating hawks and eagles, including Short-toed Eagles and a Long-legged Buzzard.

We spent a day on Lesbos, where Sappho, one of the greatest Greek poets, lived. The island is mountainous with two three-thousand-foot peaks, Olympus and Lepetymnos, dominating the northern and central portions. Some participants visited museums and some went birding. Lesbos is the best island in Greece for birding because it is situated on a major migratory flyway, making it a vital stopover for millions of land birds and water birds traveling between Europe and Africa during the spring and fall months. During our excursion, we saw Greater Flamingos, Ruddy Shelducks, European Shags, Little Grebes, Gray Herons, Black Storks, Honey Buzzards, Short-toed Eagles, Common Buzzards, Common Moorhens, European Coots, Common and Little terns, Red-rumped Swallows, Black-eared Wheatears, Eurasian Reed-Warblers, and Olivaceous Warblers. The flamingos were huddled together in a dense flock and stood in shallow water at the far end of a long pond. Some birds were preening. At times, a few flamingos flew to another nearby pond, allowing us to see their deep pink shoulders and the black trailing edges of their large wings.

Next we visited the coast of Turkey, disembarking at the coastal town of Dikili and then traveling to Pergamon, a lovely Hellenistic ruin, especially its ten-thousand-seat theater. The ancient city reached the height of its influence during the Hellenistic period, becoming the capital of the Attalid kings. During the Roman period, the city was the first capital of the Asian province, but it eventually lost this status to local rival, Ephesus. The medical doctors in our group were particularly interested in the Asclepeion, where early medicine was first practiced. It was considered a healing temple, sacred to the god Asclepius.

Set amid largely undeveloped surroundings, Pergamon offers some remarkably good birding right on the grounds of the archaeological site. We observed a number of birds both inside and outside the "walls" of the city, including Red-backed Shrikes, a Red-breasted Flycatcher, Western Rock Nuthatches, a Syrian Woodpecker, and a European Goldfinch. In a pine forest in the hills, we managed to spot a Krüper's Nuthatch, a tiny bird that has a very limited world range and occurs in Europe only, on nearby Lesbos. Similar to a woodpecker, this rare bird can be heard, faintly drumming against the tree trunks and the underside of branches as it attempts to dig out insects with its sharp bill.

On the way to Troy, Paul gave a lecture about Homer and *The Iliad*, and again we all participated in a group reading of the ancient text. I remember reading the dramatic part of this epic poem that describes the Trojan King Priam pleading with Achilles for his son Hector's body.

At Çanakkale, we disembarked and traveled a short distance to the ruins of Troy. Not much remains of ancient Troy, but the stone walls have been excavated as well as a few other parts of the ancient city. Today, Troy is located among fields and trees that hold a variety of birds. We had the good fortune to see several species, including the Eurasian Magpie, the Crested Lark, the Blue Tit, and the Oriental Greenfinch. It was thrilling to stand on the remains of the wall, look toward the sea, and imagine the Trojans seeing the arrival of hundreds of Greek ships.

After Troy, we cruised up the Bosporus into the Sea of Marmara, where we saw flocks of Levantine Shearwaters, a small shearwater of the Mediterranean. On a glorious morning, we arrived in Istanbul and disembarked. Istanbul is the most interesting city that I've ever visited, partly because it spans the water that divides Europe from Asia, but also because of the intricate layers of history that exist there. On this first trip, we visited some of the famous sites, such as Hagia Sophia and the Blue Mosque.

Later I learned an incredible story about my friend Paul Woodruff: When he was a student at Oxford, he bought a book about the Fourth Crusade written by the leader of that crusade, Geoffrey.

He took the book with him on his first trip to Istanbul and then to Vietnam, where he served in the US Army. During his military service, Paul wrote a play inspired by the Fourth Crusade, which he regarded as a misguided effort, similar to Vietnam. In Paul's play, one of the characters is named Dandolo, who was the blind Doge of Venice. Dandolo financed the crusade on the condition that they conquer Constantinople, Venice's main rival. After the crusaders conquered Constantinople, Dandolo died and was buried in the Hagia Sofia, where a stone, which we saw, read HENRICUS DANDOLO. After the Byzantine Greeks retook the city a number of years later, the soldiers dug up Dandolo's bones and threw them to the dogs.

One morning, we ascended Çamlıca Hill, the highest point of the city, which is located on the Asian side. The spot is well known among birders as the best place to observe the migration of falcons, hawks, storks, and other birds that are leaving Europe to spend the winter in Africa. From this hill, we could see the city of Istanbul, the Bosporus, and the Sea of Marmara spread out below us. Fortunately, this was a superb day to witness this marvelous migration. Most birds migrate at night. In contrast, almost all hawks migrate during the day, enabling observers to *see* migration happening. Rising thermals make it possible for the hawks to cover great distances with little expenditure of energy. They take off from their roosting spots in the morning, fly a short distance until they find a thermal, and then circle on the thermal, rising higher and higher, elevated by the updraft. As more and more hawks join the thermal, they create a "kettle" of hawks—sometimes involving a hundred hawks—all circling and moving upward. When they reach the point where the thermal won't carry them higher, the hawks set their wings and stream until they can find another thermal.

This migration was most dramatic atop Çamlıca Hill. Looking west across the Bosporus and Istanbul, we spotted a bird that was only a speck in our binoculars. As it flew closer, we could tell it was a hawk. Then, we watched it fly over the Bosporus, leaving Europe and crossing over into Asia. Eventually, it passed right over us, enabling us to identify it. I have never seen so many species of raptors at one site. The most common species were Short-toed Eagles and Common Buzzards, but we also saw Lesser Spotted Eagles, Eurasian and Levant Sparrowhawks, and even a single Goshawk.

In addition to the raptors, we spotted small flocks of White Storks, with the black trailing edges of their large wings, as well as Black Storks. Like the hawks, the storks were initially mere dots in the sky. But as they drew closer, these storks became more vivid with their distinctive red bills and long red legs. We knew that the White Storks had bred in big-stick nests in trees and specially fitted platforms on house roofs and telephone poles in towns across Europe while the Black Storks had nested in undisturbed old forests. Both species were on their way to their wintering grounds in Africa. That morning at Çamlıca Hill was one of the best mornings of birding that I ever had, a fitting end to a trip that fulfilled a long-held dream of visiting Greece and the sites that I had read about when I was teenager.

Over the years, Paul Woodruff has been an incredible resource for learning about the culture of ancient Greece, a culture that provided the foundation for western civilization. One morning, on that first trip, I asked him what was written on the famous stone at Delphi that contained the two maxims of ancient Greek culture. Paul replied, "On one side, it says, 'Know thyself.'" Paul went on to say that he interpreted this to mean know your limitations, know you're not God. "And on the other side, it says, 'Nothing in excess.'"

20

My True Obsession

Cape May Warbler
THE RAMBLE
CENTRAL PARK, NEW YORK CITY

One spring I left my house on the Bolivar Peninsula to meet a friend for dinner in Austin. While I was driving, I kept stopping on Galveston Island at small patches of woodland and thinking to myself, "If I can see just one more warbler, then I can keep this dinner appointment and not be late." I found one more warbler, and then I thought, "What about one more?" This feeling of wanting to see more is heightened for me with warblers because I know that, for the most part, I can only see these birds at certain times of the year, particularly during the spring when they are moving northward or in the fall when they migrate south. I'm also keenly aware that there are only so many springs and falls left in my life.

I can't explain why I became obsessed with these small birds, but warblers have helped me to understand the nature of obsession. It's an interesting concept to contemplate: When some behavior or object begins to dominate certain aspects of your life in such a way that you can't get enough of it. Paul Woodruff told me once that most people don't understand the notion of "enough." They always want more—more money, more love, more friends, more property, more things. Paul's point was that it's important to recognize when you do have enough of something. I definitely have a very clear idea of what enough is in most aspects of my life, but not when it comes to warblers. I can never see enough warblers. They have brought much pleasure and richness into my life.

I feel about warblers the same way Peter Matthiessen felt about shorebirds, but unlike shorebirds, which are mostly clad in shades of gray and brown, warblers are "the sprightly butterflies of the bird world," as Roger Tory Peterson once wrote. They are small birds, averaging about five inches long, with slender, pointed bills. Many of the American wood warblers, in contrast to the European warblers, exhibit brilliant plumage and patterns.

Given the beauty of warblers, it's not surprising that others share my obsession. A beautiful rendering of a Magnolia Warbler, one of the most strikingly plumaged warblers, graces the cover of the 2014 edition of *The Sibley Guide to Birds*. At High Island, on the Upper Texas Coast, between Galveston and the Louisiana border, there is a daily list of bird sightings posted in the information center. The left column includes only warblers, and the right column enumerates all other birds. It is interesting to note, however, that there are many people in the United States who have probably never seen a warbler—or even know what one is—despite the fact that warblers pass through their lives.

Many poets have written about warblers, including Robert Frost. His famous poem "The Oven Bird," originally published in 1914, features a wood warbler. The poem begins: "There is a singer everyone has heard / Loud, a mid-summer and a mid-wood bird / Who makes the solid tree trunks sound again."

Perhaps one of the most interesting stories about warblers involves President Theodore Roosevelt, who was an avid naturalist and birder from his early youth. When he was serving as president, he looked out the window during a cabinet meeting and spotted a Blackburnian Warbler. He paused the meeting so he could go outside and observe the vibrant bird more closely. In March 1908, Roosevelt compiled a checklist of birds that he had seen on the White House grounds and in and around Washington, DC, during his administration. This list included ninety-three kinds of birds and sixteen different species of warblers.

Why do warblers attract so much interest among birders? Admittedly, there are other colorful birds, such as tanagers, spoon-bills, grosbeaks, and buntings. But there is something about war-blers—the way that they move, the lightness and the intensity of life that they embody. Each species of warbler has it own personal-ity, song, and niche. Some warblers, such as the Tennessee and the Cape May, probe flowers for nectar. Others, such as the Worm-eat-ing Warbler, poke their bills into clumps of dead leaves in search of insects. Black-and-white Warblers climb up trees, circling the trunk; the Bay-breasted walks along the larger tree branches, look-ing for insects. Grace's Warblers probe their bills into clusters of pine needles to flush out insects that they then pursue and catch. Swainson's Warblers walk slowly across the woodland floor, forag-ing for insects by flicking over the leaves.

Warblers also generate a special affection because we see them so briefly. "The appreciation of warblers is a slow acquisition, since most of the species are to be seen and heard only for a few days each year, and the rarer may be seen only at intervals of several years," wrote naturalist and political scientist Louis Halle in his exquisite book *Spring in Washington* (1947). "When I say that I have been acquainted with a warbler for ten years, it may be that the sum of that acquaintance is only a few minutes."

Another great naturalist, Aldo Leopold, considered by many to be the father of wildlife management and one of my heroes, wrote about his experiences in western Mexico and his concept of *nume-non*. This term refers to a presence that permeates a specific area. Leopold's example was the Thick-billed Parrot, which lives in the pine-oak forest of western Mexico. It's a spectacular green parrot with a distinctive red crown and a loud call, resembling human laughter, that can be heard almost a mile away. Leopold believed its presence suffused the area, and the parrot's removal would cause the region to change dramatically.

When the warblers stop at High Island, on the eastern coast of Texas, the area is changed by the fact that there are a hundred to two hundred warblers resting in its woodlands. This impact is out of proportion to the species' small size. Nothing else in the bird world—at least, in North America—has this effect. When you enter a woodland on the Texas coast or any part of the Gulf Coast on the day when the wind is from the south, you immediately feel the absence of life's fullness and energy since few warblers are present. Re-enter the same woodland later on a day when the wind has shifted to the north, and it is alive with an energy that one immediately senses.

Peter wrote about the long distances that shorebirds cover on their migrations in *The Wind Birds: Shorebirds of North America* (1967): "The wind birds are strong, marvelous fliers, averaging greater distances in their migrations than any other bird family on earth." Warblers spend a significant amount of time on their migrations, too, and when they stop, the birds look for food, mainly insects, to replace the fat that they lost during their previous flight. Some warblers perform migrations that are more remarkable than that of any shorebird. The Blackpoll Warbler flies up to seven thousand miles, without stopping, over the Atlantic Ocean during the course of three days, making its autumn migration from northeastern North America to South America. In Scott Weidensaul's *Living on the Wind: Across the Hemisphere with Migratory Birds* (1999), the author writes at length about the Blackpoll Warblers' migration:

> For the next forty or fifty hours, the tiny songbirds will fly over the western Atlantic, wings buzzing at twenty flaps a second, climbing to altitudes of more than five thousand feet. They will show up on weather radar as they pass Bermuda and the Greater Antilles, glowing green specks that form diffuse blobs on the monitors, like ghosts behind the moon . . . . If a Blackpoll Warbler were burning gasoline instead of its reserves of body fat, it could boast of getting 720,000 miles to the gallon.

In order to fly these long distances, a warbler will nearly double its body mass so it has fuel for the next leg of its migration. It's one of the most remarkable feats of any animal.

Fifty-three species of warblers breed in North America. In 2008, I decided to try and see all of them. It was a special effort, but I ended up seeing forty-nine species. That year, I was co-leading

Camp Chiricahua, our summer camp in southeastern Arizona. I was also co-leading a trip, titled "Birding Across America by Train." This excursion involved birding the Adirondacks; an area near Minot, North Dakota; and the Olympic Peninsula. Each area offered me many opportunities to see warblers because I was going to be present amid the migration paths and breeding grounds of many of them. During that year, I saw warblers in Austin, High Island, the Adirondacks, Arizona, Washington state, and North Dakota. I even saw the Connecticut Warbler, which is one of the most challenging species to see because of its secretive nature, in Minot, North Dakota.

Unfortunately, I came up with the idea a little too late to see some of the birds that migrated earlier along the Texas coast, particularly the Swainson's Warbler, which is only found in the southeastern United States. I tried to see one near Bastrop, Texas; I heard the rich, musical song of the bird, but I never saw it. The Swainson's Warbler is one of the most difficult birds to see because it breeds and lives in areas with dense undergrowth and seldom gives the observer a clear view. This warbler is also less striking in its appearance with a plumage of browns and grays with a rich rufous crown.

During this effort, the last warbler I tried to see was the similarly elusive MacGillivray's Warbler with its vivid yellow chest and belly. I was staying with Bill and Andrea Broyles near Jackson Hole, Wyoming. I called a local birder, and he told me about a spot to look for this warbler, but Bill and I weren't able to find one. During my lifetime, I have seen all of the species that breed in North America, but I still hope to see them all in the space of one year. Recently, I saw Kirtland's Warbler for the first time, the rarest North American warbler. It breeds only in stands of young jack pines in northern Michigan and small swaths of Wisconsin and Ontario.

Over the years, I've witnessed many large fallouts on the Texas coast and elsewhere. One of the most remarkable fallouts that I ever observed was in Key West, Florida, on May 1, 2001. I had traveled to the Dry Tortugas with Barry Lyon to see the nesting seabirds on the small islands surrounding Fort Jefferson. We spotted some warblers there, but these sightings did not prepare us for the spectacle that awaited us in Key West. As soon as we disembarked from the boat, we started to see warblers in the bushes near the dock. That afternoon, there were warblers on the front lawn of the Holiday Inn, where we were staying. There were dozens of warblers walking or probing in patches of driftwood on the nearby beaches. There were warblers on the curbs of streets, on lawns, in parking lots, on benches, on boats, on the ledges and windowsills of buildings. There were warblers almost everywhere. In one sweep of my binoculars around the lawn of the Holiday Inn, I counted fifteen individual warblers.

I was surprised when we were eating in a restaurant and the waiter asked us, "What are all of these small colorful birds that I'm seeing all over downtown Key West?" It was evident that people who had never seen a warbler noticed that something was happening. Being obsessed with these birds, I was so taken by all this heightened activity that I couldn't sit still at the table, waiting for our food. I walked around the block because I wanted to see more warblers and more warblers and more warblers. While eating dinner, I saw Cape May, American Redstart, and three Black-throated Blue warblers on a telephone line. What was especially gratifying about this fallout was that the most abundant warblers were the Cape May, the Blackpoll, and the Black-throated Blue, all especially beautiful warblers that I very seldom see on the Upper Texas Coast.

As a warbler fanatic, I can't help but have a feeling of poignancy and sadness because there are not as many warblers now as there were ten or twenty years ago. Their numbers are decreasing because of collisions with buildings and wind towers and because of cats catching them during migrations when the birds are down low and feeding. Their habitats are being altered for agriculture. Climate changes are affecting their food sources and migration patterns. I savor these small songbirds while I can. I always hope to experience another spring when the warblers return and I get the opportunity to experience the beauty and the richness that they bring into my life.

Though Peter loved shorebirds above all else, he also loved warblers. Many times he lamented to me that he spotted fewer warblers each spring at his woodland-surrounded home in Sagaponack. He told me that he used to see ten or fifteen different species during the spring, and toward the end of his life, he was lucky to see two or three species.

Then he started visiting me at Bolivar on the Upper Texas Coast. In spring 2010, four years before he passed away, I invited Peter to give a couple of talks in Austin. I suggested that he arrive a day or two early in Houston so that Barry and I could take him to High Island on the Upper Texas Coast to look for warblers. I remember wondering if we would see many warblers with only a day or a half-day to look. If on those days the wind was from the south, there would be maybe five kinds of warblers on High Island because most of the others would have flown over the area.

Barry and I arrived at the airport in Houston a little early. I stepped out of the car and realized that the wind was blowing from the north. "How wonderful!" I thought. "Maybe we'll see some warblers." We picked Peter up and drove directly to High Island. As soon as we stepped out of the car at Boy Scout Woods, we saw warblers everywhere. Warblers searched for insects along the low branches of the nearby live oak trees, along the leaf-covered woodland floor, and in the bottlebrush bushes in front of a house across the street. We walked along the road that borders Scout Woods and then entered the network of trails that traverse the dense woodlands. We kept seeing warbler after warbler. It seemed as though the list would never end. Each time one of us spotted a different warbler, we called its name to alert the others about our discovery. "A Black-throated Green." "A Blue-winged." "A Black-and-white." "A Hooded." "A Cape May." "A Magnolia." On and on.

After a couple of hours, we very reluctantly pulled ourselves away and drove to my cottage, Warbler's Roost, which looks out onto the Bolivar Flats. Barry had brought a special kind of whiskey because he knew that Peter would enjoy sitting on the porch and looking out at the flats, savoring a drink and remembering all the wonderful warblers we had seen that afternoon. Peter was in heaven. He was so pleased to have seen all those warblers with us.

Before we departed, he wrote in my guest book (which he had given me in 2002): "I've decided to come here every spring so I can get my warbler fix." Reading that made me very happy because I thought that we would have many more times on the Texas coast together, seeing more warblers. Sadly, we only had one more spring together in Texas before Peter was diagnosed with leukemia in September 2012.

After the onset of his illness, Peter still hoped to visit High Island again. He kept telling me that he hadn't given up on the idea of returning. The spring before he died, I made plane reservations for him to travel to Texas, but then he told me that he had reluctantly decided against it because he was undergoing chemotherapy, and it was not advisable to fly. As an alternative, he suggested that I join him for a day of birding in The Ramble in New York City's Central Park. The Ramble is a thirty-seven-acre "wild garden," as described by its landscape architect Frederick Law Olmsted. Located in the center of the famous park between Seventy-Second and Seventy-Ninth Streets, The Ramble, with its leafy canopy and thriving wildlife habitat, was designed to be an area where visitors could get lost. I agreed that Peter's idea was an excellent alternative, given his health.

In mid-May 2013, we met at nine-thirty in the morning at the Boathouse in Central Park. Peter's son, Alex, and Rose Styron joined us. As soon as we entered The Ramble, we started seeing warblers. Clearly, this was a good day for birding. We saw warbler after warbler, tallying seventeen species before Alex and Rose had to leave because of other commitments. After their departure, Peter and I had a mid-morning snack at the Boathouse. Then, we returned to The Ramble for more birding. He spotted one of the most beautiful warblers, a male Cape May with its distinctive black-streaked yellow underparts. Its head is a beautiful pattern of black and yellow with an intense area of deep chestnut on its face. Peter recognized the elegant bird as it came down to drink some water in a little ravine. He was delighted that he had spotted our last new warbler for the day.

Reluctantly, we left The Ramble so Peter could catch the Jitney to return home to Sagaponack. It was hard to leave him, standing alone at the bus stop on Lexington Avenue. I didn't think about it at the time, but where I left him was only six blocks west of George Plimpton's apartment, where I had met Peter about forty years earlier.

I saw him only a few more times. In August of that year, I visited Peter and Maria in Sagaponack. Because of his illness, we took only a few short walks and drove to Mecox Bay, where there were a few shorebirds, but he rarely raised his binoculars and declined my invitation to look through the scope. Despite his deteriorating condition, Peter hoped that he would get better and be able to return to the Texas coast in spring 2014. He told me that seeing the warblers would be like an elixir. But that was not possible. He died that spring.

During one of our last phone conversations, it occurred to me to ask Peter which warbler was his favorite. After a moment of reflection, he told me it was the Blackburnian Warbler. He remembered seeing it on High Island with me. "It was perched at the top of a tree," he recalled, "with the sun hitting its orange breast in such a way that it seemed to be glowing."

21

My World

American Avocet
BOLIVAR PENINSULA
TEXAS COAST

Many of the most important events in my life have occurred in the eighty-mile stretch of the Upper Texas Coast between Freeport and High Island. It was in this area that I founded the Freeport Christmas Bird Count when I was sixteen, saw the nearly extinct Eskimo Curlew when I was eighteen, and started my company when I was thirty-five. I have spent some of the happiest days of my life in this area, enjoying the abundance of its birdlife and the migration of birds that takes place every spring and fall.

In 1998, I decided to rent a house near Crystal Beach, which is about ten miles up the peninsula from Port Bolivar. I spent a couple of weeks there, witnessing spring unfold, and I enjoyed it so much that the following spring, I rented a different house that was closer to High Island. While I was staying there, I decided that I would look for a house to buy along this stretch of coastline. Winnie Burkett, manager of the Houston Audubon Sanctuary, told me about a cottage that was for sale near the base of the North Jetty, in a small neighborhood called the North Jetty community.

I ended up buying that house in 2000. It is one of the best

decisions that I ever made in my life. Over the years, it has enabled me to become even more intimately connected to this region. I've spent time at my house during all of the seasons. I've spent time here with some of my closest friends, such as Peter Matthiessen, Robert and Birgit Bateman, Rose Styron, Bill and Andrea Broyles, Greg Lasley, Dennis Shepler, Fred Collins, John Flowers, Ron Cohen, and Greg Lipscomb, as well as with young friends such as Barry Lyon, Ben Reynolds and Jessica Gordon and their sons Eliot and Geo, Cullen Hanks, Brian O'Shea, David and Amy Sugeno, Kurt Huffman, and Peter English. Lars Jonsson and his wife, Ragnhild, stayed here before a bird-sketching workshop. During his visit, he completed a painting of some of the Avocets, with their dusky cinnamon-colored heads and black-and-white feathered bodies, on the nearby shallows in front of my house. This painting now hangs in my living room in Austin and reminds me of that time and this extraordinary area.

Warbler's Roost, as Greg Lasley named it, is a modest yellow-painted cottage on ten-foot stilts with a large porch overlooking an arm of the Gulf of Mexico that is rimmed with reeds, cane, and sedges. Inside, my cottage is merely a U-shaped room: A simple kitchen occupies one arm of the U, and three beds are arranged in the other arm. Posted on the bulletin board, to the left of the front door, are Houston Audubon High Island patches, each one featuring a different warbler, along with a checklist enumerating all the birds that have been seen at Warbler's Roost. Bird identification books and a collection of essays by Texas naturalist Roy Bedichek sit on the side table.

The porch is the highlight of the cottage—and is where I spend most of my time, particularly the early mornings. To the southwest across the ship channel, I can see the glow of Galveston most mornings before the sun rises. In the Gulf of Mexico, the distant illumination of offshore oilrigs and large ships dot the horizon and the nearby Galveston Ship Channel.

My porch also overlooks the nearby North Jetty. The five-mile jetty was built by the Army Corps of Engineers in the late 1890s, using enormous blocks of pink granite from the Llano Uplift, a geological dome of Precambrian rock in the Texas Hill Country.

(The chief engineer on the project was Brig. Gen. Henry Robert, who also wrote *Robert's Rules of Order*.) The North Jetty stops currents carrying sediment, which has resulted in the formation of large, productive salt marshes and mudflats full of decomposing plant material. This material supplies food for worms, shrimp, and other invertebrates, which are consumed by tens of thousands of birds each year.

Each day I have spent here has been different. Each has been special. The marsh—mostly spartina grass—across the inlet stretches more than two hundred yards to the narrow beach that borders the Gulf of Mexico. A series of green, brown, and russet hues make up the marshy landscape. Looking at these colors, I am reminded of two sentences written by the biologist Bernd Heinrich in *Mind of the Raven* (2007): "The colors of nature are always complementary. Nature is the standard for truth and beauty."

One recent spring morning, as I sipped my tea and watched the morning show of birds, a fleet of Brown Pelicans appeared overhead, coming from their roosting sites farther north on Galveston Bay. When I was a teenage birder in the fifties, Brown Pelicans were abundant on the Texas Coast, but by the early sixties, they had virtually disappeared. DDT concentrated in the fish they ate caused their eggshells to become so thin that they broke when an adult sat on the eggs to brood them. Since DDT was banned in 1972, the Brown Pelican population has rebounded. They are once again abundant. These pelicans were by far the largest birds I saw this morning—until a few minutes later, when eight White Pelicans flew over. They were much larger. In fact, they are among the largest flying birds in the world with a wingspread of a hundred and ten inches, almost as wide as a California Condor.

With the sun fully up, hundreds of Black Skimmers exploded from the mudflats. Black Skimmers are the only birds in the world in which the lower mandible is longer than the upper mandible. This large flock was getting restless since they will be migrating soon. Scientists call this "migratory restlessness" or in German, *zugunruhe* (*zug* means "migration," and *unruhe* means "restlessness"). There was a good chance that the flock might be gone the following day as they continued their migration.

It is always hard to leave the porch of Warbler's Roost, but that morning I decided to drive to the Johnsons' woods, which are fifteen minutes away up the peninsula. The Johnson family was one of the earliest to settle the Bolivar Peninsula, establishing their home and ranch in the 1870s when they arrived from Louisiana by boat. The family planted a large grove of live oaks after the hurricane of 1915. This grove of trees and the Johnson house were protected from subsequent hurricanes by the berm that they built between their house and the Gulf. I met Mrs. Johnson on one of my first trips to the Bolivar Peninsula in 1970. She welcomed me and my friend, Ben Feltner, and told me that we could bird her property whenever we wanted. Three years later, Ben and I decided to try and see as many birds as we could in one hour, starting at the Johnsons and ending at the Bolivar Flats. Our total that hour was 112 species, which may be a world record for the most birds seen in one hour.

After Mrs. Johnson's death, her son, Andrew, and his wife, Margo, moved into her house, and we became friends. I was even successful in getting them interested in the birds that occurred on their property, including the wide variety of migrants that took shelter there. Unfortunately, in 2008, Hurricane Ike breached the Johnsons' embankment and killed more than half of the ancient live oaks. Fortunately, Winnie Burkett planted small live oaks and mulberries along the entrance road, and these trees are providing habitat for birds.

I like to see what species are present in this small, easily surveyed woodlot so that when I return in the afternoon I would know which land birds are new arrivals. It's my version of a litmus test for migratory arrivals. Since the skies were clear during the night and the wind was from the south, I knew that there would be very few migrants at the Johnsons' place. This particular morning, there were only two Gray Catbirds, a Black-throated Green Warbler, a female Summer Tanager, and two Tennessee Warblers along with the resident Northern Mockingbirds, Great-tailed Grackles, and House Sparrows.

Before returning to my house, I checked the ponds along Rettilon Road, which leads to the beach. I saw gulls and terns on the beach as well as Piping, Semipalmated, and Snowy Plovers. Back at my cottage, the waterbirds had settled down after their morning activity. Scanning the flats with my telescope, I saw five large shorebirds sitting together. Since their bills were upcurved, I knew they were godwits, but they seemed to be too dark to be Marbled Godwits. They bathed and preened. Then one lifted a wing. It was black below with a white band in the middle. I was amazed. These were Hudsonian Godwits, the first I had ever seen on the Bolivar Flats. This godwit is much less common than the Marbled Godwit. It winters in southern Chile and breeds at the edge of the northernmost forest in Canada and Alaska. When it stops along the Texas Coast, it feeds in areas of fresh water, such as flooded rice fields. Ten minutes after I spotted these godwits, they took off and headed farther inland. I suspected that they had flown nonstop from their wintering grounds. And, indeed, research shows that this is, in fact, what they do: These godwits had flown five thousand miles and paused briefly on the flats where I spotted them.

Houston Audubon has played an essential role by purchasing property on both sides of Highway 87 near the tip of the peninsula. Winnie Burkett provided the necessary leadership in the acquisition of these areas. Despite this critical conservation work, rapid development continues, with additional large housing projects being built up and down the Bolivar Peninsula. Hopefully, more tracts of undeveloped land can be purchased in the years ahead in order to preserve vital stopover areas for migrating birds and to maintain the ambience and beauty of this marvelous region of the Gulf Coast.

After lunch, I left for High Island. At about eleven o'clock that morning, a line of dark clouds came from the north and moved out over the Gulf. There was heavy rain. The wind shifted to the north. I was hopeful that this would cause some land bird migrants to put down in the coastal woodlands. My first stop was at the Johnsons' land. Even before I stepped out of my car, I could tell things had changed since my visit that morning. There were fifteen Indigo Buntings on the dirt road that leads to their house. These male buntings were entirely blue with the color slightly richer on their heads. In the small live oaks next to the road, I spotted a warbler.

This patch of woodland and bushes had been transformed with a new energy. A Black-and-white Warbler, a Northern Parula Warbler, and a Yellow-throated Warbler searched for insects in a huge oak tree. In the nearby bushes, I spotted two of the most beautiful birds in the world—a male Baltimore Oriole and a male Scarlet Tanager. Three Eastern Kingbirds were perched on the treetops. Unlike most of the other land bird migrants that spend the winter in Mexico or Central America, these large black-and-white flycatchers had wintered in South America. Lower down in the tree, I saw an Eastern Wood-Pewee, another flycatcher that had wintered in South America. Once again, it was hard to leave, but I suspected that I would find more migrants in the more extensive woodlands at High Island.

As I got closer to the woods of High Island, the peninsula narrowed, with the waves of the Gulf of Mexico on the right and East Bay on the left. High Island's name can be misleading because the area is not surrounded by water (though it's about three hundred yards from the Gulf of Mexico). Located on the mainland, High Island's name comes from the large salt dome, about a mile in diameter, which is under the area. This dome raises the elevation to around thirty-eight feet (most of the coast is approximately five feet above sea level). The metaphorical "island" has often served to protect its residents and the trees that they planted from hurricanes and storm surges.

High Island and the forty-eight-acre Boy Scout Woods, a former Scout camp, offers optimal viewing of migrating birds, with a simple amphitheater of weathered bleachers that overlook a water drip at the knobby base of a cypress tree. For many years, Texas birders worried that owners of these woodlands would sell their property to developers, who would clear the undergrowth, cut down some of the trees, and build houses. Fortunately, my friends Fred Collins and Ted Eubanks approached Ken Burns, who was president of Houston Audubon. Together, they persuaded the Audubon board to buy Scout Woods. Subsequently, Houston Audubon was able to purchase the property known as Smith Woods and other areas of woodland. Houston Audubon receives more than twenty-thousand dollars annually from the entrance fees birders pay. By purchasing these properties, Houston Audubon established the first sanctuary on the Gulf Coast for neotropical migrants. The High Island project led to the acquisition of a thousand acres of wetlands near the tip of the Bolivar Peninsula and inspired other groups to acquire woodlands in other areas of the Gulf Coast.

As I had hoped and expected, on this afternoon in mid-April, the woods of High Island were full of migrants. Across the street from Boy Scout Woods, a dozen Orchard Orioles and fifteen Tennessee Warblers fed on the nectar of the bright red blossoms of the bottlebrush. The adult male Orchard Orioles are a unique color of dark orange below and have a black head and back. The females are greenish-yellow with two white wing bars. The young males resemble the females, except for their black throats. By posing as females, these young males can mate with a female since the older males don't realize that the younger bird is not just another female.

Inside the sanctuary, the trees were alive with warblers of ten different species, including the Black-and-white, the Northern Parula, the Black-throated Green, and the Chestnut-sided. The mulberry trees were loaded with ripe berries. Summer and Scarlet Tanagers as well as Gray Catbirds fed on this fruit. Walking the shaded trails, I spotted both Hooded and Kentucky Warblers and an Ovenbird. All were near or on the ground.

High Island is renowned for its water drips. The end of a small tube that is connected to a hose is draped over the branch of a small tree. Water drips into a shallow container. Such drips attract an almost-continual parade of birds that drink and bathe. On this day, I observed a Wood Thrush, a Northern Waterthrush, and a Common Yellowthroat using the continuous water source at Scout Woods. Then, a male Baltimore Oriole dropped down to the water. Then another and another and another until seven brilliant male orioles bathed side by side in the shallow water. I suspected they had just arrived, having flown across the Gulf, and were eager to rinse the salt spray from their feathers and quench their thirst. I was tempted to spend the rest of the day watching birds come to this drip, but Smith Woods beckoned.

Smith Woods is my favorite area on High Island. It is about three times the size of Scout Woods and has larger trees. Toward the center of the grove was once an old, dilapidated barn. Adjacent to this weathered structure is an open area, which is almost completely covered by a thick canopy of live oaks, hackberries, and honey locust trees. My friends and I named this area the "Cathedral." Over the years, some of our birding friends have had their weddings performed at this spot.

Walking toward the Cathedral from the parking lot, I spotted in quick succession a male Cerulean Warbler, a male Blackburnian Warbler, and a male Golden-winged Warbler, three of the most beautiful warblers. Along the trails, I saw more and more warblers, including my favorite—the Hooded Warbler—as well as a Blue-winged, an American Redstart, a Canada, a Bay-breasted, and others. On an excellent day, it is possible to see thirty species of warblers at High Island. On this afternoon, I saw twenty-five different kinds. In addition to the warblers, I encountered Scarlet and Summer tanagers, Swainson's Thrushes, and a Painted Bunting.

Just before leaving for Anahuac National Wildlife Refuge, I visited the rookery. A U-shaped island in what was previously a reservoir is covered with small trees and bushes, mainly Chinese tallows, rattle bushes, and salt cedars. These bushes provide nesting sites for egrets, herons, and spoonbills. I walked along a dike that borders the reservoir to several scenic viewpoints. From each one, I observed the nesting birds from a distance of only twenty or thirty yards. The most abundant birds were Great and Snowy Egrets and Roseate Spoonbills, but there were also a few Black-crowned Night-Herons, Anhingas, White Ibis, Tricolored Herons, Green Herons, and Cattle Egrets. Cattle Egrets exhibit the most dramatic change in their exterior appearance from winter to spring: In the winter, the birds are entirely white with a yellow bill and black legs. During the breeding season, the plumage of their chest, back, and upper head becomes a rich buff-orange with red legs and bill, and lavender lores (the area between a bird's eyes and the base of their bills).

I drove to the Anahuac National Wildlife Refuge, which was established in 1963 and named after a nearby town on the shores of Galveston Bay, which itself was named after a Spanish fort. (*Anahuac* means "country by waters" in Nahuatl, the ancient language of the Aztecs.) The refuge includes a thirty-four-thousand-acre area of marshlands, grasslands, and scattered groves of live oaks and willows. On the short drive from High Island to Anahuac, expansive cattle fields border either side of the largely empty two-lane road. A number of raptors and other species were perched on the evenly spaced utility poles—Red-tailed Hawks, White-tailed Kites, Crested Caracaras, and American Kestrels.

On this afternoon at Anahuac, I drove on to the two-and-a-half-mile loop that encircled Shoveler Pond. Flocks of numerous birds sunned on the shoreline or waded in the shallow waters: Fulvous Whistling Ducks, Black-bellied Whistling Ducks, Purple and Common Gallinules, Least and American Bitterns, and many others. I also observed a variety of egrets feeding along the banks of the pond, and occasionally, an alligator lethargically surfaced its rutty head, barely moving and almost blending into the blue-green water.

By the end of the day, I had returned to Warbler's Roost. The sun had begun its descent to the western horizon. About a half hour before sunset, I walked out onto the North Jetty. Many locals were also walking there, with their wheeled coolers, plastic buckets, and rods in tow, hoping to catch redfish and southern flounder. The sinking sun sent large swaths of brilliant reds, vibrant pinks, and deep lavenders across the open sky. I continued along the jetty's paved walkway, which eventually turns into large blocks of pink granite. A soft salmon glow reflected against the placid waters.

Before long, I was only a short distance from the thousands and thousands of avocets as they fed in the shallow waters. There were so many of these black-and-white birds feeding that the waters churned with their incessant activity. A Roseate Spoonbill fed along the edge of the distant reeds. Several white egrets dotted the marshy waters. Overhead, large flocks of Brown Pelicans flew by in long vees. The moon brightened in the sky, the soft pinks diminishing into the shadowy blues, while the port of Galveston was silhouetted by the sunset.

While Brown Pelicans flew overhead, hundreds of huge White Pelicans sat side by side on a distant mudflat, looking almost like a solid band of white against the beige, green, and wheat shades of the landscape. Some of the pelicans preened. Soon, these majestic birds would migrate north in large flocks. Nearby, thousands of gulls and terns roosted on the mudflats. Most of the birds were Laughing Gulls with their crisp black hoods. Some Laughing Gulls have a pinkish cast on their breasts. I saw eight species of terns, ranging in size from the very small Least Tern to the large Caspian.

The abundance and diversity of bird life that I saw while standing in this one spot on the North Jetty was amazing. As I watched thousands of birds settle down for the night and the sun set, I felt, once again, that there is no place else that I would rather be.

Epilogue

Birds have been the central focus of my life since I was a child. Wherever I am, I notice birds every day: the flash of color as a Blue Jay flies across the street in front of my house, the bright iridescent red gorget of a male Ruby-throated Hummingbird as it hovers in front of a Cardinal flower along Blunn Creek in Stacy Park, the glowing orange throat of a Blackburnian Warbler in a juniper tree next to my office.

Edgar Kincaid used to say, "Birds have it all." By that he meant that they have more attributes that attract people than any other creatures. I feel about birds the same way he did. Throughout human history, more people have noticed and been affected by birds than any other creatures. Many birds have brilliant colors, some have marvelous songs, and their migrations over thousands of miles inspire awe, wonder, and envy. The behavior of some birds is fascinating, such as the intricate dances performed by many species of manikins. Whenever I see a bird—*any* bird—I am in the moment. When I am dealing with difficulties in my life, walking in nature and seeing birds helps me put these problems in perspective. Many times I have experienced the healing power of nature through birds.

My life with birds has kept me young through a sense of wonder. I have much less interest in gadgets, popular culture, and celebrities than most people. Birds have made me observant of all aspects of nature. Every day, I notice things in nature that most people either would not notice or would regard as unimportant: the movement of clouds and the changes in their shapes and colors; a bright spot of golden light on water or on shiny leaves; the blue, green, red, and yellow colors of frost on grass when the sun shines through it; the rainbow prisms dewdrops create on spider webs; a large white egret poised, hoping to catch a fish; a Brown Pelican diving thirty feet, hitting the water and becoming partly submerged; or a brightly colored warbler searching for insects at the end of a leafy branch. These little, simple things are big things to me.

My mentors opened my eyes to birds and instilled in me an appreciation for all birds, not just the rare and unusual ones. I have traveled the world for more than fifty years and have seen some of the most striking, exotic, and beautiful birds, but I still derive as much satisfaction from seeing a brilliant male Cardinal feeding on the ground in my backyard as I did that day long ago when I looked out the window of our house on Ruth Street and watched a pair of Cardinals picking up the seeds that my mother had thrown out onto the green moss under a fig tree.

Acknowledgments

For a number of years, friends urged me to write a book describing the key events in my life. Since I am still actively involved in running Victor Emanuel Nature Tours (VENT), I knew I would need assistance to complete such a project. Jim and Hester Magnuson suggested I contact S. Kirk Walsh. After meeting her, I decided she would be the perfect person for such a task. Casey Kittrell had told me that the University of Texas Press would welcome a proposal from me for a book on my life. Kirk and I submitted a proposal in December 2014. It was accepted and we began to work on the book.

Both Kirk and Casey have been of invaluable assistance in making this book a reality. I met with Kirk almost every week that I was in Austin for almost two years. She interviewed me and then submitted a draft of each chapter. Without her help, this book would never have been written. She did important research and made excellent suggestions. My good friends Bob Fleming and Raj Singh reviewed the chapter on the Palace on Wheels. Maria Matthiessen met with Kirk and provided information on the trips she and her late husband Peter took with me. My friend Stephen Harrigan read the draft manuscript and provided valuable insights and feedback.

I am grateful for the support I received from my parents, Victor and Marian Emanuel, and my late sister, Marilyn. I am also grateful for the education and inspiration I received from my early mentors—Joe Heiser, Armand Yramategui, and Edgar Kincaid Jr.—as well as from Peter Matthiessen, Roger Tory Peterson, and George Plimpton, who helped me start VENT and also became mentors. I also wish to acknowledge longtime VENT leaders, David Wolf, Steve Hilty, Kevin Zimmer, and Barry Zimmer for their contributions in VENT's formative years and for helping keep the organization strong. VENT gave me the opportunity to travel the world and experience the richest sites in the natural world.

Young friends have played a key role in my life by helping me maintain great enthusiasm for the natural world. My time with Kurt Huffman, David Sugeno, and Peter English when they were teenagers inspired me to start youth birding camps thirty years ago. Other young friends who helped keep me young include Andrew Farnsworth, Cullen Hanks, Brian O'Shea, Ben Reynolds, and his wife Jessica Gordon, and the late Nathaniel Gerhart.

I owe a special debt to my friend and colleague Barry Lyon who attended our youth camps and later became a VENT tour leader. Subsequently, he moved to Austin to join our office team. He is now VENT's chief operating officer. He encouraged me to write this book and took over some of my duties to free up time for me to write. He also read the draft manuscript and provided suggestions that improved the book.

Some of my closest friends in the birding world have been Greg Lasley, Fred Collins, Dennis Shepler, Bob Paxton, Sarah Plimpton, Kenn Kaufman, Robert Ridgely, Pete Dunne, and the late Ted Parker. My travels with them have provided great memories, some of which appear in this book. I am grateful to all of them for their support and friendship over many years.

Suggested Readings

Halle, Louis J. *Spring in Washington*. New York: William Sloane Associates, 1947.

Heinrich, Bernd. *Mind of the Raven: Investigations and Adventures with Wolf-Birds*. New York: HarperCollins Publishers, 1999.

Kaufmann, Kenn. *Kingbird Highway: The Story of a Natural Obsession that Got a Little Out of Hand*. Boston: Houghton Mifflin, 1997. (Resubtitled as *The Biggest Year in the Life of an Extreme Birder* in 2006.)

Leopold, Aldo. *A Sand County Almanac, and Sketches Here and There*. New York: Oxford University Press, 1949.

Matthiessen, Peter. *The Birds of Heaven: Travels with Cranes*. New York: North Point Press, 2001.

———. *End of the Earth: Voyages to Antarctica*. Washington, DC: National Geographic, 2003.

———. *The Shorebirds of North America*. New York: Viking Press, 1967.

———. *The Snow Leopard*. New York: Viking Press, 1978.

———. *The Tree Where Man Was Born*. New York: Dutton, 1972.

Peterson, Roger Tory. *Birds Over America*. New York: Dodd, Mead, 1948.

Peterson, Roger Tory, and James Fisher. *Wild America: The Record of a 30,000-Mile Journey Around the Continent by a Distinguished Naturalist and His British Colleague*. Boston: Houghton Mifflin, 1955.

Sutton, George Miksch. *At a Bend in a Mexican River*. New York: P. S. Eriksson, 1972.

———. *Mexican Birds: First Impressions*. Norman, Oklahoma: University of Oklahoma Press, 1951.

Weidensaul, Scott. *Living on the Wind: Across the Hemisphere with Migratory Birds*. New York: North Point Press, 1999.

White, Gilbert. *The Natural History of Selborne*. London: B. White and Son, 1789.

Wulf, Andrea. *The Invention of Nature: Alexander von Humboldt's New World*. New York: Alfred A. Knopf, 2015.

Index

Note: The page reference "*insert*" refers to photographic insert sections.